A REVOLUTION IN SOCIAL POLICY

Other titles available from The Policy Press include:

The dynamics of modern society: Poverty, policy and welfare edited by Lutz Leisering and Robert Walker ISBN 1 86134 059 1 £15.95 pbk

Beyond the threshold: The measurement and analysis of social exclusion edited by Graham Room ISBN 1 86134 003 6 £13.95 pbk

The Gypsy and the State: The ethnic cleansing of British society (2nd edn) by Derek Hawes and Barbara Perez ISBN 1 86134 011 7 £14.95 pbk

Social insurance in Europe edited by Jochen Clasen
ISBN 1 86134 054 0 £16.95 pbk

Partnership against poverty and exclusion? Local regeneration strategies and excluded communities in the UK by Mike Geddes
ISBN 1 86134 071 0 £12.95 pbk

Setting adequacy standards: How governments define minimum incomes by John Veit-Wilson ISBN 1 86134 072 9 £11.95 pbk

All the above titles are available from
Biblios Publishers' Distribution Services Ltd, Star Road,
Partridge Green, West Sussex RH13 8LD, UK
Telephone +44 (0)1403 710851, Fax +44 (0)1403 711143

A REVOLUTION IN SOCIAL POLICY

Quasi-market reforms in the 1990s

Will Bartlett, Jennifer A. Roberts and
Julian Le Grand

First published in Great Britain in 1998 by
The Policy Press
University of Bristol
Rodney Lodge
Grange Road
Bristol BS8 4EA, UK
Telephone +44 (0)117 973 8797
Fax +44 (0)117 973 7308
e-mail tpp@bristol.ac.uk
Website http://www.bristol.ac.uk/Publications/TPP/

British Library Cataloguing-in-Publication Data
A catalogue entry for this book is available from the British Library

ISBN 1 86134 111 3

Will Bartlett is Reader in Social Policy at the School for Policy Studies, University of Bristol. **Jennifer Roberts** is Reader in the Economics of Public Health at the London School of Hygiene and Tropical Medicine. **Julian Le Grand** is the Richard Titmuss Professor of Health Policy at the London School of Economics and Professorial Fellow, King's Fund Institute.

Front cover: Photograph supplied by Dawn Louise Pudney.
Cover design: Qube Design Associates, Bristol.

Printed in Great Britain by Hobbs the Printers Ltd, Southampton.

Contents

Acknowledgements   vii

Notes on contributors   viii

List of acronyms   xii

Introduction   The development of quasi-markets in the 1990s   1

Will Bartlett, Jennifer A. Roberts and Julian Le Grand

Part One: Competitive tendering   17

one   CCT, conflict and cooperation in local authority   19
quasi-markets

Peter Vincent-Jones and Andrew Harries

two   The X-efficiency properties of competitive tendering   43

Robert McMaster

Part Two: Education   61

three   Financing of schools: a national or local quasi-market?   63

Michael Barrow

four   Educational quasi-markets: the Belgian experience   79

Vincent Vandenberghe

five   Self-managing schools in the marketplace: the experience   95
of England, the USA and New Zealand

Geoff Whitty, Sally Power and David Halpin

Part Three: Social care   109

six   How providers are chosen in the mixed economy of   111
community care

Russell Mannion and Peter Smith

seven   Markets, hierarchies and choices in social care   133

Irvine Lapsley and Sue Llewellyn

Part Four: Healthcare   153

eight   Healthcare quasi-markets in a decentralised system   155
of government

George France

nine   Purchaser plurality in UK healthcare: is a consensus   175
emerging and is it the right one?
Nicholas Mays and Jennifer Dixon

ten   Private agencies and public purposes: a quasi-market in the   201
interwar years
Noel Whiteside

Part Five: Legal aid   217

eleven   Legal aid: a case study in quasi-market failure   219
Gwyn Bevan

Part Six: Careers guidance   237

twelve   Applying market principles to the delivery of careers   239
guidance services: a critical review
A. G. Watts

Part Seven: Television   255

thirteen   Public television quasi-markets in New Zealand and the UK   257
Diana Barrowclough

Conclusion   Lessons from experience of quasi-markets in the 1990s   275
Jennifer A. Roberts, Julian Le Grand and Will Bartlett

Bibliography   291

Index   325

Acknowledgements

This book is the product of a series of seminars organised at the School for Policy Studies, University of Bristol and the London School of Economics between 1994 and 1996. The seminars were funded by the Economic and Social Research Council grant – we are very grateful for their support. The seminars enabled those who were interested in quasi-markets to come together and discuss the emerging issues. The chapters are all based on papers presented at this series of seminars. We are grateful to all those who participated in the programme so enthusiastically and to those who continue to attend the continuing programme of seminars for the support and stimulation that we have gained from their participation.

We would also like to thank those who have helped with the coordination of the seminars and have participated in producing documents for this volume. Particular thanks to Raz Govind who undertook the production of the final text and to all the contributors who were so patient and prompt in dealing with our last minute requests. Raz Govind and Jennifer Roberts would also like to apologise to their families for the lost weekends while we were producing the final version of the text.

Will Bartlett
Jennifer A. Roberts
Julian Le Grand

Notes on contributors

Michael Barrow is a Lecturer in Economics in the School of Social Sciences, University of Sussex. He has been working on an ESRC-funded research project on targeting and control of finance in local government.

Diana Barrowclough is a Fellow in Economics at St John's College, Cambridge. She lectures in microeconomics and public economics at the Faculty of Economics and Politics, University of Cambridge, where her research interests in the provision of collective goods, quasi-markets, and broadcasting were developed during PhD research.

Will Bartlett is Reader in Social Economics at the School for Policy Studies, University of Bristol. A co-editor with Julian Le Grand of *Quasi-markets and social policy* (Macmillan, 1993), his research interests cover the economics of transition and quasi-market reforms in East and West Europe. He is editor of *Economic Analysis: Journal of Enterprise and Participation.*

Gwyn Bevan is Reader in Policy Analysis in the Department of Operational Research at the London School of Economics and Political Science. He was a member of advisory groups to the Lord Chancellor's Department working on the 1994 Fundamental Review of Publicly-Financed Legal Services and the 1995 Green Paper, *Targeting need*. He began working on legal aid when at the consultancy firm London Economics. He has worked as a health economist at United Medical and Dental Schools (UMDS) and the University of Bristol, and in operation research at Warwick Business School, HM Treasury and the National Coal Board.

Jennifer Dixon is a Health Policy Analyst at the King's Fund, London, and has written widely on health policy issues in the UK. In recent years she has worked, and published, on topics as diverse as: whether there is fair funding of GP fundholders; whether the NHS is underfunded;

and healthcare reform in the United States. In 1990 she spent a year on a Harkness Fellowship studying the lack of healthcare reform in the USA. She has also spent time analysing or advising on health systems in other countries such as in Eastern Europe, and New Zealand. Originally qualifying in medicine, she practised in the NHS until 1989.

George France is a Health Economist and a Senior Researcher at the Institute for Regional Studies, Italian National Research Council, Rome and has written widely on health reform in Italy.

David Halpin is Professor of Educational Research at Goldsmiths College, University of London. He is co-author of *Grant maintained schools: Education in the market place* and *Devolution and choice in education* (Open University Press, 1998) and co-editor of *Researching education policy: Ethical and methodological issues* (Falmer Press, 1994).

Andrew Harries is a Lecturer and Research Officer in Law at the School of Financial Studies and Law, Sheffield Hallam University. He and Peter Vincent-Jones have been examining local authority contracting for blue-collar compulsory competitively tendered services in metropolitan authorities over the past six years, and are finishing an ESRC-funded project which extends this research: 'Conflict and cooperation for professional services: a comparative study'. In addition he is completing a PhD on Contract Law and contracting practice in the NHS.

Irvine Lapsley is Professor of Accounting and Director of the Institute of Public Sector Accounting Research at the University of Edinburgh. He has undertaken research across the public sector on financial planning and control issues, sponsored by government departments, charitable trusts and professional bodies. He is a member of the Research Board of the Chartered Institute of Management Accountants and of the Public Sector and Not-for-profit Committee of the Accounting Standards Board. He is Editor of *Financial Accountability and Management*.

Julian Le Grand is the Richard Titmuss Professor of Social Policy at the London School of Economics and a Senior Associate of the King's Fund. Previously he was Professor of Public Policy at the University of Bristol. He is a leading authority on the economics of the welfare state and co-edited *Quasi-markets in social policy* (Macmillan, 1993) with Will Bartlett.

Sue Llewellyn is a Senior Lecturer in the Department of Accounting and Business Method at the University of Edinburgh. Her research interests are in management control and accountability, in particular looking at the accounting practices and decision making by budget holders in the public services. She has published empirical research on these issues in both the social services and the NHS.

Robert McMaster is a Lecturer in Economics at the University of Aberdeen. He has published a number of articles on the contracting of state activities and has participated in the quasi-market group since its inception.

Russell Mannion is Department of Health Research Fellow in the Centre of Health Economics at the University of York. His research interests concern the economics of health and social policy.

Nicholas Mays studied modern history and social policy before going into the field of health services. He has worked in the National Health Service, universities and other public bodies. Since 1994, he has been Director of Health Services Research at the King's Fund Policy Institute, London. His main current research interest lies in evaluating different ways of involving general practitioners in NHS purchasing of health services.

Sally Power is Senior Lecturer in the Policy Studies Group at the Institute of Education, University of London. She is the author of *The pastoral and the academic: Conflict and contradiction in the curriculum* (Cassell, 1996) and co-author of *Grant maintained schools: Education in the market place* (Kogan Page, 1993) and *Devolution and choice in education* (Open University Press, 1998).

Jennifer A. Roberts is Reader in the Economics of Public Health at the London School of Hygiene and Tropical Medicine. Her major interests are market reforms in health sectors, economics of infectious disease and primary care. Recent research includes 'Risk, infectious disease in managed markets', ESRC Risk and Human Development Programme.

Peter Smith is Professor of Economics at the University of York, and Director of the Department of Health research programme at the Centre for Health Economics. His research interests concern the efficiency, equity and financing of the public sector, most especially in healthcare.

Vincent Vandenberghe is Researcher in Economics of Education, Institut de recherches économiques et sociales (IRES), Départment des sciences économiques, Université catholique de Louvain; Louvain-la-Neuve, Belgium.

Peter Vincent-Jones is Professor of Law, at the University of Central Lancashire. He and Andrew Harries have been examining local authority contracting for blue-collar compulsory competitively tendered services in metropolitan authorities over the past six years, and are finishing an ESRC-funded project which extends this research: 'Conflict and cooperation in contracting for professional services: a comparative study'.

Tony Watts is Director of the National Institute for Careers Education and Counselling and is Visiting Professor of Career Development at the University of Derby. His many publications include being co-author of *Rethinking careers education and guidance: Theory, policy and practice* (Routledge, 1996).

Noel Whiteside is Reader in Public Policy at the School for Policy Studies, University of Bristol. She works on changing welfare provision from a historical and comparative perspective. She is also co-editor of *Governance, industry and labour markets in Britain and France* (Routledge, 1998). She worked on the ESRC Whitehall Programme on regulation and the National Health Insurance Scheme in the interwar years.

Geoff Whitty is the Karl Mannheim Professor of Sociology of Education at the Institute of Education, University of London. His publications include *The state and private education: An evaluation of the assisted places scheme* (Falmer Press, 1989), *Specialisation and choice in urban education: The City Technology College experiment* (Routledge, 1993) and *Devolution and choice in education* (Open University Press, 1998).

List of acronyms

AMG	annual maintenance grant
APS	assisted places scheme
BBC	British Broadcasting Corporation
CBI	Confederation of British Industry
CCT	compulsory competitive tendering
CFF	common funding formula
CFH	community fundholder
CHC	Community Health Council
CTC	city technology college
DfE	Department for Education
DfEE	Department for Education and Employment
DHSS	Department of Health and Social Security
DoE	Department of the Environment
DoH	Department of Health
DRG	diagnosis related group
DSO	direct service organisation
DSS	Department of Social Security
ECR	extra contractual referral
ESCA	Eastmet Strategic Client Agency
ETS	Eastmet Trading Services
EU	European Union
FAS	Funding Agency for Schools
FEFC	Further Education Funding Council
GM	grant maintained
GMS	general medical services
GP	general practitioner
HA	health authority
HCHS	hospital and community health services
HMO	Health Maintenance Organisation
LA	local authority
LAB	Legal Aid Board
LAP	legal aid practitioner

LBC	London Borough Council
LCD	Lord Chancellor's Department
LEA	local education authority
LGA	Local Government Act
LMS	local management of schools
NAHT	National Association of Head Teachers
NFF	national funding formula
NGR	no-grade-repetition
NHI	National Health Insurance
NHS	National Health Service
NICEC	National Institute for Careers Education and Couselling
NZOA	New Zealand On Air
OLS	ordinary least squares
PBF	public broadcasting fee
PCAT	Public Choice Agency Theory
PCG	primary care group
QALY	quality adjusted life year
QB	queen's banqueters
RCNHI	Royal Commission on National Health Insurance
SEN	special educational needs
SFH	standard fundholder
SSA	standard spending assessment
SSI	Social Services Inspectorate
SSN	Servizio Sanitario Nazionale
STG	special transitionary grant
TEC	Training and Enterprise Council
TPP	total purchasing pilot
TVNZ	Television New Zealand
USL	Unità Sanitaria Locale

The development of quasi-markets in the 1990s

Will Bartlett, Jennifer A. Roberts and
Julian Le Grand

Introduction

In the area of social policy, the 1990s will be remembered as the decade
in which a major social experiment was implemented in the UK by the
Conservative governments. In nearly all areas of welfare provision, new
institutional arrangements were introduced designed to extend the
principle of markets and competition to the provision of services. At
the same time, the principle of free and universal access, fundamental to
the concept of the welfare state, was upheld. This combination of free
access at the point of delivery, combined with decentralised market-like
competition between providers of services, was the key institutional
innovation which was referred to as a 'quasi-market' (Le Grand, 1991; Le
Grand and Bartlett, 1993). Paradoxically, the ideological commitment
to markets resulted in a transformation from a 'planned economy' of
welfare towards a set of arrangements which had more in common with
models of market socialism than with free market capitalism.

The election of the Labour government may have signalled a new
trajectory for social policy, but it is clear that the new administration, no
less than the Conservative administration, is determined to reformulate
or at least reform the welfare state. The philosophy underlying the
proposed reforms is perhaps not as focused on market solutions or as
ideologically driven as that of the previous administration.

The Conservative social policy revolution was based on ideological
commitments to market principles and the belief that only by introducing

them into what was perceived as sluggish unresponsive bureaucratic apparatuses of the welfare state could efficient services, responsive to consumers' choices, be delivered. However, the ideology provided only the framework for a more pragmatic objective: to contain spiralling cost pressures in all sectors of the welfare state. Some changes were introduced almost by chance. The introduction of general practice (GP) fundholding, for example, was a quasi-market solution stumbled on partly by accident (Glennerster and Le Grand, 1995). In nearly all areas, the reforms were at first fiercely resisted by the professional cadres in the different sectors, only to be welcomed eventually by some in those same groups as a result of the increased levels of managerial autonomy and discretion that they introduced.

The proclaimed benefits of the reforms (improvements in efficiency, improved responsiveness to users, and cost containment) have proved difficult to substantiate. This was partly due to the changing resource base (increasing in health, and falling in the case of contracted out local authority [LA] services), and partly due to the intrinsic difficulties of measuring the quantity and quality of service outputs.

Nevertheless, there was a broad political consensus that the reforms would not be reversed, except at the margins, whatever party was successful at the election. The issue since the election is to decide whether this will be so: 'will the reforms be revoked, solidified in their present form, or continue along the same path, deepening the tendency for the individualisation of welfare?' Social policies are being formulated at a rapid pace and it is difficult to foresee, at this early stage, what overarching principles, if any, will determine the shape of social policy in the next decade. The election was won on a pledge to reduce inequalities, and to allow greater opportunities for the marginalised to participate in society. However, it is of interest to note that, so far, the quasi-markets in education and community care have been left almost untouched. Even in health, despite the rhetoric concerning 'the abolition of the internal market', key features of the quasi-market are to be retained, including the purchaser–provider split and GP-led commissioning (DoH, 1998).

As social policies develop they will need to be informed by consideration of the successes and difficulties experienced by the first generation of reforms. Research on quasi-market social policy has developed rapidly and the work presented in this book brings together recent findings by some of the leading authorities in the field. The chapters are all based on papers presented at a series of seminars organised at the School for Policy Studies, University of Bristol, and the London

School of Economics between 1994 and 1996, funded by the Economic and Social Research Council (ESRC). The book contains the results of the early investigations of quasi-market policies that were introduced and discussed in Le Grand and Bartlett (1993) and complements work discussing innovations in other sectors (see Deakin and Michie, 1997a). The chapters provide a wide range of opinions about the success of the quasi-market revolution based on studies carried out across the fields of competitive tendering, education, community care and health, as well as recent developments in the areas of legal aid, careers guidance and broadcasting. The book is wide ranging but, based as it is on papers presented at the seminars, it does not attempt to be comprehensive. It does not include debates relating to housing, one of the first sectors to develop along quasi-market lines, with the development of housing associations, tendered management services and more radically the sale of LA houses (Bramley, 1993). Nor does it discuss the markets that are developing in the highly regulated privatised utility services, water, electricity, gas or the transport systems. Yet lessons gleaned from the research included in this volume provide many insights that have more general application to the management of other sectors. The management of agents and the control of opportunistic tendencies that might compromise safety standards in transport, for example, has much in common with the issues raised in connection with the health sector. The research refers to the early period of the experiments in quasi-markets and the lessons from this period have, where possible, been set in the context of the emerging policy proposals of the new Labour administration.

Themes

The contributors to this book come from a spectrum of disciplines and apply a variety of approaches to the study of quasi-markets in the different sectors. Nevertheless, a common set of themes emerge from the research. One of these themes relates to the importance of trust and collaboration for welfare markets, which face particular difficulties of bounded rationality (the recognition of the cognitive limits of rational individuals), asymmetries of information (where one party has access to more information, and hence the power this brings, than the other) and opportunism (the existence of moral hazard in pursuit of self-interest). The development of trust-based contractual relations, where they are achieved, may help to reduce transaction costs and diminish the problems of inequality of access associated with the application of market type relationships.

Another theme is the importance of the institutional environment in which the new quasi-markets are embedded. The pre-existing ethos of public service in some cases carries over into the new arrangements and provides a context in which the intended incentives provided by financial autonomy are muted or even ignored. As Le Grand has observed elsewhere (Le Grand, 1997), the impact of market style incentives will depend on the motivation structure of the agents involved in decision making. Quasi-markets may operate best where they are structured to capture the positive effect of both private and altruistic motivations of welfare service providers.

A third theme is the effect of decentralisation on the spatial impact of the reforms. With the devolution of decision making and of responsibility to individual provider units, the quality and style of provision varies by location. In many sectors of welfare services it is apparent that the quality of services depends as much on where users live as on the level of need which they experience, creating both winners and losers from the reforms. This decentralisation has also provided the framework for implementation of new public management arrangements with the attendant shorter lines of command, and the greater authority and accountability inherent in these new systems. These themes run through the various contributions made to the individual sector studies in this volume, to which we now turn.

Compulsory competitive tendering

In Chapter One Peter Vincent-Jones and Andrew Harries discuss the introduction and operation of compulsory competitive tendering (CCT) in British LAs and health authorities (HAs). CCT has been applied to the purchase of ancillary services such as cleaning services for schools and hospitals, and refuse collection. Several studies have indicated that CCT has improved efficiency in this sector.

The authors argue, however, that where contracts were awarded to an internal provider (direct service organisation [DSO]) the outcome of competitive tendering was dependent on the governance structure through which the contract was organised. Vincent-Jones and Harries make a useful distinction between 'hard quasi-markets' and 'soft quasi-markets'. The former imposes a clear organisational divide between the purchaser (client) department and the provider department (DSO). The latter retains the previous organisational closeness of purchaser and provider, often locating both organisations in the same building. The authors argue that the hard version of quasi-market, which mimics an idealised private sector commercialism, creates significant problems. At the same time as arm's-length commercial relationships and competition are introduced, so the prior relationships of trust and cooperation break down, reducing potential efficiency gains. The authors argue in favour of soft quasi-market structures in which some organisational and non-contractual linkages provide a framework within which cooperative long-term contracting can take place. Such arrangements, they argue, are required to derive maximum efficiency gains from contracting out. The removal of compulsion to put work out to competitive tendering provides an opportunity for LAs to manage service contracts to obtain the best possible results from changes in public sector management. These changes evolved while structures adjusted to the changes imposed by the introduction of quasi-markets, whether the contracts were won by in-house contractors or were franchised to external providers. The 'soft quasi-market' that evolved reduced the stresses and inefficiencies of the 'hard quasi-market'. It also reduced alienation and improved responsiveness.

The empirical study described by Vincent-Jones and Harries supports many of the propositions set out by Robert McMaster in Chapter Two. McMaster provides the theoretical basis of the argument in favour of softer quasi-markets. The argument draws on Leibenstein's X-efficiency theory. The concept of X-efficiency refers to the efficiency gains which can be achieved when a workforce is well motivated and maximises efforts on particular tasks. It contrasts with allocative efficiency which refers to efficiency gains which can be achieved by a mere restructuring of resources to take advantage of differences in relative prices on the market. Allocative efficiency gains are achieved on the assumption that each resource provider in an organisation is working to some pre-set standard of efficiency. The concept of X-efficiency allows for variation in these levels of effort. McMaster argues that where CCT results in the alienation of the workforce, for example, where there is intensive monitoring based on an atmosphere of mistrust, X-efficiency may fall and the gains from CCT will be reduced below their potential level. McMaster shows how the loss of trust between purchaser and provider can lead to a loss of X-efficiency. The chapter offers an instructive perspective from which to discuss CCT. It also suggests criteria that can be used to assess the likely success of CCT policies.

Education

In Chapter Three Michael Barrow discusses funding arrangements for secondary schools in the UK. He points out that the quasi-market reforms in the UK education sector have introduced a highly regulated system, with little entry or exit of provider organisations. Schools are financed by a capitation formula, which, while designed to ensure equality, in practice introduces inequities because disadvantaged children are treated the same as their more advantaged peers. One recent innovation was to introduce a common funding formula for grant maintained (GM) schools, as a prelude to introducing a 'national funding formula' (NFF) for all schools. However, this common formula has a number of fundamental difficulties. It prevents LAs shifting resources away from secondary schools towards primary schools for fear that the secondary schools may opt out and become GM. It is argued that the promotion of GM schools is adversely affecting the 'sense of community and collegiality' in the education system. By undermining trust relationships, the introduction of competition in education, as in other sectors, is destroying the motivation and creativity of the profession. Thirdly, and most importantly, the pilot schemes studied by Barrow have revealed the difficulty of moving to a national formula on account of the large spatial redistribution of resources which would follow, creating both winners and losers and undermining the potential political support for such a policy. He discusses policy developments that have occurred since the election of May 1997. These he sees as promising a more cooperative and efficient approach to funding.

Vincent Vandenberghe presents findings from a study of the operation of quasi-markets in the Belgian secondary school system in Chapter Four. Using detailed data on individual pupil performance at school, he examines the extent to which high ability and low ability pupils are segregated. His empirical research reveals that the main determinant of segregation is the degree of market concentration of schools within education districts. Other factors such as socioeconomic discrepancies are shown to be unrelated to the degree of segregation. The findings indicate that the higher the potential for the choice of school, the greater the degree of segregation according to ability. The implication is that in

Belgium the operation of quasi-markets has led to inequality in the provision of educational services. Vandenberghe goes on to discuss the social inefficiency of segregation on the basis of ability. He suggests a number of regulatory and policy measures which could be introduced to eliminate this undesirable consequence of quasi-markets, while simultaneously retaining the essential quasi-market features of universal public provision and interschool competition.

In Chapter Five, Geoff Whitty, Sally Power and David Halpin review recent research findings in three countries (the UK, New Zealand and the USA) on the effects of increased parental choice in secondary education. The results from the three countries suggest that while there may be some benefits of increased choice in terms of increased managerial autonomy which may lead to efficiency improvements, there are also associated drawbacks in terms of adverse effects on equity. In none of the countries was there any evidence that increasing parental choice, either through introducing quasi-markets as in the UK and New Zealand, or through more participative programmes such as in some states in the USA, has had any impact at all on educational outcomes.

In many cases, the impact of the dual disciplines of performance indicators and tight budgets led instead to 'cream skimming'. This occurred as schools sought to balance their duty to less able students, who absorbed many resources and did not contribute to the visible outcomes (achievements in the league tables), against the budgetary and performance enhancing potential of high achievers.

The authors discuss the new policy initiatives of the Labour administration in a postscript to their chapter (DfEE, 1997). This addresses the removal of the assisted places schemes (APS) and the abolition of the proposed voucher scheme for nursery education. Although new titles have been adopted (for example, GM schools have become foundation schools), it is feared that status and image of the latter will allow inequalities among schools to be perpetuated unless firm guidelines are put in place.

The maintenance of the budget limits set by the Conservative government and the lack of 'ear-marked' funding for education by the Labour administration has continued to frustrate the attempts of local government to direct extra funds, however modest, towards education. LAs beset by tight budget constraints and burgeoning needs may differ in the priorities they attach to education.

Social care

Russell Mannion and Peter Smith analyse the effects of quasi-markets in community care using a theoretical framework based in the new economic sociology. This framework emphasises the social context of market transactions and the way in which social networks and trust relations modify purchasing and selling decisions. As in other quasi-markets, the reforms introduced in 1993 have encouraged LAs to separate purchaser and provider functions for services such as care of older people in need. Such services are provided either in residential homes or through home care (so-called domiciliary care). In some cases, as with CCT, discussed in Chapters One and Two, this separation of purchaser and provider is carried out within the LA itself. In other cases the provider function is externalised to independent private organisations (often in the voluntary or non-profit sector).

The question which Mannion and Smith address in Chapter Six is the way in which individuals, or social workers (care managers) acting as their agents, make choices between the different provider organisations offering services to older people in need. They develop their argument both theoretically and through new empirical evidence derived from six social services departments in the UK. Their findings stress the key role of trust in choosing a nursing home or domiciliary care provider. This is because price signals are either not available, or where they are available are not taken into consideration. There was no evidence in the study that price was in any sense traded off against quality on the basis of a utilitarian set of preferences. This was attributed to the professional ethos of social workers, who were disinclined to respond to costs and prices in the way the architects of the reforms might have wished them to. Rather, care managers were found to place a high premium on quality, an approach which appeared to restrict the provision of care to a fortunate privileged few, since fixed budget constraints prohibited the purchase of large quantities of high quality services. At the same time, since quality is hard to assess, many of the choices made were made on the basis of trust and reputation rather than hard facts.

The general argument in favour of trust-based relationships in the field of contracting, as McMaster indicates in Chapter Two, is that trust substitutes for missing markets (in which price signals are absent or ignored) where it is difficult to monitor effort. Non-trust relationships in that context involve providers who may work to a minimal set of conditions specified in the contract and hence supply minimal effort. It is argued that the development of trust supports welfare–enhancing cooperative behaviour, so that providers deliver high quality services even in the absence of (costly) monitoring and inspections. In the community care context described by Mannion and Smith, care managers' ethics induce them to ignore costs and prices and focus on quality. Yet quality is often not observable and reliance is placed on prior reputation. This suggests that a probable outcome is one in which little change in the structure of provision will take place since the more efficient providers and new entrants, who are the key agents of change, will find the contract system insufficiently attractive to motivate their activities.

Chapter Seven, by Irvine Lapsley and Sue Llewellyn, addresses the same key issue: to what extent do care managers take cost and price information into account when making referrals of elderly people with care needs to residential homes? Is such economic data typically taken into account alongside information about quality when making such decisions? Have the quasi-market reforms led to a change in behaviour which reflects the change to the 'formal rationality' of the market and away from the 'substantial rationality' of traditional public services, as desired by policy makers? Or has little change actually been made in practice? To answer these questions Lapsley and Llewellyn adopt the markets and hierarchies framework (Williamson, 1975). This stresses the difficulty of decision making when complex choices are involved due to the bounded rationality of decision makers, and the danger of them adopting opportunistic behaviour when dealing with vulnerable clients. They also question whether the culture of care has been influenced by the attempt to introduce, in new public management structures, cost-based accounting information into care managers' choice making strategies.

The authors confronted decision makers from nine Scottish regional authorities with a number of fictitious scenarios, which were nevertheless based on typical examples of real choice problems encountered in practice. These scenarios, called 'real life constructs', were offered to the decision makers in two forms. In the first stage, decision makers were confronted with choice problems based on relatively simple sets of data which then became much more complex. The choices made were observed and discussed with the decision makers to discover how far rational choices could or were being made in relation to decisions over referrals to nursing homes. The findings of the study indicated that social workers, although adhering to a professional ethic which was client centred and placed a high value on self-determination, were nevertheless beginning to incorporate considerations of cost and price into their decision-making criteria. There was little evidence that bounded rationality was a major problem facing social workers and care managers in reaching their decisions over the appropriate form of care for their elderly clients. This was largely because decision making continued to rely on standard procedures and operating methods, and there was an unwillingness to delegate budgets to field officers. While market-based forms of decision making appear to be increasingly accepted, it appears that established professional norms and the strong influence of the culture of social work on the way in which contracts are implemented, reduced their potential impact on professional practice.

Health

Reforms to healthcare systems are taking place throughout the western world, and the contribution by George France in Chapter Eight outlines the changing system of health service delivery in Italy. He uses this example to raise questions about the effect of differing institutional environments on the operation of quasi-markets. Quasi-market reforms introduced in the early 1990s have begun to transform the Italian national health services, but the precise model adopted varies from one region to another. The Italian system of government places much more emphasis on the devolution of power to regional authorities than in the UK, and this also affects the delivery of welfare services. The 20 regional authorities in Italy have administrative and legislative autonomy, although until recently funding was collected centrally and distributed to the regions through regional grants. However, new legislation introduced in the early 1990s has extended responsibility for raising revenues to the regional tier of government. Compulsory health contributions are now returned to the region of residence. Alongside this change, regions are free to develop their own system of healthcare delivery within a national reference framework, which permits regions to introduce various quasi-market methods of health service purchasing, including the use of third party reimbursement (by the local health authority), preferred provider schemes, and contract-based purchasing. On the provider side, although many hospitals are publicly owned, there has historically been a more developed private (for-profit and not-for-profit) sector in Italy than in the UK.

France explores the possible outcomes and potential problems of the regional diversity in quasi-market models. He argues that the various models will give rise to a variety of outcomes which will test the relative performance of each and may eventually lead to an evolutionary convergence towards the most successful model.

Although NHS reforms in the UK are on the surface more centrally regulated than in Italy, in practice there is considerable scope for local diversity in methods of purchasing, mainly due to the scope for discretion over the distribution of purchasing responsibilities between HAs and GP fundholders. In Chapter Nine Nicholas Mays and Jennifer Dixon analyse the evolution of purchasing in the quasi-market in healthcare. One of the major innovations of these reforms was the devolution of purchasing to family doctors. Eligible general practitioners (GPs) became fundholders, for the first time able to make purchasing decisions on behalf of their patients. However, this meant that the budget of the local HAs was reduced, affecting their ability to 'commission' services on behalf of the whole population in their locality. This dual structure of purchasing has created a tension between 'commissioning' and 'fundholding'. (This is similar to the problem of distributing budgets to GM schools described by Barrow in Chapter Three.) Mays and Dixon argue that while all the main political parties have reached a consensus on the benefits of devolved and decentralised purchasing, there is still room for debate over the form which such devolution should take. They outline seven possible models by which NHS purchasing could be structured in the future. When evaluating the various options, they take into account issues such as patient choice, ability to influence service providers, attention to transaction costs and management of financial risk. They argue that "none of the current purchasing models offer patients a great deal of choice", one of the avowed aims of the reforms.

In one of their seven options ("integrated primary care based purchasing organisations"), Mays and Dixon propose a radical model of purchasing designed to overcome this defect by allowing patients a choice between purchasing organisations, rather than between GPs. This option is rather more like the American Health Maintenance Organisation (HMO) than anything yet proposed for UK purchasing systems. In an even more radical option the authors propose that NHS and non-NHS bodies could compete for the right to manage the NHS purchasing function. In either case, larger purchasing organisations implied by such options would be more likely to be able to manage financial risk than the small GP fundholders under the present system. On the negative side, there is a concern over a possible increase in transaction costs which such options could bring about, and a likely need for a careful regulation of the proposed integrated purchasing organisations.

The chapter highlights the likelihood of further evolution of the NHS quasi-market, especially on the demand side. Since the costs of healthcare are likely to rise sharply in the future as the population ages and new technologies are more widely diffused, so the issue of appropriate models of health service purchasing and the potential need for rationing will become increasingly topical. The authors discuss their models in the context of the recent pronouncements made in the Department of Health's (DoH) White Paper, *The new NHS* (1997). They focus upon the proposed evolution of primary care groups and the phasing out of GP fundholding from April 1999.

At first glance the White Paper appears to turn back the tide of the quasi-market initiative in the NHS. It proclaims itself to be a turning point, 'It replaces the internal market with integrated care' based on 'partnership and driven by performance'. However, it places a great deal of emphasis on decentralised decision making and endorses internal management structures based on devolved budgets. Moreover, it keeps the purchaser–provider split and puts all purchasing in the hands of GP-led primary care groups. It asserts that,

> **For the first time in the history of the NHS the Government will align clinical and financial responsibility to give all professionals who make prescribing and referring decisions the opportunity to make financial decisions in the best interests of their patients. (DoH, 1997, p 9)**

However, it also proclaims a "one nation NHS with consistent standards and services" (para 8.7) and will introduce a "systematic drive to challenge and reduce unacceptable variations in all aspects of performance". It will be difficult to reconcile decentralised agreements or 'contracts' with the implementation of a 'one nation NHS'. The problems will not easily be solved by initiatives to introduce 'evidence-based medicine' or cost-effective policies, to be developed as the Purchaser Efficiency Index.

Some considerations of the X-efficiency aspects of performance monitoring (see Chapter Two) should be borne in mind when implementing such changes. The type of contract that the new Labour government does suggest (and this is new) is not one related to quasi-markets but instead one linked to the much more general social contract that it intends to implement. This is a significant movement away from the individualisation of welfare to an acceptance of the deeper structural issues that determine healthcare. It is intended to inform people about risks to health and to take "tough action – though regulation and legislation will be the exception, not the rule". Local authorities will be charged with a new duty "to promote the economic, social and environmental well-being of their areas" (DoH, 1998).

In the final chapter of this section, Noel Whiteside's historical account of the development of National Health Insurance (NHI) provides some bothersome parallels with recent debates about new Labour policies on social insurance, whether it refers to lone parents, young unemployed or the incapacitated. She describes earlier debates that sought to implement harsh thresholds for benefit, the delivery of services rather than money benefits and the perennial searches for the 'scrounger'. Her chapter also concludes that the role of competition among hospitals in the pre-NHS Britain did not improve efficiency.

Legal aid

In Chapter Eleven Gwyn Bevan analyses one of the most long-standing and hitherto least explored examples of a quasi-market in public services in the UK, that which has operated in the field of legal aid. First introduced in 1949, legal aid gives eligible individuals a free choice of provider (legal firm) with costs reimbursed by the government. This third party payment system has led to an explosion of legal aid costs, while at the same time the numbers eligible for assistance have fallen. Various attempts have been made to reduce costs by increasing regulation, and introducing standard fee rates. However, as Bevan points out, in the face of bounded rationality and opportunism these responses have failed to work, and legal firms have been provided with incentives to alter the mix of services to reduce 'cream skimming', for example, the level of provision in welfare cases, and expand work on more profitable cases, leading to potential 'cream skimming'. Bevan considers various options for reform of the quasi-market, including contracting with legal aid practitioners (along the lines of GPs in health), rationing, introducing a salaried service, and user charges. He concludes that there is a need to devise a mixed system, which involves all three options, but has a greater emphasis on the use of salaried lawyers as the key to cost containment.

The author comments on recent proposals to reform legal aid policy. Legal aid appears to be an area ripe for change. The legal aid budget is widely seen as being out of control. The current system provides incentives for solicitors to proceed only with cases likely to be successful. Solicitors and barristers seem to neglect the wider 'public good' element of law. This needs to be assessed carefully if justice is not to be compromised.

Careers services

In Chapter Twelve Tony Watts discusses the recent quasi-market reforms in the areas of careers and educational guidance. Starting in 1993, LA guidance services have been privatised to new careers guidance companies. In some cases these are conversions of the old LA services, in other cases new entrants have taken over the provision of services. The services have been let out under contract following a succession of competitive bidding rounds. They represent a new approach to public sector management based on the franchising of the right to provide a service to a management group. In some cases, under rebidding, existing providers have lost their franchise to other companies.

Watts makes the fundamental distinction between guidance services as market maker in the labour market and the application of quasi-market mechanisms to the provision of guidance services themselves. Thus far, two distinct approaches have been adopted. Firstly, for the provision of statutory client groups (school leavers), universal free services are provided under contract by the new careers guidance companies. Secondly, a much more limited service is available for adults, with a few experiments in the provision of guidance vouchers, mainly for unemployed people, organised through Training and Enterprise Councils (TECs). At the same time the new guidance companies have been encouraged to develop their adult guidance services, partly on a subsidised basis and partly on the basis of user charges. The reliance on user charges has led to a variable level and quality of services in different localities, while the voucher schemes have suffered from an absence of effective choice and high transactions costs. The most recent policy developments appear to be moving in the direction of providing free basic information services, and formally adopting user charges for further in-depth guidance of adults. The policy conflict between cost escalation and equality of access is to be solved by restricting the range of services available on a universal basis.

Guidance, as a tool that can be used to align the needs of lone parents, the young unemployed and the incapacitated with opportunities in the jobs market, has a major role in implementing the Welfare to Work policies of the new Labour government. The demand for guidance is likely to increase. Markets in guidance may feature in attempts to meet the needs of these policy initiatives.

Television

Diana Barrowclough's study in Chapter Thirteen of the quasi-market changes that have taken place in public service broadcasting in the UK and New Zealand raises issues about the nature of the 'public good' and distributional aspects of broadcasting. It also has implications for the structure of the industry and the funding of services by licensing, fees or charges. These changes are taking place in the context of very rapidly developing technologies that make national regulations and controls more difficult to operate. At present her research suggests that the structure of the TV industry is unstable and transient but the trajectory is seen to be towards more 'market'-oriented solutions.

Conclusion

Given the strict budgetary constraints that the new Labour government has chosen to adopt, debates in all sectors of social policy in the UK are bound to raise questions about priorities. Debates begun by the Conservative administration, on user charges, restricting the range of services to be provided free of charge and the possibility of introducing privately-funded pensions will continue. It remains to be seen how far the pressure on public finances will chip away at the foundations of the principle of free access to welfare services, and whether the quasi-market revolution will provide a lasting solution to the reform of the public sector.

As governments throughout the world struggle with the conflicting aims of containing the costs of ever-rising demand for social expenditure and the need to provide quality services, a variety of new approaches to managing welfare services have been mooted. In the UK, the

Conservative governments experimented with new mechanisms designed to introduce competition in what thus far remain largely publicly-funded services. Elsewhere, for example, in eastern Europe, more overtly market methods of provision have replaced systems based on state-provided services, or services provided through state-owned enterprises. In most of the countries of the European Union (EU), welfare services are based on principles of social insurance or direct state provision, although in some countries experiments with quasi-markets are beginning to be introduced, as in the Italian health system (see Chapter Eight). Experiments with competitive contracted out mechanisms have been introduced in countries such as New Zealand (see Chapter Five). With the coming to power of a new Labour government in the UK in 1997, the quasi-market system of welfare provision introduced during the last decade is coming under close scrutiny by policy makers. New directions are opening up and are under discussion. However, these new directions will inevitably be shaped and constrained by the experience so far of operating quasi-markets, and by assessments of their benefits and disadvantages. These assessments will be informed by the increasing number of research studies which are beginning to appear on these issues. The research studies presented in this book reveal the intrinsic difficulties of introducing market-type mechanisms into the provision of welfare services, particularly in regard to equity and access. However, the findings are not uniformly negative, and future reforms will need to be designed with care to ensure that the efficiency advantages of the quasi-market revolution in social policy are not discarded. The consistent finding on the importance of the institutional framework within which competition takes place, and the role of trust and collaborative working in promoting the effective provision of welfare services indicates a way forward for policy makers resolving these dilemmas.

Part One

Competitive tendering

ONE

CCT, conflict and cooperation in local authority quasi-markets

Peter Vincent-Jones and Andrew Harries

Introduction

The introduction of compulsory competitive tendering (CCT) in local government has challenged traditional assumptions about the nature of bureaucracy and the need for hierarchy, integration and planning (Walsh, 1995). While the challenge has been expressed most obviously in the growth of a mixed economy of privatisation, externalisation and 'contracting out', CCT has also had significant implications for the internal organisation of local authorities (LAs), as trading relationships have replaced hierarchical direction, and internal workforces have been exposed to competition.[1] As LAs tender for second round blue-collar services and prepare for white-collar CCT, the issue of how to organise and manage quasi-market relationships remains pressing for both policy makers and managers. This chapter examines a variety of quasi-market arrangements for the provision of buildings cleaning services in two metropolitan authorities in the north of England. It evaluates the success of these arrangements with reference to the incidence of conflict and cooperation in the contract management process. The basic argument is that the key to trusting and cooperative client–contractor relationships is the integration of quasi-markets within hierarchical structures, at either corporate or operational management levels within the organisation.[2]

Hybrid organisation

Where internal workforces have won contracts for the provision of services subject to CCT, LA organisation may be described as hybrid, involving the incorporation of quasi-market elements within fundamentally hierarchical structures.[3] For any defined activity, such as buildings cleaning or refuse collection,[4] a quasi-market is constituted through the separation of client and contractor functions, the existence of competition with potential external bidders, and the devolution of financial responsibilities. Formal mediation of the quasi-market relationship between client and contractor is provided by the contract,[5] which specifies obligations and lays down procedures for variation, monitoring, defaults, and dispute resolution. However, the quasi-market exists within a hierarchy. Client and contractor both belong to the same organisation and are subject to departmental or central controls or influences, at least to some degree. The governance of transactions is effected not just by contract, but also through a variety of hierarchical rules, standing orders and commands, backed ultimately by the discipline of individual contracts of employment. While CCT legislation and regulations establish a compulsory framework for competition, the organisational arrangements for the management and delivery of services are not prescribed. LAs have considerable choice in the hybrid structures they adopt, and in the extent of quasi-market separation and hierarchical involvement in the organisation and governance of defined service provision.

The quasi-market separation of client and contractor is necessary for competitive tendering, and implicit in the requirement for the direct service organisation (DSO) to meet certain financial objectives in the event of being awarded the contract.[6] DSOs have thus become cost centres or business units with trading accounts, enabling 'discrete audit trails' for particular activities to be traced and monitored for internal and external audit, and reports to be prepared for the DoE.[7,8] However, financial differentiation does not necessarily imply any further form of organisational separation. A 'soft' quasi-market arrangement might be one in which the 'parties' involved in providing a particular service continue to share a single organisational location, with both client and contractor for educational buildings cleaning, for example, remaining within the education department (and responsibility for other defined activities being 'dispersed' throughout the authority). A 'hard' quasi-market arrangement, on the other hand, might be one in which client and contractor are organisationally, as well as financially, separated. The most extreme example is the combination of a single multifunctional 'super-DSO' responsible for all defined activities on the contractor side, with a single multifunctional agency performing a similar role on the client side, with transactions between client and contractor being conducted along quasi-commercial lines. Intermediate forms of arrangement might involve the organisation of individual DSOs in departments separate from those of the major clients, and/or the location of the client function in a 'lead' department, usually that of the largest user for the particular service.

The implementation of CCT has also resulted in hierarchical disaggregation – the separation of client and/or contractor functions from central hierarchical involvement. The setting up of business units and cost centres, and the associated devolution of financial management and control, have tended to break down management hierarchies and to produce 'flatter' organisational structures (Walsh and Davis, 1993). In this context, two aspects of 'hierarchy' may be distinguished.[9] First, as the direct management role of the corporate centre has decreased, so its strategic role in integrating the disparate units that make up the more fragmented structure of the authority has increased. The 'central hierarchy' has to set corporate goals concerning quality, equity and customer service, and to determine policy at the broadest level. It must also coordinate and supervise the CCT process, act as a conduit for organisational learning, provide corporate support services (financial, personnel, legal, and information technology) for DSOs, and serve as final arbiter of internal disputes (Walsh and Davis, 1993). Second, a variety of smaller hierarchical structures occupy a number of sites within the authority, serving operational management or lower-level strategic functions distinguishable from those of the corporate centre. Departments, directorates, DSOs and client-agencies all exhibit aspects of hierarchical organisation. In relation to these, the terms 'strong' and 'weak' hierarchy will be used in a specific sense, to refer to the extent of integration of *operational management* of both client and contractor functions within *common* hierarchical processes.

Given this focus, the clearest example of strong hierarchical involvement is the 'twin-hatted' arrangement, already described in terms of a 'soft' quasi-market split, whereby both client and contractor for a particular service are located within the same department. Here chief officer and other senior management personnel may be so closely involved in client and contractor functions that the relationship might best be described as 'trilateral'. Every aspect of transaction management, from initial planning to implementation of the contract, monitoring, defaults and adjustments, and problem solving and handling disputes, is likely to occur within a strongly hierarchical context, even where the department is formally split into separate client and contractor divisions. The hierarchical nature of such an organisation is evident in the formal arbitration role usually accorded the chief officer, who is expected to handle disputes without reference to the ultimate central authority of the chief executive. At the other extreme, common hierarchical influence over operational management is likely to be weakest where a multifunctional 'super-DSO' contracts with a similarly agglomerated multifunctional client agency. Hierarchical management within each of these units applies to one or other, not both, client and contractor functions. Under such a fragmented arrangement, integration is provided only at a general strategic level by the corporate centre.

Hybrid governance

The parameters of transaction governance are determined in any given case by the form of hybrid organisation of the particular service: the choice of organisational arrangement opens up certain governance possibilities, at the same time as foreclosing others. The contract is always important initially, whether the service is provided externally, or internally by the DSO. Tendering regulations must be complied with, and detailed contractual information made public with regard to specification, bills of quantities, schedules of rates, and terms and conditions. However, when managing and adjusting the relationship once the contract has been awarded, a variety of uses and non-uses of contract is possible. The contract may be: used *conflictually* ('adversarially') by one or both parties; used *cooperatively*, channelling behaviour and regulating the exchange; *displaced* (in circumstances where it could have been referred to); *supplemented* by some other formal or informal governance mechanism or procedure, either because it does not provide for a particular eventuality, or because its provisions have been displaced. Where quasi-market separation and/or hierarchical disaggregation have proceeded too far, or where organisational reforms have been imposed too quickly, conflictual recourse to contract may be expected, and its inherent *limits* as a governance mechanism revealed (Vincent-Jones, 1994a; 1994b); where, on the other hand, hybrid arrangements are appropriate and have been more sensitively implemented, contract may perform a constructive and cooperative role.

Whether the contract is displaced, and what it is supplemented by, are dependent on the form of hybrid organisation of any particular service. First, where common hierarchical involvement in operational management is weak, governance must be predominantly bilateral. Formal contractual processes may be supplemented by a range of extra-contractual formal and informal mechanisms, analogous to those that operate in commercial markets. A succession of private sector studies (Macaulay, 1963; Beale and Dugdale, 1975) have demonstrated that, even where contractual planning has been strongly adopted, the management of business exchanges in practice is likely to be relational (Macneil, 1978) and heavily reliant on a variety of both extra-legal normative devices, such as customs and conventions, and completely non-normative incentives built around economic interdependence, especially in long-term relationships (see Campbell and Harris, 1993). Second, where hierarchical elements in hybrid organisation are strong, governance is trilateral rather than bilateral in character, with hierarchical processes occurring with quasi-market/contractual ones.[10] Formal hierarchical governance is implicit in the common management structure which integrates client and contractor functions within departments, with senior managers fulfilling 'twin-hatted' roles. Informally, hierarchical integration is likely to be achieved through encouraging component sections within the department towards congruent goals, so reducing opportunistic tendencies and the need for hierarchical surveillance, evaluation and direction (Ouchi, 1991).

Organising and reorganising for CCT

To minimise transaction management problems, the simplest option for LAs when organising for CCT has been to retain departmental or similar structures. This approach, which has been the preferred solution in the majority of London boroughs and metropolitan districts, is well illustrated in the case study of buildings cleaning in Westmet.[11] Although there is no evidence that efficiency gains cannot be achieved through departmental organisation, many authorities have implemented more radical client–contractor splits because of the perception that the insufficient separation of interests might lead to collusive anti-competitive practices favouring the DSO, so preventing the full benefits of competition being realised.[12] 'Harder' quasi-market arrangements, involving greater hierarchical disaggregation, are justified on grounds of potential economies of scale and efficiency advantages. However, the problem posed by the development of multifunctional 'super-DSOs' and/or super-clients is that client and contractor are dislocated from previous formal and informal governance structures, while simultaneously being placed in a novel quasi–commercial environment in which trust and cooperation have yet to be established. The potential for conflictual management outcomes is increased by a number of factors. The DSO and client may be physically relocated in separate places within the authority. There may be a change of personnel and an influx of new managers, with new management relationships having to be established and corresponding uncertainty over management roles. Previous working practices, methods of problem–handling, and lines of communication may be disrupted. Information may become 'privatised' rather than shared, because the parties calculate that secrecy serves their newly defined commercial purpose more effectively than openness. Generally, an 'us and them' mentality may be fostered by the requirements of working in a more competitive and adversarial environment. In such circumstances, as obtained in the early years of the Eastmet buildings cleaning contract, the almost inevitable result is greater reliance on formal use of contract in monitoring, varying, and regulating the exchange, accompanied by unacceptably high levels of contractual defaults, penalties and disputes.

The answer to these problems, as the case study which follows of the restructuring of Eastmet since 1990 shows, is not necessarily a return to departmentalism. Quasi–markets can be successfully organised along quasi–commercial lines, without the need for increased common hierarchical involvement in operational management, provided that appropriate bilateral relationships can be established. This requires some modification of excessively hard client–contractor structures, the development of a less adversarial culture, and more generally, recognition of the deficiencies of the naive market model of contract and quasi–markets advocated by radical reformers in the early years of CCT.

Case studies of conflict and cooperation in buildings cleaning

This analysis of conflict and cooperation in buildings cleaning will be illustrated in the case studies of the first round of tendering for these services in Eastmet 1988-90, the restructured Eastmet from 1990 to the present, and Westmet. Discussion of client–contractor relationships in education buildings cleaning has been complicated by the introduction of local management of schools (LMS). The devolution of powers to budget-holding school heads has resulted in their being treated increasingly as 'end clients', distinct from the client CCT function which continues to be exercised within the core of the LA.[13] To some extent, as will become clear, this may have contributed to an improvement in relationships where the DSO has been able to deal with school heads as 'active clients', rendering unnecessary some of the management functions previously exercised by the LA client.

Hard quasi-market/weak hierarchy: conflictual contracting in Eastmet[14] 1988-90

The political control of Eastmet metropolitan city council has swung in recent years between radical Conservative and strong Labour. The period from 1988 to 1990, covering the introduction and initial implementation of CCT under the 1988 Local Government Act (LGA), was dominated by market-oriented Conservatives intent on establishing Eastmet as an 'enabling' authority along the lines of other flagship Tory authorities such as Westminster London Borough Council (LBC).

A policy document produced after the election of the new administration in 1988 proposed bringing forward the government's timetable for compulsory tendering of defined activities, extending competitive tendering voluntarily to non-CCT services, market-testing professional and support services, and actively encouraging management buy-outs. This enabling vision was premised on a model of market relationships which demanded hard separation of client and contractor interests, reflected in an external management consultant's report which stated unequivocally that:

> **Merged client and contractor agreements produce conflicts of interest which undermine the quality of commercial decision-making. Best management practice in competitive tendering is achieved where client and contractor responsibilities are separated within different parts of the organisation (Coopers & Lybrand, 1988a, p 7).**

The report recommended that client management should be "completely separate in terms of location and executive responsibility from the commercial provider of services". Such an arrangement would allow the DSO, should it be successful in winning the bid, to be treated no differently from an external private contractor.

The separation of client and contractor functions – previously merged in departments within larger directorates – was achieved through the creation of two discrete bodies. First, all 300 white-collar and 3,000 blue-collar personnel involved in the provision of defined activities under the 1988 LGA were relocated in a 'super-DSO', Eastmet Trading Services (ETS). Each service area (such as, refuse collection, buildings cleaning, grounds maintenance) became a separate cost and business unit under the strategic management of the director of ETS. Staff now owed allegiance to a new organisation, far removed from the traditional corporate culture of the authority. The impression of independence – created among workers, politicians and client departments – was reinforced by the DSO's geographical location in new buildings, and by the encouragement of a distinctive quasi-commercial identity through the introduction of a new 'logo' and uniforms. New managers were recruited from the private sector, charged with implementing ETS's commercial vision and business plans, with price and profit supplanting the traditional concerns of budget management. The aim was that within a year ETS would either divest its individual business units (through management buy-outs or trade sales) or be formed into an 'arm's-length' company; in the meantime, the more it could operate at the margins of the public/private boundary, the more easily it could be transferred to, or be bought out by, the private sector. Its separate identity was furthered by replacing Eastmet's bureaucratic and restrictive management procedures with more flexible arrangements. This allowed Eastmet to work to its own standing orders and develop its own personnel policies tailored to the more competitive environment. ETS's need for accurate and up-to-date financial information, and for powers to vire between capital and expenditure budgets, also led to disengagement from central financial management, auditing and information systems. The relationship between ETS and the corporate centre was placed on a more commercial basis, with central services being costed and traded through service level agreements, designed to ensure that ETS only paid for what it had received. Organisational separation was reinforced by political separation, through the formation of a policy sub-committee to which the DSO was now accountable, and which (through its predominantly radical Conservative membership) ensured continuing political support for ETS's newly defined direction.

Second, the smaller number of personnel performing client management functions for defined activities were relocated within a new unit, Eastmet Strategic Client Agency (ESCA),[15] whose role included aspects of quality and budgetary control, contract monitoring and enforcement, assessment of variation claims, and strategic planning of services in accord with long-term policy objectives. Unlike ETS, which occupied a quasi-autonomous position vis-à-vis the rest of the authority, ESCA was located close to the corporate heart of Eastmet, at the apex of the administrative structure within the chief executive's department.

The separation of client and contractor roles at middle and supervisory management levels was highly disruptive of pre-existing loyalties and working relationships. Colleagues became rivals; friends became strangers. Trust based on personal face-to-face encounters and a sense of common purpose was replaced by mutual suspicion that the 'other side' was shirking its responsibilities. The alienation of ETS personnel was compounded by the perception that ESCA was performing a 'policing' function on behalf of the authority, its continued proximity to the corporate centre causing further resentment. For the buildings cleaning service, the organisational changes did not immediately affect the majority of cleaners in their everyday work, since they tended to be organised at school or end-user, rather than directorate/departmental levels. However, once ETS had won six of the nine buildings cleaning contracts, cleaners also began to feel alienated from the department and fellow workers. Operational management was now supervised from ETS, undermining the authority and responsibility of locally organised school caretakers. Both caretakers and school headteachers feared a deterioration in quality due to loss of control to a remote entity they were not even sure was part of the LA. Such fears proved justified in the early months of the contract when personnel redeployment problems, poor management structures, and lack of equipment disrupted delivery of the service. Fractures opened up between service client and contractor, between contractor and corporate centre, between cleaners and managers, and between headteachers and both service client and contractor.

The disengagement of client and contractor functions from common management structures, together with the lack of bilateral substitutes and the complexity of the new relationships, resulted in heavy reliance on contract as the only formally available governance mechanism. Since inevitable gaps left by incomplete contractual planning could not be filled by other means, managers were driven to further dependence on the contract, whose provisions were interpreted in an increasingly conflictual manner. ESCA began strictly to impose the detailed contractual specifications, including provisions regarding monitoring and penalties. ETS responded by interpreting its obligations as narrowly as possible according to the contract, and by adopting evasive and adversarial tactics. In the ensuing dispute, an internal arbitration panel, chaired by Eastmet's chief executive, heard submissions from both parties. ETS claimed that ESCA's procedures for monitoring and imposing penalties were overzealous and unfair on three major grounds.

First, the default provisions agreed within the contract were being interpreted and applied unreasonably. Alleged unreasonable practices included: awarding default points for what had conventionally, under pre-CCT working conditions, been understood to be minor omissions; monitoring, and awarding default points for, aspects of service delivery not agreed within the specification; monitoring on a daily basis tasks that were supposed to be monitored weekly; issuing default notices without carrying out inspections, or making them at the wrong time; issuing default notices without following the agreed rectification procedure, or without allowing adequate opportunity for rectification (for example, a default notice being sent out at 5.30pm with the penalty being incurred at 7am the following morning); and sending out default notices without giving consideration to valid reasons for failure to clean to the specification (for example, evening events in schools would soil areas cleaned earlier in the evening).

Second, ETS claimed that ESCA's monitoring and default procedures were contrary to commercial custom and practice in the buildings cleaning industry. In most private sector cleaning contracts, accepted good practice involved consultation over methods of issuing and calculating defaults, with some leeway being given for rectification. Also, monitoring would normally be conducted according to an agreed sampling frame, rather than carried out on a room-by-room basis, the absurdity of the latter method being that the DSO would have to achieve a compliance level in excess of 99.5% to avoid financial penalties. ETS claimed that no private contractor would have tolerated such client behaviour, which amounted to discrimination against the DSO. Given inevitable uncertainties over roles and standards in the early months of the contract, and the failure to develop extra-contractual cooperative arrangements where these did not already exist, ESCA's monitoring and default procedures were bound to produce a high level of penalties for the DSO.

Finally, ETS claimed that the financial deductions resulting from ESCA's monitoring and default procedures were not based on a reasonable pre-estimate of loss, and that the penalties of £40,000 in the first 10 months of the contract were out of proportion to the losses actually incurred. ETS argued that no private contractor would have submitted to such a regime, which was vulnerable to legal challenge. Citing legal authority,[16] ETS used common law reasoning to show that the financial compensation provisions in the contract were 'penalty' rather than liquidated damages clauses, and therefore legally unenforceable. The central contention was that, whereas the contractual specification outlined 10 tasks in respect of which payments might be deducted for failures in performance, ESCA had been monitoring and applying default points against 16 different activities. ETS again argued that it was being discriminated against because of its status as internal contractor, and that the only factor preventing successful court action was the absence of separate legal personality.

ESCA submitted in reply that the system for monitoring and defaults was the only available means for disciplining the contractor for performance failures, and ensuring that the authority's fiduciary duties were discharged and not left open to challenge by external audit. It said that the total deductions amounted to little more than 1% of total contract payments, therefore representing good value for money. Nevertheless, the panel was not prepared to accept the high price in terms of deteriorating relationships and poor morale within the authority, whatever the purely financial arguments, and the arbitration was resolved in favour of ETS, with ESCA having to refund 90% of penalty deductions.[17] The dispute proved to be a defining moment in the organisation of buildings cleaning provision within Eastmet, signalling the failure of radical quasi-market reforms and an acknowledgement of the need for more cooperative relationships. If ESCA's room for manoeuvre was limited by its structural position and role, and if conflictual contracting was at least to some degree the logical outcome of the hard client–contractor split, then the problem was fundamental and could only be addressed by further organisational reform.

Soft quasi-market/weak hierarchy: bilateral cooperative contracting in Eastmet from 1990 to the present

Labour gained political control of Eastmet after the local elections in 1990, on a pragmatic platform of protecting internal provision (and the employment prospects of 4,000 DSO workers) and ensuring that the quality of service and of customer relations matched what might be offered by private sector competitors. A number of factors lay behind the change in direction, which involved reversing the competition strategy developed since 1988: the realisation of the negative consequences of attempting to impose hard quasi-commercial relations; political sympathy for public service ideals and mistrust of superficially attractive market-based alternatives; recognition of the need to retain workers' skills within the authority in order to achieve its broad strategic objectives; and the realisation of the dangers posed by LMS, in that headteachers had a free choice in deciding whether to have Eastmet's buildings cleaning and grounds maintenance services, and so might threaten the viability of internal provision by contracting directly with the private sector if standards were not dramatically improved. The need to gain the loyalty of headteachers was regarded as particularly important. To achieve this it was necessary to create a more responsive management structure, which would allow more direct communication between service providers and end clients, and permit the development of more trusting and long-term relationships.

A review by the new administration concluded that the main problems lay with the client rather than the contractor side. To allow the DSO to 'get closer to the customer', it was decided that ESCA should be disbanded. A small, corporate competition unit was retained. Its responsibilities were to: manage the approved list of contractors; develop best contract practice through standard forms; draft service specification in close consultation with end clients; disseminate information on the latest policy changes (such as, secondary legislation, DoE circulars and the Chartered Institute of Public Finance and Accountancy [CIPFA] codes of practice); and standardise the management of contract packaging, evaluation, letting and award. Operational client functions (such as monitoring, managing default procedures, dealing with variations, invoicing and financial management) were returned to the respective directorates. For general buildings cleaning, each directorate for whom the service was provided nominated a client officer with whom ETS could liaise. For schools cleaning, since LMS had devolved financial and other management powers to headteachers (most schools having decided not to opt out of the service provided by ETS), each of the headteachers became an individual client point.[18]

Although the DSO remained organisationally separate and relatively autonomous, it was realised that client-side reorganisation was insufficient in itself to improve the buildings cleaning service, and that some change in practice and attitudes on the contractor side was also necessary. ETS was encouraged by the corporate centre to improve its tarnished image with end clients by adopting a less 'commercial' and more conciliatory approach, which would support the case for reletting contracts to the DSO when the second round of tendering began. The corporate centre played a large part in overseeing the changes in the early months of the reorganisation. It also helped to reintegrate the strategic interests of ETS within the authority's broader corporate strategy. It did this by clarifying its mediating role should relations between ETS and end clients deteriorate, by encouraging pragmatism and realism in relationships with the aim of avoiding disputes, by checking that variation and default procedures were being used correctly, and by reviewing the DSO's financial position on a monthly basis to ensure that targets were being achieved. At the political level, more effective mechanisms for accounting for ETS's performance were introduced, so that reports were now made directly to specialist service committees (for example, in schools buildings cleaning to the Education Committee) rather than to a general sub-committee as had previously been the case.

These organisational reforms have led to a significant reduction in conflict, and to the general displacement of contract as the principal means of ensuring and adjusting performance. In part, the improvement has been due to better communications and the 'getting closer to the customer' philosophy, allowing end clients greater input into the design of contract specification (for example, with regard to task description, frequencies and quality thresholds), and greater participation in the management and delivery of services. The most radical change in governance has occurred with respect to monitoring and default procedures. Once ESCA was disbanded, ETS became more visible to end clients through a more clearly defined structure of site supervisors, area supervisors, and area managers, with more direct channels for communicating problems over service delivery. The emphasis shifted from third party enforcement to contractor self-monitoring, with service quality being guaranteed through improvements in ETS's training and management structures. For the second round of tendering, and for contracts agreed with individual headteacher clients, ETS was required to conform to the widely accepted quality control and assurance system BS 5750. This system has been complemented by other extra-contractual governance mechanisms, such as consumer (end client) satisfaction surveys and neighbourhood forums. The result has been a less adversarial method of monitoring and dealing with problems relating to service quality. Rather than solutions being sought in the detail of contractual specification and in rigid adherence to contract conditions, the contract is displaced and supplemented by processes which encourage the contractor continuously to make improvements, without the need for recourse to punitive default procedures.

Contractual procedures for variation have been more closely followed, although the more cooperative use of contract since reorganisation is again explained partly by the more direct relationship that now exists between ETS and end clients. Whereas previously ESCA had administered variations in task and cost due to changes in floor coverings, frequency of cleans, and use of rooms, end clients now raise their own variation orders. These are sent to ETS for costing, and returned to end clients for checking and authorisation. The costing procedure is complex and relies on inputting relevant data into a computer database so the price can be adjusted according to the change in task.

Although strong emphasis is placed on the contract as a planning mechanism, and planned procedures for variation are generally adhered to, effective performance is achieved through displacing the contract and supplementing it with other forms of governance. This flexibility has helped to develop trusting and cooperative relationships between ETS and end users. Since the reorganisation, there have been no disputes requiring 'external' mediation. Despite considerable central intervention in the transitional restructuring period, which brought to the fore some of the hierarchical aspects of hybrid organisation, the role of hierarchy remained 'weak' in the sense that there was still no *common* operational management structure which would integrate client and contractor in a direct trilateral relationship. Instead, the corporate hierarchy, or strategic centre, was concerned primarily with establishing the relational conditions under which bilateral cooperation could develop, and with discouraging opportunistic behaviour and ensuring fair play between the parties.

Strong hierarchy/integrated quasi-market: trilateral cooperative contracting in Westmet

Prior to CCT, Westmet's buildings cleaning service was the responsibility of five separate service departments, with the Education Department employing the majority of cleaners. The service was packaged for competitive tendering as five contracts, with existing staff, organisational and managerial structures being retained rather than reorganised prior to submission of the internal bid. Contract preparation, specification, tendering, evaluation and award were carried out by the corporate centre, ensuring standardisation with other CCT services and conformity with legislation. Although two contracts were awarded to small local companies employing around five operatives each, the other three were won in-house, including the high value schools cleaning contract, for which there had been no private sector bids. The following discussion focuses on the organisation and governance of the school buildings cleaning service.

The continued location of client and contractor within the Education Department, with minimal change in working practices, reporting procedures and managerial responsibilities, may be described as a 'soft' quasi-market integrated within a common hierarchical management structure. Client and contractor interests were formally separated for financial purposes, to enable the tracking of income and expenditure for internal and external audit, and the preparation of annual reports to the DoE. There was also a degree of organisational separation in that some designated staff had more client-oriented responsibilities (fleshing out the specification, carrying out reactive monitoring and service development), while others exercised contractor functions (line management for cleaning supervisors, training, and staff development). However, there was a blurring of roles, with operational managers on client and contractor sides occupying the same or adjacent office space, and routine collaboration over problems of interpretation and implementation. Also, the assistant directors remained 'two-hatted' in their responsibilities, with the director of the department, rather than the authority's chief executive, exercising the formal arbitration role. From the outset the view within Westmet was that further clarification and separation of the client role would only be necessary in the event of the contract being won by the private sector.

Organisational continuity allowed pre-existing cooperative practices to persist, and enabled the parties to draw on a reservoir of trust and goodwill. Problems that arose in the early stages of implementation of CCT could be resolved informally, without the need for excessive reliance on more formal processes. For example, headteachers had been worried initially that staff redeployment and reorganisation might result in loss of quality in the cleaning service. Client officers responded by bending over backwards in the help, reassurance and advice they gave, with the result that headteachers came to appreciate the value of the client function, and rapidly gained confidence in the new system. Once teething problems had been addressed, informal governance remained a feature of the Westmet contract, encouraged by the short lines of communication inherent in the structures that had survived reorganisation. All parties involved in the schools building cleaning service – school heads, caretakers and cleaners, as well as service client and contractor – still felt a sense of 'belonging' to the Education Department, which they trusted to look after 'their' interests.[19] When operational cleaning problems arose, cleaners and caretakers cooperated to prevent the departmental hierarchy becoming formally involved, with flexibility and speed of response being usually achieved through face-to-face or voice-to-voice channels. Where a complaint was brought to the attention of the client officer carrying out reactive monitoring, the problem would typically be dealt with by telephoning the appropriate cleaning supervisor or caretaker, or by an office chat with the contractor managers, without the need for paper-passing or any further formal action. For example, the common complaint that tables had not been cleaned was dealt with through involving all concerned parties, without reference to the contract. If the problem persisted (most cleaners would wipe more regularly than the contractual specification if requested to do so) the usual practice was for the client to review a cleaner's workload, and indicate to the headteacher where time savings might be made. The generally cooperative environment contributed to a high level of organisational learning, which minimised uncertainty and disruption in the transition from one form of organisation to the other.

The persistence of informal hierarchical norms and working practices under CCT enabled gaps in the buildings cleaning contract to be cooperatively filled; planning failures that had proved disastrous in the Eastmet contract were unproblematic in Westmet. While contractual planning was relatively complete as regards specification (price, quantities, frequencies, locations, materials, personnel) and delivery (monitoring, variations, defaults, disputes resolution and termination), many aspects of performance nonetheless remained unclear. The standard of cleanliness required of the successful contractor was vague: "locations should be cleaned to a standard which is in all respects to the entire satisfaction of the Council", with the caveat that the client will not deduct payment for 'minor' deficiencies (such as failure to empty a wastepaper basket) unless these occur regularly. The case studies of Eastmet and other authorities show how the wide discretion left to officers in interpreting such terms could lead to adversarial practices, either through opportunistic client use of contract terms, through grudges held by staff who have an 'axe to grind' because they resent their new roles under CCT, or through the professional/technical experience of officers ("contracts are technical documents no different from those I have interpreted for engineering road repairs").[20] However, the cooperative organisational arrangements within Westmet have avoided such outcomes: there is little risk of opportunism in such a soft quasi-market; staff roles have remained substantially similar despite some reorganisation and retraining; managers in key positions have neither incentive nor experience to implement inappropriate legalistic regimes.

Although the client, through caretaking supervisors, carries out low-level monitoring as laid down broadly within the contract conditions, the many gaps in the contract have meant that in practice the details of monitoring procedure have had to be developed post-award. The contract is supplemented by random pro-active monitoring (approximately 10 per week) on those sites that have incurred high levels of headteacher complaint. However, since the contract specifications are not explicit on standards, these are worked out with reasonable reference to past practice, central directives, and the requirements of health and safety and other relevant legislation. A basic report form is used to record site visits, with ticks and crosses denoting whether rooms have passed or failed. An opportunity to rectify poor performance is given prior to default, the usual practice being for supervisors to convene a meeting or contact by phone all those affected so that the problem may be resolved without formal action having to be taken. Again, such procedures are not specified in the contract plan. Flexibility, reasonableness and common sense allow past cooperative working practices to continue, with caretakers, for example, helping cleaners if there has been an evening function making the school dirtier than normal, so that headteachers will be satisfied and the risk of failing a morning inspection avoided.

Not surprisingly, since there have been few problems that could not be resolved informally, the procedures laid down in the contract for defaults and penalties (based on a sliding scale of deductions should the number of default points in any given year or month reach a certain level) have been generally redundant. In circumstances where the formal default procedure *could* have been used due to technical breach of contract, this outcome has generally been avoided, such that the contract may be described as having been displaced as well as supplemented as a governance mechanism. Rather than using the elaborate contractual default procedure, deductions from payment to the DSO for defective performance are determined according to a semi-formal (extra-contractual) system based on fairness to both client and contractor. The issue is rarely one of simple compensation, or of literal interpretation over whether or not a 'breach' has occurred; the parties recognise that the formal procedure with its tariff of compensation might take the personal element out of the transaction, encouraging bad faith and mistrust, and undermining departmental solidarity. So in all these cases – with regard to standards, monitoring and defaults – 'cooperative trilateral' solutions to potential problems have predominated, based on well-established practices that existed prior to CCT. This has resulted in minimum disruption and maximum quality of service delivery in the new environment.

The only example of procedures laid down in the contract being closely followed in practice concerns variation. Contractual variations are the formal means whereby the constantly changing demand for cleaning services can be registered and costed, allowing financial adjustments to be made to the contract price in a predetermined manner, and satisfying the DSO's legislative audit and reporting requirements. The function of accounting for so many complex monetary gains and losses requires the use of a computerised management system as specified in the contract. This could not be achieved informally or extra-contractually.[21] Cooperative exchange has been achieved by using contract sparingly and in ways that have complemented, rather than superseded, existing formal and informal governance. There have been no disputes of significance, and certainly none requiring formal resolution, so the director of the Education Department has not been called on to perform an internal arbitration role.

Conclusion

In LAs where the adoption of hard quasi-market structures has resulted in transaction–management problems, a more sophisticated understanding has arisen of the organisational conditions that enable trusting and cooperative relationships to be developed. The case studies show how services may be provided satisfactorily by DSOs through either trilateral or bilateral client-contractor arrangements.[22] On either basis, contracts may play a positive role in clarifying responsibilities, improving accountability, communicating information, channelling potential conflict, and improving service quality through better specification. However, the case studies also suggest that good client–contractor relationships are likely to be characterised by *flexible* resort to, and displacement of, contract – which may be supplemented in the case of trilateral organisation by formal and informal hierarchical governance, and in the case of bilateral organisation by extra-contractual quasi-market governance.[23]

Irrespective of how quasi-markets are organised, efficient and effective service provision is likely to be heavily dependent on the maintenance of trusting and cooperative relationships. The easiest way to encourage such relationships and reduce transaction management costs within LAs would be to abolish (perhaps subject to the attainment of efficiency targets) the requirement for retendering, or at least to increase the periods between compulsory tendering.[24] Even with the relaxation of CCT, it appears highly likely that quasi-markets will continue to be a feature of LA organisation into the 1990s and beyond.[25]

Postscript

The Labour government's intention to abolish CCT was announced in a written Parliamentary Answer by the Minister for Local Government on 2 June 1997. Under the new Best Value framework which is to replace CCT (see DETR, 'Best Value criteria' and 'A framework for Best Value in England', 14 November 1997) councils will be required, inter alia, to set standards, to establish mechanisms for monitoring and evaluating service provision, to maintain trading accounts, and to allow stricter public audit and comparability with other local authority providers through 'benchmarking'. Balanced against the new mandatory requirements will be greater flexibility for councils to decide how services should be provided, in contrast to the restrictive specification of process that applies under CCT, but with powerful central government sanctions for failure to meet new standards. The question that follows from the conclusion to our chapter is how this policy movement away from overt compulsion is likely to impact on the competitive internal contracting arrangements that have developed under CCT.

Our provisional answer is that there are unlikely to be significant practical changes in the role of contract and competition in the internal provision of local authority services, at least in the short term. The reasons are various. CCT will run in parallel with the Best Value framework in 40 pilot local authorities for two to three years before the details of the abolition of CCT and its replacement are finalised. The transitional period is likely to see mutual interpenetration of new and old ideas and practices, with much of the discipline associated with CCT being retained in less prescriptive form in the Best Value authorities.

The new framework, if implemented as presently conceived, is likely to have the effect of imposing informally a range of regulatory, monitoring and enforcement constraints that are not dissimilar to the formal requirements that operate under CCT. It may be argued that Labour's current policy on the role of competition in local public services provision is characterised by continuity with the past rather than by any radical disjunction, and that this continuity will be reinforced practically through the transitional arrangements.

Generally, the Best Value guidance makes explicit a presumption in favour of 'open competition' as against other public management tools, such as benchmarking, that might also be used to demonstrate improvements in service performance. Contract might be expected to continue to play a significant role under the Best Value framework as the natural adjunct to voluntary competitive processes. Quite apart from central government pressures, local authorities are likely to want to retain and develop contracting arrangements that potentially permit a degree of control over service provision that might not be available were more radical service-providing alternatives to be adopted, involving the complete transfer of functions outside the public sector and/or their vesting in independent companies.

Acknowledgements

We are grateful to Eoin Reeves for acting as discussant at the seminar, and to those who contributed and subsequently commented on the paper. This chapter is an abridged version of an article which appears in *Local Government Studies* (Vincent-Jones and Harries, 1996b). This chapter draws on work undertaken in connection with a research project for which the support of the ESRC is gratefully acknowledged (R000 236416).

Notes

[1] Most services subject to CCT under the 1988 LGA are 'internally' provided. Although DSO success measured by the proportion of contracts won declined from 75% in December 1991 to 60% in December 1995, the proportion of contract value awarded internally according to the later survey was still 75% – see Local Government Management Board (1995).

[2] It will be assumed that high levels of trust and cooperation are indicative of optimal service provision, and correspondingly that conflict and the absence

of trust are suggestive of both dynamic and operational inefficiency – see Deakin and Wilkinson (1996). While the high costs of managing and adjusting conflictual transactions might be outweighed by financial savings in some cases, there is likely to be a strong association between trust/cooperation and efficiency. A high level of contractual conflict is also likely to be culturally damaging in terms of antagonistic relations within the organisation, and to detract from the quality of the service (through interruptions, poor morale, and so on) to the ultimate consumer. For a development of Zucker's (1986) distinction between 'process-based' and 'institutional-based' trust in the local government context see Seal and Vincent-Jones (1996).

[3] Following the development of Coase's seminal observations on markets and firms as alternative means of organising transactions in the 'new institutional economics' (for example, Williamson, 1985), there appears to have been relatively little application of the transactions-costs perspective either in relation to hybrid forms (but see Powell, 1990; Schanze, 1991; Stinchcombe, 1985; Thorelli, 1986; Williamson, 1991a) or in specific regard to the public sector. For a theoretical discussion of 'internal hybrid' organisation within LAs, see Vincent-Jones and Harries (1996b). 'External hybrid' organisation occurs where the form of institutional arrangement, in addition to being neither hierarchy nor market, is also intersectoral (that is, 'intermediate between' public and private sectors). Obvious examples are joint ventures in which the LA shares ownership and control with a private firm. Hybrid organisation may also obtain in situations where there is no common ownership, and where the parties are more completely separated: management buy-outs, in which entire parts of the authority are in effect privatised, may also satisfy the definition where the new business continues to use the same premises, workforce and facilities as existed prior to the transfer – see Vincent-Jones (1996).

[4] Defined activities under the 1988 LGA Section 2(2) are refuse collection, buildings and other cleaning, school and welfare and other catering, vehicle maintenance, and ground maintenance. Further activities included by order of the Secretary of State exercising powers under Section 2(3) are: sport and leisure services management (added in 1989); on-street parking, security, vehicle fleet management, housing management, legal, construction and property services (all added in 1994), and information technology, finance, and personnel (added in 1995).

[5] Although the contract is not legally enforceable in internal transactions, because the DSO lacks separate legal personality, there appears to be no

material difference in the role of contract in internal and external exchanges – see Walsh and Davis (1993) paragraph 2.31.

[6] The Secretary of State has the power to determine financial objectives under the 1988 LGA Section 10(2). DoE circular 19/88 requires a 5% rate of return for all defined activities except buildings cleaning, which must break even. Under DoE circular 12/94 ('Financial objectives specifications 1994') the objective of breaking even is further specified as including "a capital financing charge of 6% of the value of fixed assets used in the provision of the service".

[7] 1988 LGA, Section 11.

[8] The DoE became the Department of the Environment, Transport and the Regions [DETR] in 1997.

[9] A further aspect of hierarchy – the ultimate control exercised by central government through the DoE and the Secretary of State – will not be considered specifically here. The 16 years of Conservative government, previous to Labour coming to power in May 1997, have seen a vast increase in the powers of the central state at the expense of local government – see Loughlin (1994); Vincent-Jones (1996).

[10] On the importance of hierarchy in M-form and similarly disaggregated organisations, Simon has commented:

> **A major use of authority in organisations is to coordinate behaviour by promulgating standards and rules of the road, thus allowing actors to form more stable expectations about the behaviour of the environment (including the behaviour of the other actors). (1991, p 39)**

[11] 'Westmet' metropolitan authority serves a population of around 210,000 encompassing a mixture of rural/farming and inner-city/industrial constituencies, and has 11,500 employees organised in 10 service directorates.

[12] Central government controls aimed at eradicating anti-competitive practices and stimulating competition have been extended following the provisions excluding 'non-commercial considerations' in the awarding of contracts under the 1988 LGA section 17. See DoE circular 10/93 'Competition in the provision of local authority services' and Local

Government (Direct Service Organisations) (Competition) Regulations 1993 (SI 1993/848).

[13] Although in theory school heads are free to opt out of LA buildings cleaning provision, in practice most have opted in, making use of the authority's client CCT function to avoid the higher transaction costs of contracting independently.

[14] 'Eastmet' metropolitan authority serves a population of 490,000 mainly inner-city constituencies, and has 20,000 employees organised in nine service directorates.

[15] The strategic client agency employed around 30 personnel divided into four sections: administration, cleaning and catering services (such as, school and welfare catering, other catering, and buildings cleaning), leisure management, and technical and environmental services (refuse collection, street cleaning, grounds maintenance, and vehicle maintenance).

[16] *Dunlop Pneumatic Tyre Co Ltd v New Garage and Motor Co Ltd* [1915] AC 79.

[17] The hybrid nature of the authority's role is well illustrated in this internal arbitration process. On the one hand, the panel is supposedly independent, hearing submissions and reaching decisions as if it were a court, and as if the 'parties' were legally separate entities. On the other hand, the panel represents the apex of the hierarchy of which client and contractor are both a part, and may be expected to make decisions on the basis of administrative and policy criteria only indirectly connected with the specific issues in contention. However, faced with the threat of further internal disintegration, hierarchical considerations prevailed over quasi-market ones. ETS's use and understanding of legal arguments shows how the logic of a 'hard' quasi-market split pushed the contractor in this instance to the edges of the boundary of public sector organisation.

[18] In a sense, the effect of LMS was analogous to a 300-fold increase in Eastmet's directorate structure. Subsequent secondary legislation (1988 LGA [Defined Activities] [Exemption] [Small Schools] Order 1992) reduced the number of client points by exempting primary schools from CCT. However, such schools have in practice invited ETS to provide their buildings cleaning, thereby avoiding the substantial transaction costs involved in employing their own contractors and drawing up new management systems.

[19] That such cooperation cannot be taken for granted is evident in the case study of Northern Metropolitan, another authority within the current research programme. Here cleaners and caretakers were more clearly separated, with caretakers protecting headteachers' interests and cleaners identifying with departmental DSO interests. Conflicts and tensions multiplied here as personal trust in previously close supervisory relations was eroded – see Vincent-Jones and Harries (1996a).

[20] This occurred in Northern Metropolitan (n 19 supra) where officers with engineering contracting backgrounds were brought in to perform monitoring tasks.

[21] There have been approximately 60 formal variations per year since the contract began. However, even here there have been many instances of displacement of the formal variation procedure, as occurred in the case of the problem of dirty tables referred to above.

[22] In one sense the experience of buildings cleaning in Westmet and the restructured Eastmet was similar, in the trend towards schools becoming 'active clients' in the contract management process, and in the corresponding declining role of the authority service client. However, important differences remain: within Eastmet, the DSO operates with a quasi-commercial ethos and enjoys substantial autonomy from the rest of the authority, whereas within Westmet, service clients, contractor, cleaners and end client have remained departmentally integrated.

[23] The present study provides specific support for one of the main conclusions of Walsh's research, that "the major factors making for effective contract management were trust, problem resolution, and a proper mixture of formality and informality" (Walsh and Davis, 1993, para 9.5).

[24] There is already some evidence of such a softening of competition policy in the recent decision to extend blue-collar contract periods to between five and 10 years, and in the greater flexibility LAs now have in choosing which areas of newly defined white-collar services should be exempt from the compulsory programme – see the 1988 LGA (Defined Activities) (Specified Period) (England) Regulations (SI 1995/2484).

[25] For greater elaboration of an argument in support of this claim, see Vincent-Jones (1996).

TWO

The X-efficiency properties of competitive tendering
Robert McMaster

Introduction

During the past few years the provision of state services has been subject to radical change. This has essentially been characterised by the loosening of the state monopoly over the delivery of welfare activities. Compulsory competitive tendering (CCT) of certain health and local authority (LA) activities has been followed by 'quasi-market' (Le Grand, 1991) reforms in health, education and housing. The theoretical basis of these reforms is the *agency-orientated* public choice models of state provision or bureaucracy referred to hereafter as 'public choice agency theory' (PCAT).

In a seminal contribution, Niskanen (1968; 1971) applied standard economic assumptions to non-market institutions and showed that such institutions are inherently allocatively inefficient relative to competitive markets. However, unlike private monopoly firms, monopoly state providers produce *too much* output. Later refinements to Niskanen's basic model de-emphasised the weighting of this finding, highlighting instead the intrinsic X-inefficiency of state services (where X-efficiency refers to the gains in efficiency achieved by a well-motivated workforce which maximises effort on particular tasks) (for instance see, Migue and Belanger, 1974; Orzechowski, 1977; Peacock, 1983). PCAT theorists base their findings on two primary assumptions: that bureaucratic agents display the tenets of *homo economicus* (basically man is an egoistical, self-interested, utility maximiser), and that information is asymmetrically distributed in their favour (Mueller, 1989). Self-interested bureaucrats will exploit this advantage to the detriment of service users. The PCAT approach perceives the efficiency problem of state provision to be a result of underlying agency difficulties (for an outline of agency theory see Fama and Jensen, 1983). Correspondingly, PCAT asserts that introducing the market mechanism through competition for delivery of services will alleviate information asymmetries and constrain agents' discretionary potential, that is, impede their ability to shirk and other cost-raising activities to their benefit. Quasi-markets adjust bureaucrats' incentives in an efficient manner; the agency problem is resolved.

There is a strong a priori case for asserting that such a course of action would lead to improvements in X-efficiency. Leibenstein and Maital define X-efficiency as,

> ... [T]he failure of a productive unit to fully utilise the resources it commands and hence attain its efficiency frontier – the maximum level of output possible under prevailing resources and circumstances. (1994, p 252)[1]

Moreover, X-efficiency is sensitive to influences which are both internal (motivation and orientation of workers) and external (competitiveness of the environment) (Leibenstein, 1989). By subjecting state bureaucracies to external competition, external conditions adjust in an efficiency-enhancing manner and the prevailing informational asymmetry is eliminated.

The growing empirical literature on the contracting out of state activities, prima facie, makes the PCAT case compelling. The vast majority of those studies have identified significant cost savings as a consequence of competition, and private delivery, over a range of local and health authority activities. These include residential care, hospital domestics, and refuse collection (see, among others, Domberger et al, 1986; 1987; 1995; Knapp, 1986; Milne and McGee, 1992; Szymanski and Wilkins, 1993). These results suggest that there is an extremely attractive case for pursuing market-orientated policies in other areas of state activities that are not currently subject to any form of competitive process.

This chapter questions the robustness of the X-efficiency predictions of the PCAT model. PCAT implicitly assumes a pervading conflict of interest between principals and agents and low-trust relations. These presumptions are challenged within the context of Leibenstein's X-efficiency framework. In this chapter it will be argued that the role of conventions and trust are important influences on agents' motivation, effort and hence X-efficiency. Beyond the standard economic account of utility maximisation the PCAT model includes little about motivational influences. Consequently, the model offers no more than a special case of a more general phenomenon. From here the chapter applies the central argument to the context of competitive tendering (CT). It contends that the process of CT adjusts prevailing conventions, and by so doing can act as a signal of distrust. Far from increasing agents' effort, an inappropriate implementation of CT can demotivate agents and crowd out X-efficiency.

X-efficiency and trust: an interpretation of Leibenstein

Effort and conventions

Leibenstein (1966, p 406) argues that agent effort is a principal internal influence on X-efficiency. Effort is composed of four elements: *activity* (A), *pace* (P), *quality* (Q), and *time* (T) (Leibenstein, 1975, p 589). Activities constitute the employee's task, pace is the rate at which work is performed, quality refers to the standard of output, and time relates to the time pattern of work. These elements are not mutually exclusive and each element may, as Frantz (1988, p 75) observes, display feedback properties. For instance, the pace at which tasks are performed can entail quality ramifications. The 'choice' of a particular level for a given element carries implications for other aspects of effort. Effort is composed of APQT bundles, which are variable depending on the influences on the individual. Each APQT bundle is associated with a productivity value, which is the agent's contribution to the value of output and may be known or unknown, and a utility value for effort expended. Individuals are assumed to derive satisfaction from the expenditure of effort, as well as income gained (Leibenstein, 1976, p 102; Shen, 1985, p 393). The choice of effort is likely to involve some individual discretion as "[t]he individual must in some way choose or interpret the job" (Frantz, 1988, p 75). An individual's intertemporal utility will influence the choice of effort made, (see Shen, 1992). In other words, employment relations are sufficiently incomplete as to permit individual employees some latitude in interpreting not only what constitutes performance in some circumstances, but also relevant inputs, or effort (see Fox, 1974; Simon, 1991).

According to Leibenstein (1976; 1979) and Frantz (1988) actors interpret their jobs in terms of effort positions, where satisfaction exhibits diminishing returns as effort increases. Near the plateau of the effort-utility contour lies an agent's inert area. The individual is assumed to consider that every effort-utility level below the inert area is inferior to those within the area. This implies that in circumstances of low effort the individual is dissatisfied, in effect bored, and it is beneficial for the individual to increase effort. The reverse holds for greater effort levels beyond the inert area. Leibenstein (1975; 1979) holds that agents' effort positions will tend to remain within inert areas, since the costs of moving will be considered to be greater than or equal to any gain in satisfaction. Frantz (1988) observes that the inert area is analogous to imperfections in the human sensory system, where awareness of the environment is reduced due to habitual behaviour or routines. Individuals are resistant to any change that threatens the inert area, given established preferences. A shift in the effort-utility contour caused by, for instance, more intensive vertical monitoring, by an agent's superiors, would be resisted if this shift resulted in an effort position outside of the actor's inert area. The upper bound of the inert area is assumed to lie below the X-efficient effort level (Frantz, 1988). As noted, external pressure, via the competitive process, is seen as the catalyst of inducing internal pressures consistent with efficient effort positions.

Peer group influences, hierarchical relations, and historical influences, such as specific working method, act as constraints to agents seeking their own inert areas. More recently, Leibenstein has claimed that agents will generally adhere to those determinants since individuals:

> **... care about how others feel about their behaviour, and care about the sanctions that others may impose on them if they choose effort levels that are very different from historical effort levels or average observed effort levels. (Leibenstein, 1984, p 82)**

In other words, individuals display loyalty and some mutual value set (Simon, 1991). The institutional space agents inhabit influences their behaviour. Individual effort is influenced by (institutional) conventions, emulation, as well as discretion (Leibenstein, 1987, p 607).

The relationship between effort and conventions represents a considerable shift in emphasis in Leibenstein's work. In his 1975 *Bell Journal of Economics* and 1979 *Journal of Economic Literature* papers, and in *Beyond economic man* (1976), he adopts a highly individualistic approach; no reference is made to the role of institutional conventions. However, his 1984 *Journal of Institutional and Theoretical Economics (JITE)* paper on conventions suggested a loosening of this individualistic position. By recognising conventions, Leibenstein admits that forces beyond the individual are involved in *moulding* as opposed to constraining individual preferences. It also carries with it important considerations for Leibenstein's assertion that competition is the sole conveyor of efficiency. Disruptions to conventions can lead to *less* effort, as discussed below. Frantz's (1988) explicit recognition of the role of habits and routines reinforces this view.

Although Leibenstein does not explicitly state the dominant influence on effort, a case could be argued for assigning this role to conventions (see Shen, 1992, for an alternative approach based on individual utility). Leibenstein perceives conventions as coordination games and regularities in behaviour, where individuals prefer, expect, and, conform to the regularity. Conventions influence an individual's effort position in the same way throughout history, and through the observed average behaviour of peers (emulation). Any significant departure from those norms is likely to lead to the imposition of sanctions on the deviant individual. In this way, conventions influence the parameters of an individual's inert area. In other words, the existence of sanctions prevents individuals from freeriding,[2] thereby limiting the scope of individual discretion, and maintaining the convention. Such conventions, Leibenstein (1989, p 266) argues, will be persistently sub-optimal since no individual may gain from any shift to an 'optimal' convention.

Trust

Leibenstein (1987, p 606) argues that conventions are a partial solution to trust deficits particularly in employment relations characterised by incompleteness. Conventions convey mutual limited trust, confined to the bounds of a specific situation within a certain value range.

Trust has three distinct characteristics: it enhances efficiency; it is sensitive to 'substitutes'; and it cannot be traded (Leibenstein, 1987, p 600). This draws from Arrow's (1974) well-quoted passage on the importance of trust as an externality ensuring economic activity. Leibenstein does not define trust, but his use of the concept is consistent with much of the literature. His application is compatible with the definition of trust given by Fox (1974), Rowley and Elgin (1985), and Zucker (1986) in terms of the diminution of uncertainty, where actors have confident expectations regarding the conduct of other actors. It is also compatible with Khalil's (1994, p 339) observation that trust has to do with intention or motivation. It is consistent with Simon's (1991) view that trust must involve some degree of reciprocity, and mutual value orientation, and Dasgupta's (1988) contention that trust is acquired over time, but can be demolished instantaneously. For instance, Leibenstein (1987, p 603) states that where trust is feigned and detected it would be 'almost impossible' to establish future trust with the individual(s) concerned.

Even in situations of limited trust the foregoing is applicable within the confines of established conventions. This argument is not unique to Leibenstein; it is emphasised in the relational exchange literature. Goldberg (1980) and Macneil (1982) observe that where contracts are incomplete a considerable amount of resources will be allocated to the establishment of conventions, that is, in constructing a vehicle for conveying trust.

Trust, as conveyed by conventions, is considered by Leibenstein to be particularly effective in promoting efficiency since moral hazard is either diminished or eliminated. This is because *peer-group* benchmarks and sanctions potentially mitigate against freeriding. Intuitively, in the context of Alchian and Demsetz's (1972) team production, the efficiency properties of trust are especially important. However, Leibenstein does not comment on the ability of the process of trust to diminish adverse selection of a provider. Dasgupta's (1988) point as to the time characteristics of trust is of relevance here. Since trust is fragile and takes time to establish, and has to involve some mutual value orientation, then adverse selection problems are avoided to some extent.

Given this, the dilution of trust accompanied by its substitution by more formal behavioural constraints – such as insurance, monitoring, sanctions, rewards for performance fulfilment, litigation, as well as various combinations of those 'substitutes' – risks inefficiency. Specifically, there are three principal costs: opportunity costs of transactions forgone; ex post facto contractual difficulties associated with behavioural uncertainty (moral hazard); the costs of trust substitutes, (Leibenstein, 1987, p 604). Arguably, the imposition of any of the foregoing trust substitutes can be interpreted as a signal of *dis*trust, with a consequent reduction in efficiency. It is not immediately obvious that Leibenstein attaches any particular weighting to any one of the foregoing substitutes. However, within the context of the employment relation, it can be argued that he views trust as being more sensitive to monitoring than to potential sanctions *associated with conventions*. He states:

> [M]onitoring is likely to diminish or eliminate trust. In this connection who carries out the monitoring and in whose interest it is carried out are important questions. (Leibenstein, 1987, p 604)

In the context of the employment relation, monitoring, and accompanying sanctions, are most likely to be vertical, whereas sanctions derived from conventions are associated with the individual's peers, (Leibenstein, 1987, p 609). In other words, *intensive* monitoring infringes on the reciprocity property of trust to a much greater degree than conventions which convey trust. This point will be returned to in the following section.

Leibenstein's analysis of trust contrasts with PCAT, where a low-trust syndrome is tacitly assumed. Effort is assumed as a disutility to individuals who extract utility from shirking (see, among others, Fama and Jensen, 1983). Since there is no role for conventions in PCAT, effort is solely determined by either constraints to discretionary behaviour (in the form of penalties) or by manipulating individuals' incentive sets so that they are complementary to the interests of the principal's (residual claimant). By contrast, Leibenstein's recognition of conventions appears to offer a more generalised approach, where the restrictive low-trust assumption can be relaxed. The following section develops this more fully in the context of competitive tendering activities for health authorities (HAs) and LAs.

Whither competitive tendering?

CCT commenced in 1983 with various instructions to the HAs to tender for so-called hotel services (catering, domestics, and laundry), with the extension of the initiative to other ancillary activities, such as portering and patient transport either implemented or proposed. LAs were mandated to tender for specified services by the 1980 Land Planning Act. CCT was introduced and extended by the 1988 and 1992 Local Government Acts (LGAs). Among activities designated for CCT were catering, various types of cleaning, refuse collection, and selected managerial activities.

Health and local authorities and the provision of services

Since its inception, the NHS in the UK has been subject to various organisational initiatives all of which, until the 1980s, tended to retain the dominating influence of clinicians and the Hippocratic ethos, particularly in operational matters. The Hippocratic ethos essentially emphasises a clinician's, especially a doctor's, duty of care to his/her patients. Patient welfare is paramount, the raison d'être of clinicians. A similar welfarist ethos is also claimed to pervade the activities of LAs, but is manifested in a more disparate fashion. For example, Dunleavy (1991, p 242) argues that "[state] agencies are expected to foster desirable social objectives". Examples include generous employment practices, a client orientation that involves 'acting in the spirit of the law', and 'thoroughly investigating grievances and complaints'.

The conventional view of the Hippocratic/welfarist ethos has been challenged by Hartley (1990), who argues that authorities often deliver 'Rolls Royce' service standards that do not necessarily benefit patients, but primarily benefit providers. Hartley (1990, p 185) draws attention to the purchase of expensive sophisticated medical equipment of little additional benefit to patients, but which gives clinicians satisfaction by applying new technology. In Hartley's view, there is a valid efficiency-based argument for reducing the influence of clinicians. Recent initiatives, such as the development of the internal market, appear to have reduced embedded clinical influence in the face of increased reliance on the price mechanism accompanied by greater managerial influence (see Strong and Robinson, 1990; Reed and Anthony, 1993). This argument extends to LAs, where an increased role for the price mechanism will lead LAs to a more efficient location on their cost–quality frontier.

CCT represents an increase in the role of the price mechanism, but, a priori, has less direct influence on the position of the core bundle of activities. However, there may be an indirect influence through the relationship between ancillary and core activities, although differences are likely to be observed between HAs and LAs. Specifically, the provision of LA services is more disparate than the supply of healthcare. Refuse collection and teaching have little in common in terms of delivery, whereas HA activities are more site specific.[3] Ascher (1987) notes that certain health ancillary activities complement aspects of core activities. She emphasises that domestic work and portering are ancillary services with a close relationship to nursing; domestics, porters and nurses are perceived to be part of a team, especially in patient recuperation. Arguably, this implies that the Hippocratic ethos pervades some ancillary services. Core and ancillary activities in the health service share common values, and hence, conventions. This raises two points relating to X-efficiency theory: APQT bundles are influenced by the Hippocratic/welfarist ethos, and established APQT bundles are supported by trust.

Given the persuasiveness of the Hippocratic ethos it can be argued that actors engaged in ancillary activities will be well disposed to the well-being of patients. Whynes argues that, generally, in the public sector,

> **[i]ndividuals ... genuinely care for those who demand their services, and ... are willing, in the normal course of their duties, to offer more than the minimum. (1993, p 444)**

Simon (1991) asserts that this property is not only confined to the public sector; individuals display loyalty traits in any organisation. He states:

> **The question is not whether freeriders exist – much less employees who exert something less than their maximum – but why there is anything *besides* freeriding. Why do many workers ... exert more than minimally enforceable effort? (Simon, 1991, p 34)**

This is similar to Akerlof's (1982) well-cited argument that effort in employment relation is a "partial gift". He draws on examples from case studies of the 'general phenomenon' of agents exceeding any stipulated performance standards, *without* remuneration. 'Gifts' are given according to established conventions (Akerlof, 1982, p 555).

In the context of HA ancillary activities the foregoing suggests that established conventions, manifesting the Hippocratic ethos, will produce a particular APQT range. In particular, those ancillary services more closely associated with the clinical delivery of care will display activities (A) that provide informal assistance to nursing staff. Activities such as the comforting of postoperative patients, assistance with bed baths and lifting of patients, and even the arranging of flowers contribute to patient well-being (Ascher, 1987). Ancillary staff may also be aware of the quality (Q) of the activities they engage in, although important subjectivity biases may distort the deliverer's, as well as consumers', view(s) of performance (Walsh, 1991). Ancillary services less closely associated with core activities, such as laundry and ground maintenance, are unlikely to demonstrate similar scope in their activity bundles. However, Ascher (1987) reports that, in general, NHS ancillary services are not prone to restrictive practices, whereas equivalent LA activities have been (see for example, Domberger et al, 1986).

Breton and Wintrobe (1982) consider that all *intra*-bureaucratic exchange is supported by trust-based property rights. Following Leibenstein's (1987) observations on trust, the Hippocratic ethos can be arguably viewed as an effective conveyor of trust. Parties certainly demonstrate a high degree of mutual value orientation, as healthcare delivery is characterised by relatively high-trust collaborative relations (Reed and Anthony, 1993). While trust, within and between different activities, ensures the *effective* delivery of healthcare, it may also carry with it considerable cost-raising properties in the manner indicated by Hartley (1990). Given state fiscal constraints the Hippocratic ethos may be inconsistent with moves to diminish such constraints, by exerting inflationary pressure on costs.

As noted the fragmented delivery of LA services may not engender the same degree of orientation across the body of LA activities. In certain services there is extensive documentation on the rigidity of provision, refuse collection being the most cited, suggesting a low-trust syndrome (Fox, 1974), and excessively narrow routinisation, or strict task demarcation and inflexibility (Nelson and Winter, 1982). Resource costs in this case are less justifiable as they may represent the appropriation of economic rent by agents. Certainly, this may be the case where a non-personal service is delivered, since the provider may be divorced from service users and less appreciative of the nuances of any welfarist ethic. Following Dunleavy (1991), the providers of such services may perceive themselves to be beneficiaries of any underlying welfare ethos.

Process of competitive tendering

The advocates of CCT maintain that the implementation of the policy will release resources tied up in the 'inefficient' delivery of support services (see, for instance, Carnaghan and Bracewell-Milnes, 1993). In essence, the implementation of CT involves an increased role for the price mechanism not only in the allocation of resources, but in the setting of behavioural norms. At the risk of oversimplification, the prerequisites for this increased role involve the creation of cost centres, ex ante service specification, ex ante screening processes as part of the process of intertemporal rivalry, and the establishment of more sophisticated ex post facto monitoring mechanisms.

Each of these elements contributes to the attenuation in the perceived information asymmetry between principals and agents. The establishment of cost centres not only generates additional information, but creates a vehicle for the more efficient allocation of resources in the provision of support activities (Carnaghan and Bracewell-Milnes, 1993). Information is also generated by ex ante screening of perspective contractors, and their suitability can be adjudicated by the contracting authority. In this way, the risk of adverse selection in the competitive process is diminished.

Ex ante service specification provides information on the nature of tasks to be contracted, and the standards of output desired. Tightly specified contracts are viewed as advantageous if price competition is to be decisive in the award of tenders (Hughes, 1990), and as a means of mitigating against moral hazard. However, it is well documented that the specification process will be incomplete. Williamson (1985) is prominent among those who have emphasised that the bounded rationality of agents precludes the complete ex ante specification of future contingencies in relation to intangible activities, such as clinical services in the health service and legal services in the LAs. Bonus (1986) and Alchian and Woodward's (1988) discussion of *plasticity*, the extent that a supplier has legitimate discretionary potential, also indicates the nature of the impediments to complete ex ante specification, concerning both inputs and performance indicators. Walsh (1991) and Whynes (1993) argue that the specification of performance exhibits inordinate difficulties, even for relatively routine (non-plastic) tasks, since the development of indicators is in its infancy. Domberger et al (1987; 1995) note that in the event of performance measurement being unattainable, as in defining 'cleanliness' in domestic/cleaning contracts, specification can be elucidated in terms of inputs. In other words, APQT bundles are stipulated. A result of this may be that contracts become more complex and lengthy, implying an increase in monitoring costs, needed to ensure compliance (Domberger et al, 1987, p 48).

However, input measures are likely to be a poor proxy for performance (Borland, 1994), particularly in the presence of *activity plasticity*. Frantz (1988) has also cautioned against the ex ante specification of APQT bundles for several reasons. He considers that to pre-set an APQT bundle requires an inordinate amount of knowledge, entailing potentially considerable search costs in acquiring this knowledge. The non-transferability of tacit knowledge further impairs the exercise (see Nooteboom, 1992; Binmore and Samuelson, 1994). 'Working-to-rule' is likely to lead to considerable rigidity, reducing the flexibility required to accommodate environmental changes effectively and efficiently (North, 1994). Frantz also draws attention to the demotivational effects of prohibiting employees from deciding how best to perform a task. Interestingly, Frantz further contends that the ex ante stipulation of APQT bundles for non-managerial workers also entails a similar presetting for management. He states:

> Their [managers'] APQT bundle must also be pre-set so as to ensure that the APQT bundles of the non-managerial employees are pre-set and adhered to. And who, one might ask, pre-sets the APQT bundle of the managers? (Frantz, 1988, p 76)

In other words, the old aphorism, *quis custodiat custodes?*

Some propositions

Ex post facto monitoring is generally recognised, particularly in PCAT, as a prerequisite for contractor compliance. As noted, meterability is variable being influenced to some degree by *activity plasticity*. Specifically, if ex ante specifications are incomplete then monitoring can only be partial. If agents are assumed to display the characteristics of homo economicus, then a redistribution in shirking activity would occur from monitorable to non-monitorable activities (Whynes, 1993; Frey, 1993).[4] Other impediments include interpretation difficulties caused by noise, that is, exogenous influences on the flow of information (see Dunsire et al, 1988) and the non-transferability of knowledge (see Nooteboom, 1992).

The efficiency rubric of PCAT turns on an assumption of prevailing low-trust vertical, and horizontal, relations. Relaxation of this assumption makes the issue of efficiency and tendering less obvious. Following Leibenstein's (1987) observations on trust and conventions, the CT of ancillary activities represents an adjustment to established conventions, and consequently, an erosion of trust. Specification and more sophisticated monitoring mechanisms seek to adjust prevailing APQT bundles associated with the Hippocratic/welfarist ethos, at the margin at least.

Specification of services involving either output performance, and/or input methods implies that the primary function of tendered activities will form the focus. Informal arrangements within the parameters of Hippocratic/welfarist conventions may not be amenable to the norms of tendering activity. More generally, Ouchi (1980, p 139) contends: "Traditions are implicit rather than explicit rules that govern behaviour. Because traditions are not specified, they are not easily accessible …".

Specification narrows the scope of ancillary activities (A), and may alter the time pattern (T) of agents' tasks, which may entail more binding pace (P) requirements. Quality (Q) ramifications may result (for contrasting evidence see Domberger et al, 1995; McMaster, 1995). Even in the absence of tight specifications, say in a 'menu auction regime',[5] APQT bundles are likely to exhibit some form of adjustment. This is, after all, consistent with the basic notion of X-efficiency improvements, *in a low-trust scenario*. New behavioural norms stress a greater consciousness of costs, and the need to operate within budgets (Tirole, 1994). However, unlike some non-*plastic* LA activities, such as refuse collection, by adjusting the governing norms of HA ancillary staff, and hence their APQT range, those workers become disengaged from core activities resulting in potential losses in operational synergies.[6]

Implementing a more formal and intense monitoring mechanism is, arguably, the most visible signal of a new set of norms. As noted, Leibenstein (1987) considers monitoring to be a *costly* substitute for trust, which diminishes the sense of trust, although he does not fully explore the rationale underpinning this position, except to emphasise the fragility of trust as an input. Ouchi (1980) and Frey (1993) provide more explicit accounts of trust sensitivity and organisational changes. Ouchi (1980, p 136) argues that transaction costs are traceable to a "demand for equity"; parties have a sense of fairness within the bounds of prevailing conventions. Equity, as influenced by convention, is analogous to a property right. Changes to existing conventions that are perceived to adversely affect particular individuals, or groups, without adversely affecting colleagues or superiors will be read as being unfair, and an infringement of existing property rights. Some form of resistance may well result (Nelson and Winter, 1982). Monitoring ancillary services closely associated with core activities arguably falls into this category. To subject an element of a team to a system involving more sophisticated monitoring activities can be interpreted as a signal that superiors no longer have complete confidence in agents' disposition to their stipulated tasks.

Frey (1993) advances this aspect further by contending that more intensive monitoring can alienate individuals from their tasks. He concludes:

> [i]ncreased monitoring raises the marginal utility from shirking as the agent's 'bad conscience' is absolved by the breakdown of trust with the principal. Thus, to some extent monitoring '*crowds out*' work effort'. (Frey, 1993, p 665)

In other words, more intensive monitoring is analogous to an attenuation in prevailing property rights as defined by convention. Individuals, ex post facto, are less well disposed to their tasks as a feeling of dislocation from organisational goals may accompany the change in monitoring. By reducing work effort, more sophisticated monitoring can be counter-productive, as agents switch from commensurate to perfunctory effort. Absenteeism may also increase (Frantz, 1988). In effect, the process of CCT far from generating X-efficiency improvements, by eliminating shelters from a competitive environment, may induce X-inefficiency by alienating agents otherwise well disposed to their tasks.

However, this alienation need not necessarily induce agents to switch from commensurate to perfunctory effort. Agents may be hostile to the shift in behavioural norms, but maintain loyalty to the essence of the Hippocratic/welfare ethos. On the other hand, their ability to display loyalty traits may be impaired by new APQT range patterns. This presumes that there is no wholesale change in the incumbent labour force delivering services post-tender. The experience of CCT in both HAs and LAs suggests that incumbency is not radically altered (see, for instance, National Audit Office, 1987).

From the foregoing it is possible to generate propositions regarding the conditions required for implementing CT to promote X-efficiency.

Remoteness

Where activities are remote from the core bundle of activities then the likelihood of synergy losses associated with any change in governing conventions, through adjustments to agents' APQT range, is slight. Peripheral activities are less likely to be influenced by prevailing conventions at the core. For example, as noted, educational conventions are unlikely to impact on street cleaning. Hence, vertical disintegration where an activity is remote from the core bundle of activities, or services, poses less disruptive potential than subjecting a core activity to rivalry.

Low trust

If vertical relations in those activities are not supported by high-trust relations, then periods of intertemporal rivalry may reduce actors' propensity to shirk, and hence, stimulate effort. However, this presumption is sensitive to the behavioural assumptions employed. It assumes a conventional agency homo economicus situation, where agents are ill-disposed to their task(s). Relaxation of this perspective reveals the possible scenario that intertemporal rivalry may engender a low-trust situation deteriorating further, lowering morale and adversely impacting on agents' effort levels. X-inefficiency is generated in this latter scenario.

Routineness

As noted, the more routine, and less *plastic* activities are the greater the meterability of those activities. Individual discretion is limited, and the risk of performance non-compliance is reduced. It is possible to specify agents' APQT bundles more fully and contract for the activity. In this way the potential adverse impact of a low-trust scenario is, to some extent, avoided. However, following the general thrust of the argument, the range of activities where discretion is minimised may be limited, especially in the health service. Recall Fox's (1974) argument that even in the most seemingly routine tasks there is some discretionary potential. Frantz's (1988) cautionary note concerning the fixing of APQT bundles resonates. It is unlikely to be the case that stipulating APQT bundles will eliminate agents' discretionary potential; agent morale and effort will still impact on X-efficiency.

If any one of those conditions is absent, or difficult to attain, it can be argued that the X-efficiency properties of CCT are less clear cut than the proponents of the initiative would predict. In the absence of all of those conditions, implementing the policy will generate *X-inefficiencies*. Given this, and the intrinsic features of the delivery of HA and LA activities, it may be the case that certain LA activities more readily fulfil those conditions than HA activities.

Conclusion

The analytically appealing causal link running from CCT to improvements in X-inefficiency as presented by PCAT, seems, a priori, to provide a compelling rationale for CCT in particular and quasi-markets in general.

However, this chapter has argued that PCAT turns on two restrictive assumptions – the absence of conventions, and a low-trust syndrome.

Relaxation of those assumptions muddies the water. The clear-cut predictions of the PCAT model seem to be a specific case of a more general phenomenon. The link between rivalry and X-efficiency is more convoluted than PCAT indicates. In the context of CCT for health ancillary activities X-efficiency may be sensitive to adjustments in established conventions and trust. This may be especially pronounced in those services closely associated with core activities.

The process of CCT, in the health service, can be seen to change the prevailing Hippocratic ethos in those activities subject to the initiative. This suggests that agents' established APQT range will be subject to potentially significant change. The adjustment is likely to narrow the activities of staff and could engender synergy losses. By infringing trust-based property rights, commensurate effort may give way to perfunctory effort and X-inefficiency is generated. This is not to say that in all circumstances CCT is undesirable from an X-efficiency perspective. For example, given the delivery characteristics of certain LA services, such as ground maintenance and street cleaning, CCT may encourage improvements in X-efficiency. The central point of the argument presented here is that the X-efficiency properties of CCT are more complex than mainstream models indicate. Careful consideration must be given to the role of conventions and trust as efficiency ensurers, otherwise CCT, far from resolving any perceived agency problem, will introduce one.

An ancillary motivation of this chapter was to generate a number of testable propositions. Unfortunately, this will not be a straightforward task since many of the concepts employed are not directly amenable to conventional quantification techniques. It is imperative that researchers analyse these issues and do not confine themselves to analyses of comparative cost levels that may overestimate benefits from tendering and fail to recognise the insidious nature of the contract state.

Acknowledgements

I would like to thank Giovanni Guidetti, Clive Lee, David Newlands, John Sawkins, Robin Milne, and the participants of a lively session at the Third ESRC Quasi-Markets Research Seminar held at the London School of Economics during September 1995. The views expressed in this chapter are my own.

Notes

[1] For neoclassical critiques of X-efficiency theory see Stigler (1976) and De Alessi (1983). Frantz (1988, 1992) provides a very readable rebuttal. Hodgson (1991) illustrates the nature of the heterodox critique.

[2] Ultimately freeriding, with respect to effort, by individuals will lead to a Prisoners' Dilemma (PD) situation (Leibenstein, 1984, p 268). Leibenstein argues that if effort is partially quantifiable then employers may have some ability in associating wage levels with effort; a minimum wage for minimum effort. The freeriding employee minimises effort in the anticipation that others will not, so that the firm generates sufficient revenue to secure their job. The employer, on the other hand, may desire to minimise wage costs. Both face a dilemma. By minimising effort the employee may face reductions in her/his wages, and presumably utility, whereas the employer cannot attempt to minimise wage costs without reducing effort, and hence, productivity and profits. Effort conventions avoid this PD situation.

[3] The importance of site is well illustrated by Vincent-Jones and Harries (1996b). In their investigation of quasi-markets in LAs they recorded instances of senior management in schools attempting to defend the positions of school cleaners subject to the CCT initiative. Clearly, actors may have perceived that they were involved in providing a package of welfare services, therefore a welfare ethos may have been pervasive.

[4] An argument presented by Dobra (1983), in the context of bureaucratic provision, suggests that monitoring activity will be effective in promoting efficiency. Dobra claims that the supply of shirking is not infinite, nor is the supply of monitoring zero. Rational monitors will specialise in monitoring agencies with the greatest propensity to shirk, as detection costs are relatively low. In the basic PCAT model bureaux with the largest budgets will be subject to the greatest supply of monitoring. The robustness of Dobra's argument is extremely sensitive to plasticity. He tacitly assumes that bureaucratic activities are not plastic; in the light of the discussion in the text this seems a particularly restrictive assumption.

[5] A menu auction allows competing bidders the opportunity to bid not only in terms of price, but also in terms of service specification. In effect, an auctioning authority may set a number of broad parameters regarding the service requirements they desire, with rival bidders

endeavouring to provide more focused specifications and an accompanying price. Menu auctions thereby provide a number of dimensions for rival bidders to compete on the basis of 'value for money'.

[6] Kay (1982, pp 39-40), drawing from Ansoff, defines synergy as the "effect which can produce a combined return on the firm's resources greater than the sum of its parts. This has frequently been expressed as 2 + 2 = 5 since the firm's combined performance is greater than the simple aggregate of parts". Synergies can be categorised into sales, operating, investment, and management. Operating synergies refer to shared facilities, personnel, overheads, learning curves, and inputs. Disengaging ancillaries from core activities potentially involves separating, and hence losing, personnel and input synergy sources.

Part Two

Education

THREE

Financing of schools: a national or local quasi-market?
Michael Barrow

Introduction

During the past decade the mechanisms used to fund education in the UK have changed dramatically, at all levels, but particularly for schools. These alterations have occurred alongside other changes such as the introduction of performance league tables for secondary schools and the National Curriculum for pupils aged 5-16. As far as finance is concerned, there has been a general move in the direction of formula funding of schools with an associated reduction in the discretion allowed to local education authorities in allocating resources. A parallel system of finance for grant maintained (GM) schools has been created, in which the intention is to move away from funding based on local decisions about spending levels and towards a 'common' funding formula. This common funding formula (CFF) began in April 1994 in five pilot areas in England. It was proposed that this should be replaced by an national funding formula (NFF).

These reforms transformed the way in which the education 'market' worked. The education market in the UK has some distinctive characteristics. These suggest that the market cannot be analysed in the same way as most goods markets. The main characteristics are that:

- the incentives for profit maximisation or cost minimisation are muted and it is difficult for any party to appropriate any economic rent that may arise, at least in cash terms;
- the market is competitive in so far as there are many schools, but growth, mergers, entry and exit are all difficult;
- a school may have some spatial monopoly power since a major cost to consumers is travel time;

- schools in the state sector cannot compete on price but do compete to a limited extent on (perceived) quality, recently sharpened by the introduction of performance league tables;
- most schools have little choice over the quality of inputs (that is, they are non-selective), over the level of output or price;
- the market is regulated by government (both central and local) because of factors such as the externality effects of education, and targets in relation to equity.

This chapter examines the workings of this regulated market and evaluates the reforms of the Conservative administration. Central to this is the study of the allocation of resources by formula, either by the local management of schools (LMS) formula, the CFF which applies to some GM schools, or the proposed NFF, for GM schools. The research is based on policy documents obtained from both central and local government, and on interviews conducted with education finance officers in six local education authorities.

The chapter begins by describing the changes that have taken place in education, with emphasis on the introduction of the CFF. It then analyses and evaluates the reforms.

Funding reforms in education

The four phases of reform are:

- LMS – the switch to formula funding for all local education authority (LEA) schools;
- GM status – the opportunity for schools to opt out of LEA control, since 1988, and become 'self-governing', receiving funding from the then Department for Education (DfE) initially and now from the Funding Agency for Schools (FAS);
- the introduction of the CFF for GM schools – this was introduced in five pilot LEAs (Bromley, Calderdale, Essex, Hillingdon and Gloucestershire) in 1994-95 and extended to 21 in 1995-96;
- proposals for an NFF for GM schools (see DfEE, 1996a).

Local management of schools

Since the LMS reform has been extensively described elsewhere (see Levačić, 1992a; 1992b; Thomas and Bullock, 1992; Bartlett, 1992). This chapter will pick out the key features that are relevant for the study of quasi-markets.

Before the introduction of LMS the market was a 'command economy' as far as resource allocation was concerned. This may alternatively be described as input-budgeting or a curriculum-led approach. The budget of a school, which was not separately identified, was based on the cost of its inputs, such as teachers. However, some LEAs were experimenting with decentralisation and devolved budgets before LMS appeared.

The Conservative government's objectives for the LMS reform were to make clear to parents and governors the basis of the calculation of resources to schools, and to give schools the freedom to take expenditure decisions which matched their priorities and to retain any savings. LMS may be referred to as output-budgeting, or a pupil-led approach to funding. A school's budget was determined by output measures such as age-weighted pupil numbers, special educational needs (SEN) assessments and other factors usually outside the immediate control of the school or the LEA, such as premises-related costs.

In introducing this approach, central government significantly restricted LEA's ability to allocate resources or to discriminate subjectively between schools. Despite this, most authorities tried to devise a scheme which closely replicated the previous pattern of provision (see Coopers & Lybrand, 1988b). Many LMS schemes include age-weighting factors to four decimal places for just such a reason and some also include such items as 'A'-level factors which had the effect of favouring grammar schools.

However, some reallocation of resources did occur: from smaller to larger schools; to those with rising rolls from those with falling rolls; and from those with generous staffing complements to those with relatively fewer staff. LMS schemes were largely designed to reflect the status quo rather than being based on some objective notion of the costs involved in teaching different types and ages of children.

LMS turns the school into a type of self-managed firm, with little or no control over the level of activity, the price of output, capital input, or the quality of (child) input, but able to decide on labour and other inputs.

Grant maintained status

The government's key objectives in creating the opt-out route were to increase choice and diversity within the state sector and thereby improve standards in schools. GM schools' budgets were still initially determined by the LMS formula, but paid by the then DfE and the money recovered from the LEA. The formula allocation to GM schools is known as direct annual maintenance grant (AMG) or LMS replication. Approximately 85% of each school's budget was allocated by formula (the exact percentage varied between LEAs). GM schools also received a percentage add-on which was meant to pay for services provided free to LEA schools (those not distributed by formula). This was known as central AMG, and the percentage add-on varied from 5.9% to 22.1% at primary level to 4.7% and 16.5% at secondary level (1994-95 figures). The percentage add-on depended upon the extent to which funding was delegated in the LEA - the more that was delegated by formula, the lower the percentage add-on.

A quirk of the formula was that the percentage add-on was calculated with respect to the *previous* year's level of delegation. Since LEAs were generally increasing the level of delegation from year to year the percentage add-on overcompensated GM schools for the value of free central services foregone. This hampered further delegation since LEAs did not want to redistribute resources away from 'their' schools towards the GM sector. Other grants paid to GM schools reflected school meals subsidies, transitional costs of becoming GM and capital costs.

Although the government argued that opting out should be financially neutral in its effects on a school and its former LEA there have been numerous claims that GM schools have been financially advantaged in many ways. The most notorious example is that of 'cash protection' for GM schools, a mechanism whereby the central AMG add-on is protected, in cash terms, from one year to the next (although this has subsequently been modified, see below). Since the extent of funding delegation had been increasing year by year the central AMG should normally have fallen. Because of cash protection this did not happen and GM schools received some element of 'double funding'. For example, one school in one of the sample authorities benefited in this way to the extent of £100,000 per annum on a budget of £1.6m, that is 6.25% of its budget. In another authority it was estimated that every GM school had cost the LEA an extra £150,000 on average because of the percentage add-on system.

Favourable funding available per GM school depended on how many there were – the more that opted out, the fewer additional resources, such as, capital grants, available per school. This gave the greatest benefit to schools opting out early, and perhaps, in part, explains the slowing of momentum of opting out. In the 12 months to March 1995 only 13 secondary schools opted out, compared with 112 in the previous year.

Common funding formula

The aim of the CFF was to provide a stable, long-term basis of funding for GM schools as an alternative to the system based on LEA decisions about LMS schemes and budgets. It also aims to "be as simple as possible for parents and schools to understand".

The CFF was announced in the White Paper *Choice and diversity* (DfE, 1992) and was introduced in five pilot LEAs chosen by the Secretary of State for Education. The five were chosen on the basis of the number of GM schools in each LEA and whether the LMS scheme and budget could be considered to provide a reliable basis for the calculation of the AMG. The CFF initially applied only to secondary schools, although there were proposals for introducing the formula to primary schools.

Despite the aim, the CFF was, perhaps inevitably, highly complicated, as the following description demonstrates. There were essentially six steps to the calculation:

- The starting point for the CFF was the LEA's standard spending assessment (SSA) relating to schools. This was despite the fact that government ministers often stated that SSAs, used to distribute Revenue Support Grant to LAs, were *not* intended as an indicator of what should be spent on education.
- From the SSA a percentage was deducted to cover the LEA's continuing responsibilities for such items as nursery schools, educational welfare and psychology. This 'top-slice' varied between 10.59% (Calderdale) and 22.80% (Gloucestershire). The calculation of the top-slice was a complex, 15-stage procedure which was essentially based on the LEA's actual expenditure on such items. The calculation involved data which the then DfE accepted could not be replicated by LEAs. However, as one LEA document commented, "the figures appear reasonable based on a simple pro-rata approach".
- The remaining sum was divided between primary and secondary sectors, based on the previous year's split of expenditure, to give a secondary total available for distribution.

- The secondary total was then divided among all local schools, GM and LEA, using the CFF. The CFF is unique to each authority, so its title is a misnomer: it is not 'common'. For example, the pupil age-weightings are based on the LMS weightings in each of the pilot areas and the five different formulas also contain different factors, for example, for split sites. The age weightings can differ substantially between areas. For example, Hillingdon paid 38% more than Gloucestershire per Key Stage 3 pupil (ages 12-14), while at age 16+, Bromley paid 53% more than Calderdale (1994-95 figures).

- Step five established a cash floor for each school (including LEA schools) to ensure that its cash allocation was no less than it received in 1993-94, adjusted for pupil numbers. For LEA schools the 1993-94 allocation was what they would have received if they had been grant maintained. The revised CFF allocation for each school was then the maximum of its initial CFF figure or the cash floor. If the total now distributed exceeds the secondary allocation derived at step three, all budgets are scaled down to fit, so a type of damping mechanism operates.

The DfE consultation paper claims that "these arrangements should provide a measure of protection for *all* schools" (1993, p 9, emphasis added). However, this calculation was purely notional so far as LEA schools were concerned, as the same paper admits further on: "For LEA secondary schools these budgets will remain notional since their funding will continue to be determined by reference to their LEA's LMS scheme." (p 10).

Some GM schools continued to benefit from cash protection (from the replaced AMG mechanism). Following representations from LEAs and others the government decided to phase this out. For 1994-95, cash protection was 90% of the 1993-94 figure, less any 'winnings' made under the CFF. These winnings were defined as the revised CFF allocation minus the cash floor, or zero, whichever is the greater.

All hope of parents and schools understanding the methodology probably disappeared at an early stage.

- The final step of the calculation was a link to LEA budgets. This ensured that GM schools retained the benefit of LEA spending above SSA, despite their opted out status. The sum of the budgets of all secondary schools was calculated according to the current

AMG methodology and if this total was greater than the CFF-derived total then the CFF budgets of GM schools were uprated by the relevant percentage. CFF-derived budgets of LEA schools were not uprated at this point. If the LEA budget was less than the CFF-derived total, no adjustment to GM schools' CFF-derived budgets was made. Thus the funding procedure required *all* schools' budgets to be calculated according to *both* LMS and CFF.

There was clearly an asymmetric effect within these procedures. Effectively, if the LEA spent below its secondary education SSA then GM schools' budgets were based on SSA. If spending was above SSA, GM schools' budgets were based on spending. In either case, GM schools received a budget based on the higher figure. Since LEA schools' budgets were calculated via the LMS formula, the CFF calculations were purely notional for them.

This was clearly a complicated process and its impact was not immediately obvious. In one of the sample authorities where the process was examined in detail, most elements of the procedure had little effect, the most important being the cash floor and cash protection items which had the biggest effect on those who opted out early on. Many of the vagaries of the CFF were described as "small beer, irritations" by one LEA officer interviewed. In many instances, GM schools would get less via the CFF than via the LMS formula (before the protection elements work through). The two formulas per se did not favour one sector or the other, they just gave different results.

National funding formula

The argument for an NFF is that GM schools' funding should not be tied to LA decisions about the size of the education budget. An NFF would be consistent with the National Curriculum, the teachers' national pay scales and the national system of inspection.

A discussion paper (1996a) from the DfEE (which replaced the DfE in 1995) raised all the usual issues about constructing a formula: the objectives of simplicity, transparency, stability and fairness, alongside practical issues such as transitional arrangements. The paper was perhaps more interesting because of the issues it did not cover and for illustrating the complications of parallel funding systems. The whole question of the overall level of funding and of its split between sectors was ignored, the paper's arguments and modelling work being concerned only with the distribution of an existing sum between individual GM schools.

Some example calculations in the paper illustrate the problems of replacing a locally-based system with a national one. For example, GM schools in Lambeth would lose on average 17% of grant while those in Sutton would gain 11%. This occurred because of the simplicity of the proposed NFF which was less sensitive to local issues, in particular to measures of additional or SEN. Sutton's GM schools, almost all selective, already obtained excellent academic results and hardly seemed in need of additional resources, certainly compared to Lambeth. One LEA officer (not from Lambeth), while expressing respect for the work of DfEE officers, suggested they were 'number crunchers' inevitably lacking sufficient local education knowledge.

It seems unlikely that changes of such magnitude would be tolerated by schools. The above figures were averages for each LEA, the gains or losses to individual schools could be larger – the DfEE paper shows a range from +17.43% to -22.26%. It seems likely that such changes would involve strong pressure from 'losing' schools to have the chance to opt back in to LEA control, not possible in 1995. It seems unlikely that a simple, transparent, national formula can replace the myriad of local schemes without substantial gains and losses.

Did the quasi-market in education work?

One obvious problem with this method of funding education was the tension between national and local influences, between the CFF and LMS schemes. Each of these formulas was fairly non-problematic per se, but it was the interaction between them that raised difficulties. This was vividly highlighted by the decision about how much to spend on education and about the split of this sum between primary and secondary sectors.

Formula funding highlighted the disparity of funding between the two sectors, now well known by schools, governors and even parents. The secondary sector was well funded compared to the primary sector – in 1993-94 the former obtained 56% more per pupil than the latter and many have questioned whether this was justified. The House of Commons Select Committee on Education (1993-94) recommended a common pupil–teacher ratio across the two sectors, for example. Pupil teacher ratios in 1993 were 22.4 in the primary sector, 16.1 in the secondary (DfE, 1994a).

However, the CFF funding arrangements made it virtually impossible for an LEA to switch resources from secondary to primary sector, even if it wished to. Any GM school was guaranteed a CFF budget based on at least the LEA's secondary education SSA. Hence, if an LEA spent less than its SSA it gave an incentive for the LEA schools to opt out. If it spent more than its secondary SSA it could not reduce it to help fund the primary sector since GM budgets were protected by the 'floor' described earlier. The cost would then have to fall on the LEA secondary schools which would then have an increased incentive to opt out.

Some further consequences of the CFF also follow. An LEA spending below its secondary education SSA was effectively forced towards it because of the opt-out threat. As a result, secondary spending would rise. This had a knock-on effect in the following year, when the education SSA was split (for the purpose of calculating the CFF) between primary and secondary sectors on the basis of the previous year's spending (when the secondary share was increased). This would reduce the share going to the primary sector and to the LEA's continuing responsibilities, unless expenditure on these was raised at the same time. To avoid this, the shares of education expenditure going to the different sectors were effectively frozen. Any policy decision which an LEA might have wished to make about altering the balance of funding was effectively ruled out. In an authority which was at its overall capping limit (such as Calderdale, one of the CFF pilots) an enforced increase in the education budget implied reduced spending elsewhere, possibly significantly so since education formed a large part of the overall budget.

What should be a policy decision was effectively blocked by the detailed operation of the funding formulas. The government view was summarised in a DfE memorandum to the Education Select Committee (1993-94):

> **The relative size of the primary and secondary control totals and the implied per pupil allowances within them reflects the latest information available about the pattern of LEAs' actual spending at national level. It is not intended to reflect a view of the appropriate balance of spending within the educational component of the SSA between the primary and secondary sectors. Nor is it interpreted as such by LEAs. Budget decisions affecting the ratio of spending between primary and secondary pupils are entirely a matter for individual LEAs. (DfE, 1994b)**

This would no longer be the case with the CFF in place. All of the interviewees stated that spending was increasingly determined by the SSA figure and was moving towards it. In addition to the above arguments, one interviewee reported that the local council was moving towards a "no taxation without representation" position. The council spent above its SSA, but councillors were asking why they should ask local taxpayers to fund expenditure items over which the council had little or no control. In another LEA, the council was turning towards the areas where it still had control – under-fives and adult education, for example. All the interviewees revealed that they were trying to put more money into primary education yet were limited to using 'growth money' to do this.

The quasi-market in education altered the incentive structure, in both positive and negative ways. The fact that a school's budget was fixed and any savings could be used may have encouraged greater efficiency. This was evident in the fact that schools built up significant balances, approximately £500m at the end of 1993-94. However, the incentive was reduced if LEAs (and central government) used the levels of balances as an excuse to reduce funding in subsequent years. Government ministers publicly commented on the high levels of balances in some schools and our LEA interviewees expressed similar comments. One LEA officer said that her council had felt that schools would be able to cope with cuts to the education budget by making use of their balances. This argument was correct for the average school, but would cause problems for those with low balances. A wide variation between schools in the level of balances may have protected all schools from cuts to the education budget.

While encouraging greater efficiency in individual schools, the balances could have had adverse effect on the efforts of LEAs. Although unspent balances were held in LEA bank accounts (for LEA schools) and earned interest, they could not be used by the LEA for other purposes. Since, LAs could not borrow for revenue purposes they must hold separate balances in addition to those held by schools. The pooling of risk was hampered and economies of scale in holding balances were not exploited as they were formerly.

Incentives to individual schools were not compatible with overall efficiency in other instances and some management of the market may have been desirable. One example of this was inefficient entry into the market, in this case the opening of new sixth forms. By law, high schools (those taking pupils up to 16 years old) may set up small sixth forms without this constituting a 'change of character' and thus requiring permission. According to one interviewee this had reached the edge of legality in some cases, or even gone beyond it. Schools did this because of the increasing demand for sixth form education, its financial benefit to the school and to raise status. Many of these sixth forms were too small to be effective, yet could not be closed down by the LEA because of the threat that they might opt out. Proposals in the White Paper (DfEE, 1996b) gave greater freedom to GM schools to open sixth forms and nursery provision, potentially exacerbating this problem.

The opt-out option made it more difficult for LEAs to close surplus places and to reorganise provision. One LEA found it difficult to close its middle schools and move to a transfer system at age 11 because of the opt-out option. The LEA officer interviewed claimed that the governance structure in education had made the task 'impossibly difficult'. In the one sample LEA where there were no opt-out schools, reorganisation had taken place in the early 1980s before the GM option existed.

The substantial rise in pupil exclusions is another example of schools responding to financial incentives, which may not be for the overall good. Although the school loses the funding for that pupil, it may be less than the costs imposed by that pupil on the school. One interviewee reported that the financial arrangements made such matters more difficult for the LEA to deal with – a GM school might exclude a child without the LEA's knowledge. The LEA would learn of this only when the child turned up at another (LEA) school.

Examples of 'opportunism', where a school takes advantage of a situation to further its own interest to the disadvantage of other schools, were also apparent. Whereas both assets and debt passed to hospital trusts under the NHS reforms, with a requirement to pay interest and dividends, only the assets passed to GM schools. Any debt remained with the LA and continued to be a burden on the local taxpayer. Since LEA schools were not required to service their assets, there is equity between sectors in this sense, but so far as schools as a whole were concerned capital was a free good, which led to inappropriate incentives.

GM schools had the incentive to opt out with as large an asset base and as little debt as possible. Two schools in one sample LEA studied opted out while in deficit under the LMS arrangements, but promised to reimburse the money, a type of 'gentlemen's' agreement. One of the schools also ordered a large amount of equipment just before opting out. The deficits were not repaid in full (an initial payment was made) and the Secretary of State for Education refused to authorise repayment (the law has now been changed and deficits are repaid). In this case, the LEA refused to pay for the equipment so this was a cost that fell on the school, but this matter was still in dispute.

The LEA also had an incentive not to invest in schools which it believed would opt out. Two sample authorities placed a block on investment if a school decided to ballot on GM status. This was done openly and with the knowledge of the schools concerned. One school balloted part way through an LEA-funded capital works programme. The council completed the work to which it was contractually committed, but not the rest. Another LEA took a more neutral attitude to opting out and did not block investment when a ballot was announced; there was a variety of attitudes to opting out within the ruling Conservative group on the council which led to the neutral policy stance.

There were also some incentives to finance small amounts of capital works from revenue finance. For example, if there were mid-year receipts which boosted the budget, these could be spent on LEA schools if confined to capital items, but would be shared with GM schools if spent on revenue items. This discretion could be exercised at the margins of expenditure but was not extensive, partly due to the committed nature of much expenditure. Small amounts of revenue funding were also spent on capital items.

Another example of opportunism was the misreporting of the take-up of school meals by GM schools in Hampshire, leading to them receiving increased funding. An FAS inquiry found that three schools had 'untypically high' numbers of pupils taking school meals and it removed £25,000 from their budgets. It would have been impossible for this to occur under the old 'command economy' arrangements and it was arguable that it would be unlikely to occur under LMS alone (without any opted-out schools) when a greater atmosphere of collegiality prevailed. One interviewee considered that the GM option had destroyed 'a good deal of the sense of community and collegiality' in education.

There were also examples of LEAs benefiting by opportunistic behaviour and some of our interviewees regarded the whole GM experience as an example of such behaviour by central government.

The sheer complexity of the funding arrangements could lead to important but inadvertent redistributions of resources. As an example, one sample authority has always funded its schools on headteachers' estimates of pupil numbers, with a retrospective adjustment the following year if necessary. The CFF was similar, except that for 1994–95 only the DfE did not make provision for retrospective adjustment (for GM schools). This meant a £400,000 windfall for the GM schools which had overestimated pupil numbers. Some LEA schools had done the same but the LEA could and did make retrospective adjustments. If these adjustments had not been made the education budget would have been overspent by £250,000.

Funding formulas are also intended to ensure a reasonable degree of equity between schools, something which could not be guaranteed under the previous system which was less transparent. Equity might be defined in an analogous way to that implicit in local government equalisation grants – a school's need to spend in order to achieve a standard level of achievement. However, it is extremely unclear what level of spending is implied. Should the aim be to equalise exam results (surely impossible), or opportunity, or inputs? As a result, spending levels can differ enormously between LEAs and different LMS schemes distribute resources in different ways.

The proposal to introduce an NFF further illustrates the problem. As shown above, it implies a potentially huge redistribution of resources between authorities and schools and would pose an extremely difficult political problem for government. The losers' complaints are likely to drown out the winners' celebrations. Perhaps the conclusion is that there is no 'correct' definition of equity and that the finer details of funding formulas are irrelevant. Schools and LEAs may well prefer a regime of stability within which they can plan with some confidence to an uncertain one which offers a spurious promise of equity. Unfortunately, LMS, the CFF and the NFF produced substantial redistributions which were perceived as unfair (except, perhaps, by the winners) and only added to the sense of uncertainty.

Conclusion

The education quasi-market largely relies on formulas to allocate resources, instead of prices and consumer preferences. Unfortunately, a number of factors, principally related to multiple agencies and parallel allocation mechanisms, inhibit the effective working of such a market.

The substantial increase in the complexity of funding arrangements led to some unintended yet important consequences, as the discussion of the balance of funding between primary and secondary sectors demonstrated. It was extraordinary that such an important policy decision was effectively short-circuited by the minor details of a funding formula.

The complexity of the continually changing arrangements also encourage opportunism by a number of players in the education market. This may be promoted by the creation of two different types of school, altering the atmosphere of the market and reducing the moral inhibitions on cheating.

Equity between schools is also important but becomes more difficult to ensure as schools become more heterogeneous. Unfortunately, the funding reforms had questionable effects on equity and added to the uncertainty facing schools. Equity is difficult to define (as the variety of different funding formulas suggest) and so efficiency and stability should perhaps be given higher priority.

Despite these arguments, it appears that formula funding can work. LMS itself has proved popular with schools and LEAs. The Association of Metropolitan Authorities (1994) called it one of the major success stories of the late 1980s and early 1990s. The CFF formulas themselves were also relatively uncontroversial per se. This was because they were devised locally, not nationally, and were sensitive to local issues. The problems appear to arise where constraints have been imposed from the centre, such as the protection of central AMG or the calculation of the CFF based on which was the larger out of the SSA or the local education budget.

The future in 1995 did not look bright. The NFF highlighted the contrast between national and local decisions about education finance and left the government to make fundamental decisions such as the balance of funding between primary and secondary sectors of education.

Postscript

The election of May 1997 effectively put an end to the opt out option for schools and with it some of the political controversy over funding. The Education Bill (May 1998) currently before Parliament will create four new categories of school: community (mainly ex-LEA), foundation (ex-GM), aided (ex-voluntary aided or 'church' schools) and community special (former LEA and GM special schools).

The new government has promised fairness in funding for the different types of school and all are financed by LMS arrangements from 1999 onwards (the NFF idea seems to have disappeared), although there is likely to be greater delegation of funds to schools, along the lines of the former GM arrangements. The government has also stated that the focus is to be on standards rather than structures, so that the LEAs' role will be to challenge schools to improve standards, rather than to control them. All this seems a welcome improvement.

There are still some important funding issues but the omens are that these might be dealt with in a cooperative and efficient manner. The commitment to reduce class sizes to a maximum of 30 at Key Stage 1 (5 to 7-year-olds) implies increased expenditure in some local authorities, financed either from other key stages, from other services or from central government (which has promised some extra money for this). This would have been more difficult to achieve under the former arrangements.

There are also moves towards a convergence of funding for 16 to 19-year-olds, between those educated in LEA-funded schools and those in Further Education Funding Council (FEFC) funded colleges (see Barrow, 1997, for details). One LEA is already using a formula based on FEFC principles (which include, for example, an element of funding related to pupil achievement) and others are considering it. In Weston-super-Mare there is a cooperative arrangement over school sixth form provision. The school's sixth form is run in partnership with the local Further Education college and funded by the FEFC. The LEA has representatives on the college's board of governors. There are other proposals (by the Local Government Association, for example) for increased representation of college governors on LEA education committees and LEA representatives on college governing boards.

All of this augurs well for the future functioning of the education quasi-market. There appears to be more of a balance between competition (over standards achieved) and cooperation (over funding issues). It may not be perfect but it is an improvement over the rather pointless funding disparities that went before.

FOUR

Educational quasi-markets: the Belgian experience
Vincent Vandenberghe

Introduction

For several decades the Belgian education system, including primary, secondary and tertiary education, has been primarily based on a quasi-market principle (Le Grand and Bartlett, 1993; Glennerster, 1991). The system can be defined briefly by the combination of school choice, financed by per capital public payment for each student. It corresponds to the 'voucher' idea initially promoted by Friedman (1962).

This institutional arrangement, which can also be found in The Netherlands (James, 1986), is a response to a philosophical and institutional conflict between the Roman Catholic Church and the secular State. Both institutions have historically claimed their right to control education and other semi-public services, but neither has been in a position to impose its conception. Although the religious and philosophical context explains the origin of the Belgian or Dutch quasi-market, growing secularisation suggests that its current raison d'être is to ensure free choice for parents and students (Glenn, 1989; Billiet, 1977).

Yet, educational quasi-markets are no longer a Belgian or Dutch curiosity. Free choice and market-oriented schools are the subject of discussion and policy in many countries, particularly in the United States (Friedman, 1962; Clune and Witte, 1990; Chubb and Moe, 1990; Bowles and Gintis, 1993). Quite surprisingly, the US still maintains a system of attendance zones – the 'zoning' regulation – which amounts to imposing a public school on the basis of each family's residence. In other words, if parents want to benefit from the public school system (that is, free access to school), they have no choice but to send their children to the school located in their neighbourhood. New Zealand and Australia abandoned the 'zoning' principle during the 1980s (CERI, 1994). Several European countries, where public education traditionally offers little or no parental school choice, are moving towards increased choice of school. Radical quasi-markets reforms were introduced in the United Kingdom during the late 1980s and in Sweden in the early 1990s (Miron, 1993). In other European countries such educational reforms are at the forefront of political debate.

Quasi-markets appeared in different contexts and for various reasons. They have been adopted by governments seeking alternatives to public monopolies or quasi-monopolies as a method of producing and delivering. As explained by Bartlett et al (1994), quasi-markets can be used to regulate and finance education, healthcare, community care services, social housing and other public services. This generalisation and widespread diffusion of quasi-markets is a sufficient reason to analyse them more thoroughly, both theoretically and empirically.

This chapter contains a brief presentation of educational quasi-markets in Belgium. It exposes empirical results suggesting that Belgian quasi-markets are synonymous with segregation by ability: the greater the extent to which school choice district wide, the more important is segregation along the ability line. It then explains why ability segregation should be seen as a source of inefficiency. The central argument is that segregation can be synonymous with misallocation of non-monetary inputs: the peer effects. The chapter concludes with an analysis of the regulatory strategies that could be implemented to prevent segregation and improve efficiency of educational quasi-markets.

Do Belgian quasi-markets cause interschool segregation?

Reflecting a common concern about school choice, the first research questions asks whether quasi-markets, as they exist in the French-speaking community of Belgium, are associated with segregation along the 'ability' line (contrary to most US studies, the work on segregation carried out for this study does not primarily refer to situations where inter-racial exposure is low). This exercise does not attempt to estimate the impact of quasi-markets (school choice more specifically) on educational achievement since data that would enable an examination of these questions is not available. The focus is limited to 'ability' segregation between schools (interschool segregation). However, segregation can be synonymous with both inequity and inefficiency.

Interschool segregation is explored at district level. The average size of a district ranges from 20 to 40 square kilometres. The data refers to secondary education in the French-speaking community of Belgium; both elementary and higher education are excluded from this analysis. The secondary education system counted, in 1991-92, a total of 334,509 pupils enrolled in one of the 650 schools (inequally) distributed across the 21 districts forming the territory of the French-speaking community of Belgium.

The data used in this study – centred on the year 1991 – comes from several sources. The most important is the Ministère de l'éducation, de la recherche et de la formation (1993). The data this Ministry releases consists of a distribution of pupils by year of birth and by district, by school inside the district, and by grade and academic track inside the school. It allowed the computation of grade-repetition indexes showing the extent to which pupils registered in a particular school, at a certain grade, in a certain academic track, have been forced to repeat some of their previous grades because of unsatisfactory results. It has been shown elsewhere (Vandenberghe, 1996) that the presence of a large number of pupils with a grade-repetition record in a school is correlated with variables suggesting that this school concentrates on low-ability pupils. Although teachers are not a priori very coordinated when evaluating pupils, they seem to be relatively 'coherent': they apparently impose grade-repetition sanctions to pupils with a low human capital endowment; pupils who are native of a non-European Community country, and pupils who are more violence prone.

Assumptions tested

The first hypothesis of this study is that ability segregation could be exacerbated by the extent of school choice in the district. People with a no-grade-repetition (NGR) record, acting as proxy for high-ability pupils, would be isolated from the rest of the population more systematically when options, for them and the others, are more numerous. The strategy adopted to test this assumption is by measuring the structure of the local quasi-market using a Herfindahl index,[1] or other measures of concentration, and examining the impact on segregation.

This then allows a second assumption to be tested: whether the interschool segregation indicates the intensity of pre-existing human capital disparities among inhabitants of the district. The underlying assumption is that high-ability people tend to isolate themselves more when the socioeconomic or ability gap between them and the rest of the population grows.

Ordinary least squares (OLS) results

The dependent variable used in the study is the level of disparity between the proportion of pupils with an NGR inside each district (d), and schools organising the same grade (i = 1 to 6). Its statistical measure is based on the dissimilarity index (Rumberger and Willms, 1992). This index $D_{d,i}^{k=0}$ in Table 1) gives the proportion of the sub-group, the pupils who have repeated a certain number (k) of grades, that would have to change schools in order to achieve an even distribution across schools operating in the district. Appendix A gives a mathematical definition of the dissimilarity index. The higher the dissimilarity index, the higher the interschool segregation.

Interschool segregation is not influenced by the ability gap

Ordinary least square regression results (see Table 1) are of great interest. All variables describing the pre-existing socioeconomic discrepancy inside the district have non-significant coefficients in all equations estimated. The coefficient of the income inequality proxy $(\textbf{GINI}_d)$ is positive but insignificant (similar results are derived when using the coefficient of variance variable [**CVAR**]). The intermunicipality unemployment rate dissimilarity $(\textbf{DU}_d)$ has a negative but insignificant coefficient (the assumption here is that unemployed people belong to the low-ability group of the population). Similarly, coefficients are insignificant for intermunicipality dissimilarity concerning the proportion of active persons with a university degree $(\textbf{DUNIV}_d)$ (the assumption here is that people with a university degree are part of the high-ability segment of the population). The same conclusion can be made concerning the proxy of the ability gap among pupils $(\textbf{AGAP}_{d,i}^{k=2})$; see Appendix B for a detailed presentation of this index. Its coefficient in regression equation 4 is insignificant. Thus, interschool segregation, all other things equal, does not seem to be more important in districts where socioeconomic disparities and ability differences are apparently more accentuated.

Interschool segregation is exacerbated by the importance of school choice

By contrast, a significant part of interschool variance in terms of NGR history is explained by school concentration indexes. Regression equations 1 to 3 are computed with the Herfindahl index ($H_{d,i}$). The coefficient of the Herfindahl variable is negative and significant: t-ratio is high in absolute value. The higher the concentration on the local quasi-market, the lower the dissimilarity between schools. In equation 1, an increment from H = 0.1 (10 schools of equivalent size) to H = 0.11 (9.09 schools of equivalent size) leads to a 1.039 point drop of interschool dissimilarity. However, equation 3 reveals that part of this effect can be attributed to a higher intraschool, between the tracks, dissimilarity effect.

In equation 1, the effect of higher concentration on interschool dissimilarity is partly incorporated into the coefficient of the intraschool dissimilarity variable ($\mathbf{WDINTRA}_{d,i}^{k=0}$). As in several other countries, the secondary educational system in the French-speaking community of Belgium incorporates different specific academic tracks (general, technical and professional). These tracks significantly reduce the level of interaction between pupils inside schools. Pupils attending different academic tracks generally attend different classes and have almost no contact with each other. Once intraschool dissimilarity is taken into account, the Herfindahl index's coefficient is reduced by approximately 40%. Equation 3 reveals that the higher the intraschool dissimilarity the lower the interschool dissimilarity inside the district. The coefficient of ($\mathbf{WDINTRA}_{d,i}^{k=0}$) in equation 3 is indeed negative and statistically significant. This observation reinforces the position of those who claim that school desegregation is not 'the end of the road'. Greater attention should be paid to segregation occurring *within* the school, between academic tracks and also, what it has not been possible to measure here, between classrooms inside each track.

Previous results are confirmed by equation 5, where the Herfindahl index is replaced by the inverse of the number of schools organising a particular grade ($\mathbf{CONC}_{d,i}$). In equation 5, the coefficient of this simple concentration index is negative and statistically significant. An increment from $\mathbf{CONC}_{d,i}$ =0.1 (10 schools of equivalent size) to $H_{d,i}$ = 0.11 (9.09 schools of equivalent size) leads to a 0.735 points drop of interschool dissimilarity.

Finally, grade dummies (i = 1-6) have a significant influence on interschool dissimilarity. Coefficients of grade dummies superior to 1

Table 1: Explanation of interschool dissimilarity in terms of secondary education pupils with a no-grade repetition record ($D_{d,i}^{k=0}$) (French-speaking community of Belgium) (all grades for the school year 1991-92) (OLS regression coefficients [t-statistics])

Dependent variable: $D_{d,i}^{k=0}$
Dissimilarity index of pupils with an NGR record

(k=0), in district d, grade i	Regression 1	Regression 2	Regression 3	Regression 4	Regression 5
Constant	0.340*	0.276*	0.408**	0.461**	0.416**
	(2.456)	(2.128)	(2.983)	(22.211)	(3.045)
$AGAP_{d,i}^{\psi=2}$: Ability-gap index				-0.006	
				(-1.021)	
$GINI_d$: Gini index measuring district-wide income inequality	0.195	0.204	0.020		0.005
	(0.920)	(1.063)	(0.097)		(0.023)
DU_d: Intermunicipality unemployment rate dissimilarity index	0.008	0.006	-0.040		-0.045
	(0.058)	(0.050)	(-0.369)		(-0.416)
$DUNIV_d$: Intermunicipality dissimilarity index for proportion of active persons with university degree	0.122	0.118	0.149		0.158
	(0.943)	(0.967)	(1.320)		(1.409)
$H_{d,i}$: Herfindahl concentration index	-1.309**	-1.060**	-0.626**	-0.697**	
	(-8.699)	(-10.410)	(-4.918)	(-6.326)	
$CONC_{d,i}$: Simple concentration index (1/number of schools organising the grade)					-0.735**
					(-5.147)
$WDINTRA_{d,i,j}^{k=0}$: Intraschool dissimilarity index pupils with an NGR record (k = 0)			-0.434**		-0.445**
			(-4.457)		(-4.930)

i = 2: school organised grade 2	0.042* (2.602)	0.063** (3.899)	0.062** (3.907)	0.066** (4.189)
i = 3: school organised grade 3	0.090** (5.987)	0.153** (8.293)	0.149** (8.383)	0.136** (8.840)
i = 4: school organised grade 4	0.079* (5.317)	0.139** (7.154)	0.138** (7.224)	0.140** (7.439)
i = 5: school organised grade 5	0.086** (5.484)	0.138** (8.388)	0.1361** (8.448)	0.136** (8.261)
i = 6: school organised grade 6	0.065** (3.387)	0.114** (5.910)	0.113** (5.741)	0.115** (6.075)
N (number of observations)	126	126	126	126
R^2adj (part of total variance explained)	0.564	0.623	0.622	0.628

N (number of observations): 126

R^2adj (part of total variance explained): 0.420

** Denotes a significance at 5%

* Denotes a significance at 10%

NGR = no-grade repetition

(the regressions are centred on grade 1) are all positive and statistically significant in equations 2 to 5. Maximal interschool dissimilarity seems to occur at grade 3 and grade 4: compared with grade 1, the dissimilarity index is inflated by 10 points or more. The shift from grade 5 to 6 seems to be synonymous with less interschool dissimilarity. This could be the consequence of before-graduation drop-outs. In other words, taking dissimilarity at entrance grade 1 as a benchmark, higher grades are synonymous with greater dissimilarity, irrespective of the value of the concentration index ($H_{d,i}$ or $CONC_{d,i}$). Dissimilarity seems to be systematically 10% higher at grade 3, and beyond, than at grade 1.

It could be concluded from this that 'cream skimming' occurs. However, it should be remembered that evaluation is left to each school's discretion in the French-speaking community of Belgium. Hence, the observation of an increasing dissimilarity along the grade scale may hint at 'cream skimming'. Each end-of-term examination could be used by the most selective schools to 'improve' their relative position. However, this conclusion needs to be tested more systematically.

Conclusion

The empirical work, centred on the quasi-market of the French-speaking community of Belgium, contains strong evidence that school choice, measured by low Herfindahl concentration indexes or other proxies of school choice, exacerbates 'ability' segregation: the less concentrated the local quasi-market, the more dramatic interschool segregation. When controlling for the importance of ability and socioeconomic discrepancy among children and inhabitants of a district, the same results were found. The structure of the local quasi-market exacerbates segregation - all other things being constant.

Should we be worried about ability segregation?

Allocation of individuals with different characteristics between schools, neighbourhoods or firms is traditionally presented as a social choice problem reflecting individual or collective preferences. Some economic argument should be introduced into this delicate debate since it relates to efficiency more than equity. The hypothesis presented in this chapter is that peer effects, also called contextual effects, are central to human capital production.

Peer effects: the idea

Peer effects reflect the idea or hypothesis that the knowledge a child assimilates during a school year depends directly on the characteristics or actions of their comrades. In other words, education is one of those numerous human activities characterised by social spillovers. The incorporation of social interaction as a determinant of the production process (for example, human capital accumulation), while not new from the perspective of sociology, is relatively recent in the context of economic theory (Brock and Durlauf, 1995; Bénabou, 1996). The concept is far from being specific to educational problems. Recent empirical evidence, highlighting the importance of social interaction, has been developed in several contexts: teenager pregnancy; drug addiction; intergeneration and ghetto poverty (Jencks and Meyer, 1987; Corcoran et al, 1990; Dynarski et al, 1989; Evans et al, 1992).

In the educational context, Coleman et al (1966) were the first to defend the social interaction idea. Since Coleman, several empirical studies have come to the same conclusion: the quality of social interactions heavily influences educational achievement (Summers and Wolfe, 1977; Henderson et al, 1978; Duncan, 1994; Dynarski et al, 1989). Using Scottish data, Willms and Echols (1992) estimate that the peer effect ranges from 0.15 to 0.35 of a standard deviation. This suggests that a child with national average ability moved from a school where the mean ability is one half of a standard deviation below the national average to a school where the mean ability is one half of a standard deviation above the national average, has an expected attainment about one quarter of a standard deviation higher. This is a substantial effect.

Peer effects: the stakes

If peer effects matter, allocation of heterogeneous individuals between strictly delimited entities becomes a critical issue as regards to efficiency. Allocation of heterogeneous individuals relates to 'productive' efficiency problems: the production of human capital is directly affected by the way heterogeneous individuals are allocated. An objective consisting of maximising the total stock of human capital can be compromised if individuals are inappropriately allocated among schools. However, the same is true with a more egalitarian objective aiming at equalising educational achievement. The cost of this policy is potentially influenced by the way in which peer effects are allocated among schools.

It can be shown analytically (Vandenberghe, 1996) that desegregation will be preferable to segregation when:

- the presence of an additional high-ability pupil in school 1 generates a peer effect (an improved teaching climate) that does not offset the negative consequences of the presence of an additional low-ability pupil in school 2. In other words, the peer effect function is concave in the proportion of high-ability pupils;
- low-ability pupils are more sensitive to peer effects than their more able class mates;
- peer effects have a decreasing marginal productivity.

It would be expected that the third of these conditions would be verified because peer effects, as with any other input, probably have a decreasing marginal productivity beyond a certain threshold. Empirical work tends to suggest that the two other conditions are verified at the primary and secondary level at least. As regards the first condition, Henderson et al (1978) claim on the basis of their results for French-speaking Canadian pupils that:

> **A mixing of weak and strong students within a given population will enhance performance of the overall student population. Although the strong students will lose as result of the mixing, the *concavity* of the peer group effect will ensure that the decrease in the achievement of strong students relative to a stratified classroom situation will be smaller than the gain of the weak students, though the loss may be substantial.**

A more recent study, focusing on primary education (Leroy-Audouin, 1995), concludes that the second condition is also verified: low-ability children are more sensitive to peer effects than their more able counterparts. This result seems to be confirmed by a more recent study carried out by Gamoran and Nystrand (1994) on secondary education US data.

Nonetheless, several studies conclude that the idea of social spillover apparently suffers some limitation when multiracial mixing is at stake (Winkler, 1975; Brooks-Gunn et al, 1993). In the American context, young black men apparently need racial homogeneity to be successful at school. They benefit from their 'high achieving classmates' only if those are black men or black women (Duncan, 1994; Link and Mulligan, 1991).

How to regulate quasi-markets?

What type of regulatory and financing framework should a social planner, in the educational quasi-market, adopt to enhance efficiency, that is, maximise human capital coming out of schools? Correspondence between social priorities and each school's interest cannot be taken for granted. Inefficiency cannot be eliminated simply by 'informing' the decentralised decision makers and schools on recruitment choice (perfect desegregation according to the results presented above) or effort levels that are socially desirable.

Incentives for schools

Cream skimming deterrence scheme

If school zoning is discarded, the alternative policy consists of using the financing formula to incite schools to revise their recruitment strategies. The regulator can steer recruitment practices simply by making the per-pupil amount allocated to schools conditional on the socioeconomic composition of the school (the human capital endowment of the recruited pupils). This variable is probably publicly known or, at least, observable at a limited cost. Conditional allocation could, for example, correspond to the suppression of financial subsidy to schools insufficiently 'mixed'. In that extreme situation, school heads would obviously modify their recruitment policy.

Output-based formula

Once schools are totally dissuaded from 'skimming off the cream', the regulator has solved only one part of the problem. The new equilibrium is probably synonymous with poor accountability. On a quasi-market, the level of peer effect from which a school benefits is possibly the main source of teachers' payoff. A teacher is sensitive to the aggregated characteristics of their pupils: the level of peer effects enters into their utility function. The teacher wants to maximise the level of this local social spillover in the school or classroom simply because this is synonymous with greater comfort. If the allocation of peer effects is totally prescribed by the regulator, schools might lack the minimal incentive to deliver effort. Several studies have suggested that a lack of effort or accountability could considerably alter the performance of educational systems (Chubb and Moe, 1990; Bowles and Gintis, 1993). In the UK, for example, the Conservative government presented quasi-markets as a crucial necessity to fulfil requirements imposed by citizens' interests, that is, efficiency and accountability. If the accountability problem is serious, the regulator must presumably complement the cream skimming deterrence mechanism used by some output-based financing formula.

Refined output-based formula: yardstick competition

However, residual inefficiency potentially persists. A regulator who does not know the parameters of the cost function cannot appropriately decide on the level of per-pupil expenditure. These limitations can be circumvented by a yardstick competition mechanism (Shleifer, 1985), allowing schools to decide on their effort level and their per-pupil cost/ expenditure (assuming that the per pupil expenditure was a priori fixed by the regulator). In a district with two schools, for example, where school 1's revenue is based on its relative performance in terms of output and per-pupil cost, the higher its effort, the higher its per-pupil income; the lower its cost, the higher its income. However, simultaneously, the higher the effort of school 2, the lower school 1's per-pupil income and the lower school 2's cost, the lower school 1's income.

It can be demonstrated analytically that a combination of cream skimming deterrence and yardstick competition embedded in the financing scheme can generate the first best outcome (Vandenberghe, 1996).

Incentives for high-ability families

The regulator's problem is more complex than simply imposing their social priorities on schools and teachers: they probably have also to impose them on *strategic* parents. In Belgium, parents can group together to establish a new school and receive public money for this provided they respect some basic conditions: enrolment size must be significant, teachers hired must have the appropriate diplomas, and the school must accept the annual visit of a government officer. The constitution imposes upon the State to finance private educational initiatives. A 'public choice' perspective would indicate that parents are political clients, that they can dismiss politicians, regulators or boycott their fiscal duties when displeased with an educational policy. Even if the cost of attending a desegregated school is extremely limited, bypass, if feasible, is likely to occur. Private parties are sensitive to peer effects when these are beneficial to their children. Yet, they most likely ignore the social benefits or costs of their individual decision: they ignore the effect of their school choice on the quality of peer effects in the rest of the educational system.

Bribes for high-ability individuals

To persuade families of high-ability pupils voluntarily to attend desegregated schools, their contribution to cost should be inferior to that of families of low-ability pupils. If the social planner is not sensitive to distribution issues, at least for the parents' generation, it can be demonstrated that this policy is welfare improving. By definition, high-ability families are compensated and preserve their utility level but low-ability individuals are also better off in the long run, even if in the short run their contribution to cost is raised. The human capital surplus their children obtain by attending the same schools as their more able peers more than offsets the extra financial cost they bear. This educational policy seems a priori politically unacceptable. This is probably true. But one should bear in mind that mechanisms that somehow implement it already exist, particularly in the US. So-called public 'magnet schools', for example, implicitly offer 'bribes' to middle class and upper class families which are extremely mobile and easily shift from one district to another. Instead of busing black children to predominantly white schools, the 'magnet' schools philosophy is to incite 'bright' (mostly white or Asian) children to attend urban schools where black or low-ability pupils are overrepresented. The bribe, in this case, takes the form of unique programmes benefiting from a higher per-pupil funding level. By attending those schools, pupils benefit from programmes and teacher–pupil ratios that are unavailable in the rest of the public school system. Higher education suppliers (colleges) do the same much more explicitly. A common practice consists of awarding 'merit' grants (to be distinguished from more classical 'social' grants) to high-ability students in order to attract them in colleges with a predominantly low-ability intake.

Commensurability problem

However, some major limitations exist. Bribery is optimal only if there is perfect commensurability between money and disutility entailed by desegregation. But can money really 'buy' disutility attached to the presence of 'different' pupils? So far, it has been assumed that the 'difference' among pupils was synonymous with ability differentials. Yet, people do not only differ in terms of ability but also in their beliefs, cultural sensitivity, ethnicity or political conviction. People can be of equal ability but dramatically diverge when it comes to moral and religious values. This simple observation raises questions that go beyond economic reasoning.

Further reflections

This analysis of educational quasi-markets conveys the message that the role of public authority in western societies is bound to evolve. Its traditional role of money collector and welfare provider based on both a progressive tax system and various forms of conditional, targeted or unconditional transfers shows some limitations. Inefficiencies, either non-internalised externalities or inequalities, occur despite the public nature of many financing mechanisms. Modern western societies have to cope with coordination challenges requiring more than public financing. Adequate answers call for new forms of intervention which are probably more complex to implement. In the last section of this chapter, for example, it has been suggested that the regulator's fundamental problem is to influence the allocation of heterogeneous individuals in order to fully exploit social interactions and promote accountability.

Note

[1] The Herfindahl index ranges from 0 to 1. The lower this index, the lower the concentration of the educational quasi-market in the district, that is, the larger the number of schools of relatively similar size organising the same grade of secondary education. Similarly, the higher this index the smaller the school choice parents and pupils enjoy in the district.

Appendix A:
Dissimilarity index

Dissimilarity index defines as:

$$D_{d,i}^k = \frac{1}{2.EL_{d,i} \cdot P_{d,i}^k (1 - P_{d,i}^k)} \cdot \sum_{j=1}^{N_{d,i}} EL_{d,i,j} \cdot | P_{d,i,j}^k - P_{d,i}^k |$$

where:

- $EL_{d,i,j}$ is the number of pupils in school j at grade i in district d;
- $EL_{d,i}$ is the total number of pupils at grade i in district d;
- $P_{d,i,j}^k$ is the proportion of pupils in school j at grade i, in district d, who have repeated k times;
- $P_{d,i}^k$ is the proportion of pupils at grade i, in the whole district d, who have repeated k times;
- $d=1...21$, the district index;
- $i=1...6$, the grade index;
- $j=1...N_{d,i}$, the school index with $N_{d,i}$ the number of schools organising grade i in district d;
- $k=0, 1, 2, \geq 2$, the grade-repeating-record index.

We see from the numerator of this index that segregation depends on the discrepancy between the proportion of sub-groups in each school and the overall proportion of those sub-groups in the district ($P_{d,i,j}^k - P_{d,i}^k$). Note finally that the denominator standardises the index so that it ranges from 0 to 1. We insist that the dissimilarity measure is not influenced by the district's average proportion: a district with a high average proportion of pupils with some grade-repetition record has no particular reason to have a high dissimilarity index. It is the dispersion around this average that determines the importance of dissimilarity.

Appendix B:
Ability gap among pupils

In order to describe ability disparities (or the 'ability gap') among children of the district, we need to characterise pupils with an NGR record (supposedly high-ability pupils) and the others (low-ability pupils). Our information is limited. We have no way of characterising the first category. Hence, we essentially use the information available concerning pupils with some grade-repetition record to build our measure of the ability gap. Among these pupils some have repeated 1 grade, while others have 2 or more grades. We make the assumption that the higher the number of grades repeated the less 'able' the pupil. Technically speaking, the ability gap will be measured by the following index:

$$AGAP^{\psi}_{d,i} = \sum_{k=1}^{3} \mu^{k}_{d,i} \cdot (k)^{\psi}$$

with

- $k=1, 2, \geqslant 3$, the grade-repetition record index;
- $d=1...21$, the district index;
- $i=1...6$, the grade index;
- $\mu^{k}_{d,i}$ the proportion of pupils who repeated k grades among the total number of pupils with a grade-repetition record ($k \geqslant 1$);
- $\psi \geqslant 1$ the extra weight we put on 'big' grade repeaters.

FIVE

Self-managing schools in the marketplace: the experience of England, the USA and New Zealand

Geoff Whitty, Sally Power and David Halpin

Introduction

This chapter reviews recent evidence concerning the progress and effects of the currently fashionable 'parental choice' and 'school autonomy' agendas in contemporary education policy in England, the USA and New Zealand (based on findings from the authors' own ESRC-funded projects [nos C000230036, C000232462, R000231899, R00023391501] on autonomous schools in England, and their work on similar developments in the USA and New Zealand together with a review of other relevant research in all three countries). In considering parental choice, a particular focus will be those policies that claim to enhance opportunities for choice among state schools (the term used to describe publicly-funded and publicly-provided schools in England and New Zealand; the term 'public schools' will be used to describe such schools in the USA) and those which use public funds to extend choice into the private sector. In the context of this chapter, school autonomy refers to moves to devolve various aspects of decision making from regional and district offices to individual schools, whether to site-based professionals, community-based councils or a combination of both.

The discussion will concentrate on the ways in which the interaction between these two sets of reforms is contributing to the creation of quasi-markets. Levačić (1995) suggests that the distinguishing characteristics of a quasi-market for a public service are "the separation of purchaser from provider and an element of user choice between providers" (p 167). She adds that there usually remains a high degree of government regulation. Most commentators similarly see quasi-markets in education as involving a combination of parental choice and school autonomy, but together with a greater or lesser degree of public accountability and government regulation.

Advocates of these policies argue that they will lead to increased diversity of provision, better and more efficient management of schools, and enhanced professionalism and school effectiveness. Some proponents, notably Moe (1994) in the USA and Pollard (1995) in the UK, have argued that such reforms will bring particular benefits for families from disadvantaged communities, who have been ill-served by more conventional arrangements. However, critics suggest that even if the reforms enhance efficiency, responsiveness, choice and diversity (and even that, they say, is questionable), they will almost certainly increase inequality between schools.

Before looking at some of the initial research evidence on these matters, the nature of the policies pursued in the three countries will be outlined. (Within the UK, our analysis refers to England. Different education legislation applies in Scotland and Northern Ireland. There are also some minor differences between England and Wales.)

Parental choice and school autonomy in England, the USA and New Zealand

In England, prior to the 1980s, the vast majority of children were educated in state schools maintained by democratically-elected local education authorities (LEAs) which exercised political and bureaucratic control over their schools but also often provided them with considerable professional support. After the Conservative victory at the 1979 election, the Thatcher and Major governments set about trying to break the LEA monopoly of public schooling through a series of Education Acts passed in the 1980s and early 1990s.

Although the introduction of the National Curriculum and its associated system of testing can be seen as a centralising policy, most of the measures have been designed to enhance parental choice and transfer responsibilities from LEAs to individual schools. The earliest of these include the assisted places scheme (APS), which provided public funding to enable academically able children from less well off homes to attend some of the country's elite private schools (see Edwards et al, 1989).

Later, the government sought to create new forms of state school entirely outside the influence of LEAs. City technology colleges (CTCs) were intended to be new secondary schools for the inner city, with a curriculum emphasis on science and technology, run by independent trusts with business sponsors. The grant maintained (GM) schools policy enabled existing state schools to 'opt out' of their LEAs after a parental ballot and run themselves with direct funding from central government. Subsequent legislation, which permitted schools to change their character by varying their enrolment schemes, sought to encourage new types of specialist schools and made it possible for some private schools to 'opt in' to the state system.

Local management of schools (LMS) gave many of those schools that remained with their LEAs more control over their own budgets and day-to-day management, receiving funds determined by the number and ages of their pupils. The open enrolment scheme allowed state schools to attract as many students as possible, at least up to their physical capacity, instead of being kept to lower limits or strict catchment areas so that other schools could remain open. This was seen as the necessary corollary of per capita funding in creating a quasi-market in education. In some respects, it was a 'virtual voucher' system (Sexton, 1987), which was expected to make all schools more responsive to their clients and either become more effective or go to the wall.

Taken together these measures were widely expected to reduce the role of LEAs to a marginal and residual one during the next few years. However, fewer schools than anticipated left their LEAs. In 1995, while claiming to have already increased diversity and choice, the then prime minister John Major looked forward to the day "when all publicly funded schools will be run as free self-governing schools". He believed in "trusting headmasters (sic), teachers and governing bodies to run their schools and in trusting parents to make the right choice for their children" (*The Times*, 24 August 1995).

By contrast with England, New Zealand in the 1980s was a somewhat surprising context for a radical experiment in school reform, let alone one associated with a conservative agenda. Unlike in England and the USA, there was no widespread disquiet about educational standards in the state school system nor were there the vast discrepancies in school performance that contributed to a 'moral panic' about urban education in the other two countries. The initial reforms were introduced by a Labour government, albeit one that had enthusiastically embraced monetarism and 'new public management' techniques in the mid-1980s

(Wylie, 1995). The education reforms, introduced in October 1989, led to a shift in the responsibility for budget allocation, staff employment and educational outcomes from central government and regional educational boards to individual schools. Schools were given boards of trustees that have effective control over their enrolment schemes, with even lighter regulation than currently exists in England. However, Wylie (1994) argues that other aspects of the New Zealand reforms "offer a model of school self-management which is more balanced than the English experience". This is because they put "a great emphasis on equity [and/or] on community involvement [and/or] on parental involvement [and/on] partnership: between parents and professionals" (p xv). Neither the costs of teacher salaries nor of some central support services were devolved to individual school budgets, although there have subsequently been moves in this direction since the election of a conservative administration in 1990. Only 3% of New Zealand schools were in a pilot scheme for 'bulk funding' (or devolution of 100% of their funding including teachers' salaries), but a 'direct funding' option was opened up to all schools in 1996 for a trial period of three years. Unlike the English funding formulae, which fund schools on the basis of average teacher salaries, the New Zealand scheme is based on actual teacher salaries and a given teacher:student ratio. Alongside these reforms, National Curriculum guidelines were introduced but these were far less detailed and prescriptive than the English model and paid more attention to minority Maori interests. The extension of choice into the private sector begun in 1995 with the announcement of a three-year pilot of a New Zealand equivalent of the APS, leading to claims that "it marks the start of a move towards a voucher system in which schools compete for parents' education dollar" (*Wellington Evening Post*, 28 September 1995).

In the USA, the limited role of the federal government in relation to education makes it more difficult to generalise about the nature and provenance of policies designed to enhance parental choice and devolve decision making to schools. The more significant decisions are taken at state and district levels. While a few states, such as Minnesota, have state-wide choice plans, many initiatives have been more local. Wells (1993) demonstrates the huge variety in origins and likely effects of the various choice plans that have been mooted or implemented in the US during the past few years. Similarly, American specialist or 'focus' schools have very different origins and purposes (Raywid, 1994; Hill et al, 1990). They include long-standing specialty schools, such as the Boston Latin

School and New York's highly academic Stuyvesant High School, magnet schools associated with desegregation plans, alternative schools, which are sometimes based on progressive pedagogic principles, and private Catholic schools. The nature of charter schools and that of site-based management within school districts also varies considerably (Wohlstetter et al, 1995).

Devolution and choice in the US enlists significant support from progressive forces, particularly among those representing minority ethnic groups. The mixed evidence about the efficacy and effects of desegregation and magnet schools in the 1980s (Blank, 1990; Moore and Davenport, 1990) has sometimes led to the conclusion that enhanced parental voice and choice, rather than more concerted political intervention, will provide the best chance of education salvation for minority parents and their children. Moe (1994) goes so far as to claim that the best hope for the poor to gain the right "to leave bad schools and seek out good ones" is through an "unorthodox alliance" with "Republicans and business ... who are the only powerful groups willing to transform the system" (p 33). For this reason, some aspects of the current reform agenda have developed a populist appeal well beyond the coteries of conservative politicians or even the white populations to which they usually appeal.

In so far as it is possible to generalise, the New Zealand reforms have ushered in a more thoroughgoing experiment in free parental choice in the state sector than has been tried in England. Also, both these countries have gone further in this respect than all but a few school districts in the USA. In terms of freedom from local bureaucratic control, New Zealand schools had most autonomy and those in the USA the least. Within England, GM schools had the most autonomy, but even LEA schools, which virtually all now have local management, have considerably more autonomy than most US schools. As for freedom in financial management, schools in England operating under LMS currently have more resources under their direct control than even New Zealand schools, apart from those of the latter participating in the 'direct funding' option. In the USA, financial devolution within school districts has not gone nearly as far as it has in either England or New Zealand. In that respect, little of the American experience of site-based management is directly relevant to the claims made by advocates of more radical supply-side reforms.

Equity considerations have had different degrees of influence in the three countries. For example, 'race' has been a much more influential issue in the USA and New Zealand than it has in England, where a government minister dismissed concerns about the possibility of racial segregation with the statement that her government did not wish "to circumscribe [parental] choice in any way" (*The Times Educational Supplement*, 1988). 'Race' has influenced policies in New Zealand, in terms of funding and community influence, and in the USA, in relation to funding and enrolment policies, far more than it has in England.

The limited evidence available about the effects of policies designed to encourage parental choice and school self-management in these three countries will now be considered.

Research on the effects of quasi-markets in education

In England, a national study conducted by Birmingham University and funded by the union National Association of Head Teachers (NAHT) was generally positive about the impact of LMS but conceded that direct evidence of the influence of self-management on learning was 'elusive'. The team's initial survey (Arnott et al, 1992), showed that the vast majority of headteachers agreed with the statement that 'local management allows schools to make more effective use of their resources'. However, a majority also felt that meetings were being taken up by administrative issues which lessened their attention to students' learning. They were thoroughly divided on the question of whether 'children's learning is benefiting from local management'. It was therefore rather unclear to what their concept of greater effectiveness actually related.

The results cited here came mainly from headteacher respondents, whose authority has been greatly enhanced by the self-management reform. It may be significant that the relatively few classroom teachers interviewed by the Birmingham research team were far more cautious about the benefits of LMS for pupil learning and overall standards. An independently funded study (Levačić, 1995) found headteachers generally welcomed self-management even where their school had lost resources as a result of it, while classroom teachers were sceptical about its benefits even in schools which had gained in resources. Levačić concludes that although local management enhances cost-efficiency, there is "a lack of strong theoretical argument and empirical evidence" to show that it improves the quality of teaching and learning, as claimed by the government (Levačić, 1995, p xi).

In the final report of the Birmingham study (Bullock and Thomas, 1994), relatively more headteachers claimed improvements in pupil learning, but significantly these seem to be associated with increased funding rather than self-management per se. While the Birmingham team concluded that self-management was broadly a successful reform, they argued that more evidence was needed on the relationship between resourcing levels and learning outcomes. This seems particularly important in that the schools most affected by budgetary difficulties, and therefore least likely to report a positive impact on pupils' learning, were often those with pupils from disadvantaged backgrounds.

The Birmingham study echoes some of the concerns expressed by Le Grand and Bartlett (1993) in their study of quasi–markets in social policy. Bartlett (1993) points out that, although parental choice has been increased by open enrolment, "the door is firmly closed once a school [is full]". He goes on to say that

> **by encouraging an increasingly selective admissions policy in [over–subscribed] schools open enrolment may be having the effect of bringing about increased opportunity for cream-skimming and hence inequality. (p 150)**

Furthermore, he found that

> **those schools which faced financial losses under the formula funding system tended to be schools which drew the greatest proportion of pupils from the most disadvantaged section of the community. (Bartlett, 1993, p 149)**

Whatever gains may have emerged from the reforms in terms of efficiency and responsiveness to some clients, there are serious concerns about their implications for equity.

The danger of 'cream skimming' is demonstrated in an important series of studies at King's College London on the operation of quasi-markets in London. In an early study, Bowe et al (1992) suggested that schools were competing to attract greater cultural capital and hoping for higher yielding returns. Subsequently, Gewirtz et al (1995) have shown schools seeking students who are "able", "gifted", "motivated and committed", and middle class, with girls and children with South Asian backgrounds being seen as particular assets in terms of their potential to enhance test scores. The least desirable clientele include those who are "less able", have special educational needs (SEN), especially emotional and behavioural difficulties, as well as children from working class backgrounds and boys, unless they also have some of the more desirable attributes.

There is certainly evidence that some schools discriminate against children with SEN (Feintuck, 1994). Bartlett (1993) argues that this will only not happen if the market price varies with the needs of the client. Funding formulae need to be weighted to give schools an incentive to take more expensive children. The current premium paid for children with SEN may not be enough, if it makes the school less popular with clients who, although bringing in less money, bring in other desirable attributes. Bowe et al (1992) and Vincent et al (1995) give examples of schools making just this sort of calculation.

The academically able are the 'cream' that most schools seek to attract. Such students stay in the system longer and thus bring in more money, as well as making the school appear successful in terms of its test scores and hence attractive to other desirable clients. Glennerster (1991) suggests that, given the opportunity, most schools will want to become more selective because taking children who will bring down scores will affect their overall market position. This is especially so when there is imperfect information about school effectiveness and when only 'raw' test scores are made available as is currently the case in England. Schools with the highest scores appear best even if other schools are more successful at enhancing achievement.

So long as schools tend to be judged on a uni-dimensional scale of academic excellence, many commentators have predicted that rather than choice leading to more diverse and responsive forms of provision, as claimed by many of its advocates, it will reinforce the existing hierarchy of schools, based on academic test results and social class. Those parents who are in a position to choose are selecting those schools that are closest to the traditional academic model of education that used to be associated with selective grammar schools. Even new types of school tend to be judged in these terms. Research has shown that many parents choose CTCs not so much for their hi-tech image, but because they are perceived as the next best thing to grammar schools or even elite private schools (Whitty et al, 1993).

In this situation, those *schools* that are in a position to choose often seek to identify their success with an emphasis on traditional academic virtues and thus attract those students most likely to display them. Many of the first schools to opt out and become GM were selective, single sex and with traditional sixth forms and this gave the sector an aura of élite status (Fitz et al, 1993). A few GM comprehensive schools have reverted to being overtly academically selective. Furthermore, Bush et al (1993) suggested that 30% of the GM 'comprehensive' schools they investigated were now using covert selection. GM schools have been identified as among those with the highest rates of exclusion of existing pupils and among the least willing to cater for pupils with SEN. To that extent they can hardly claim to have increased parental choice across the board (see Power et al, 1994).

Walford (1992) argues that, while choice will lead to better quality schooling for some children, the evidence so far suggests that it will "discriminate in particular against working class children and children of Afro-Caribbean descent" (p 137). Smith and Noble (1995) also conclude from a review of the evidence that choice policies in England are further disadvantaging already disadvantaged groups. Although schools have always been socially and racially segregated to the extent that residential segregation exists, Gewirtz et al (1995) suggest that choice may well exacerbate this segregation by extending it into previously integrated schools serving mixed localities. Their research indicates that working class children and particularly children with SEN are likely to be increasingly 'ghettoised' in poorly-resourced schools.

The Smithfield Project, a major government-funded study of the impact of choice policies in New Zealand, suggests that much the same type of social polarisation is taking place there (Lauder et al, 1994; Waslander and Thrupp, 1995). In another New Zealand study (Fowler, 1993), schools located in low socioeconomic areas were found to be judged negatively because of factors over which they had no influence, such as type of intake, location and problems perceived by parents as linked to these. Wylie (1994) has noted that schools in low income areas are more likely to be losing students to other schools. If we could be sure that their poor reputation was deserved, this might be taken as evidence that the market was working well with effective schools reaping their just rewards. However, as in England, judgements of schools tend to be made on social grounds or narrow academic criteria and with little reference to their overall performance or even their academic effectiveness on value-added measures. The funding regime makes it extremely difficult for schools in disadvantaged areas to break out of the cycle of decline. Wylie's study of the fifth year of self-managing schools in New Zealand (Wylie, 1994) identified schools in low income areas, and schools with high Maori enrolments, as experiencing greater resource problems than others.

Such research suggests that many of the differences between schools result from factors largely beyond the control of parents and schools, except for the power of advantaged parents and schools to enhance further their advantage and thereby increase education inequalities and social polarisation. This is not necessarily an argument against choice, but it is clear that procedures for selection to oversubscribed schools need reconsideration. Significantly, the Smithfield Project found that only in one year, where allocations to oversubscribed schools were based on 'balloting' (or drawing lots), did social polarisation between popular and unpopular schools decrease.

Wylie (1994; 1995) reports that the combination of choice and accountability measures has led to schools paying more attention to the attractiveness of physical plant and public image than to changes to teaching and learning methods other than the spread of computers. It has also led to increased attention to the information about school programmes and children's progress which reaches parents, changes that Wylie says "are clearly not without value in themselves". However, she also notes that

> **they do not seem able to counter or outweigh factors affecting school rolls which lie beyond school power, such as local demographics affected by employment, ethnicity, and class. (Wylie, 1995, p 163, citing Gordon, 1994; and Waslander and Thrupp, 1995)**

In the USA, despite the early association of public school choice with racial desegregation, there are considerable concerns about the equity effects of more recent attempts to enhance choice, especially as there is no clear evidence to date of a positive impact on student achievement. What evidence there is about the effects of choice policies on student achievement and equity continues to be at best inconclusive (Plank et al, 1993), despite claims by advocates of choice that "the best available evidence" shows that parental choice improves the education of all children, especially low income and minority students (Domanico, 1990).

Even some of the more positive evidence from controlled choice districts, such as Cambridge (Rossell and Glenn, 1988) and Montclair (Clewell and Joy, 1990), which seemed to show gradual overall achievement gains, is now regarded by Henig (1994) as methodologically flawed making it difficult to attribute improvements to choice per se.

Although choice has not always led to resegregation as its critics feared, improvements in the racial balance of Montclair and Cambridge schools were most noticeable during periods of strong government intervention. Henig goes on to argue that the much vaunted East Harlem 'miracle' (Fliegel with Maguire, 1990) has "escaped any serious effort at controlled analysis" even though it has had a special role "in countering charges that the benefits of choice programs will not accrue to minorities and the poor" (p 142). Not only have the apparently impressive gains in achievement now levelled off or even been reversed, it is impossible to be sure that the earlier figures were not merely the effect of schools being able to choose students from higher socioeconomic groups from outside the area or, alternatively, the empowerment of teachers.

The American evidence with regard to private school choice is also contentious, but relevant to the concerns of this study in view of current demands for an extension of the use of public funds to permit students to attend private schools. Much of the controversy centres around the various interpretations of the data from the high school studies of Coleman et al (1982) and, in particular, the work of Chubb and Moe (1990). Henig (1994) argues that the small advantage attributed to private schools is a product of the methodology used. Lee and Bryk (1993) also suggest Chubb and Moe's (1990) conclusions are not supported by the evidence as presented. Nevertheless, Bryk et al (1993) claim on the basis of their *own* work that Catholic schools do impact positively on the performance of low income families but they attribute this at least as much to an ethos of strong community values antithetical to the marketplace as to the espousal of market forces.

The evaluation by Witte et al (1994) of the controversial Milwaukee private school choice experiment, which enables children from poor families to attend private schools at public expense, concludes in its fourth year report that "in terms of achievement scores ... students perform approximately the same as Milwaukee Public School students". However, attendance of choice children is slightly higher and parental satisfaction has been high. For the schools, "the program has generally been positive, has allowed several to survive, several to expand, and contributed to the building of a new school". Yet some of the stronger claims made both for and against this type of programme cannot be sustained by the evidence, as it is a small and narrowly-targeted programme and certainly not a basis on which to judge the likely effects of a more thoroughgoing voucher initiative.

The Milwaukee programme overall has not hitherto been oversubscribed and, although students are self-selected, the schools involved have not been in a position to exercise choice. Elsewhere, the combination of oversubscription and self-selection in explaining apparent performance gains through private school choice suggests that equity is a major issue as it is in England and New Zealand. Smith and Meier (1995) use existing data to test the school choice hypothesis and conclude that "competition between public and private schools appears to result in a cream skimming effect" and that there is no reason to expect that the same will not happen with enhanced public school choice.

Conclusion

Some advocates of devolution and choice have argued that the indifferent performance of the reforms so far is merely evidence that they have not gone far enough (Tooley, 1995). However, the studies reported here suggest that marketisation is unlikely to produce the benefits for the poor that some of its most vocal supporters suggest it would. Whatever gains are to be had from handing decision making to parents and teachers (and they seem to be far fewer than the advocates claim), it seems that more rather than less regulation will be required if equity is to remain an important consideration in education policy. The key issues are likely to remain political ones, which need to be pursued at a political level.

Part of the challenge must be to move away from atomised decision making to the reassertion of collective responsibility without recreating the very bureaucratic systems whose shortcomings have helped to legitimate the current tendency to treat education as a private good rather than a public responsibility. While choice policies are part of a social text that helps to create new subject positions which undermine traditional forms of collectivism, those forms of collectivism themselves failed to empower many members of society, including women and minority ethnic groups. We need to ask how we can use the positive aspects of choice and autonomy to facilitate the development of new forms of community empowerment rather than exacerbating social differentiation. As Henig says of the USA,

> **the sad irony of the current education-reform movement is that, through over identification with school-choice proposals rooted in market-based ideas, the healthy impulse to consider**

**radical reforms to address social problems may be channelled
into initiatives that further erode the potential for collective
deliberation and collective response. (1994, p 222)**

In this context, it may be possible to identify progressive moments within
policies that foster devolution and choice. This potential was recognised
in some of the early moves towards devolution in New Zealand, but the
recent evidence suggests that it is proving increasingly difficult to realise
progressive moments at school-site level in a situation of diminishing
resources and when the broader political climate is pointing firmly in
the opposite direction. Atomised decision making in a highly stratified
society may appear to give everyone equal opportunities, but transferring
responsibility for decision making from the public to the private sphere
can actually reduce the possibility of collective action to improve the
quality of education for all. While some forms of devolution and choice
may warrant further exploration as ways of realising the legitimate
aspirations of disadvantaged groups, they should not be seen as an
alternative to broader struggles for social justice.

Postscript

In England, there were early indications that the change of government
would bring significant changes in policy. 'High quality education for
the many rather than excellence for the few' was the initial slogan. The
phasing out of the APS in the first piece of educational legislation of the
new Labour government, and the abolition of the nursery voucher scheme
suggested that privatisation (at least in its overt sense) was not the favoured
path of the government and that resources could – at least in principle –
be redistributed. Another rhetorical shift represented specialist schools
as a community resource rather than a privileged escape route for those
attending them, implying that a degree of collective responsibility for
the education of all children was to replace rampant competition between
schools. The key term was to be 'partnership' between different
stakeholders, including an enhanced although limited role for LEAs in
matters of planning and quality.

In practice, even these moves have probably been more symbolic
than anything else. Beyond that, the key elements of the Conservative
settlement, at least with regard to the compulsory years of schooling,
have largely stayed in place. It appears that we are still to have that

admixture of state control and market forces, combining a National Curriculum and assessment system with quasi-markets based on local management, diversity and choice. Labour, in the words of Michael Barber (1997), now head of the DfEE's Standards and Effectiveness Unit, seeks to "link its traditional concern with equality with a new recognition of diversity" (p 175).

The government has chosen to maintain the current distinction between LEA-maintained, voluntary-aided and GM status in the (initially) renamed forms of 'community', 'aided' and 'foundation' schools. Even if most GM schools identify themselves as comprehensive schools, they are more likely than LEA maintained schools to have sixth forms, relatively high proportions of middle-class pupils, and correspondingly low proportions of working-class and black pupils. Conservative efforts to present these schools as academically superior to others may have been intellectually dishonest in the absence of comparative data on 'value-added' performance, but they have almost certainly influenced public perceptions.

The proposals in the White Paper (DfEE, 1997) to identify 'foundation' schools even more closely with GM schools than was envisaged by Labour in opposition make it likely that the existing status hierarchy will be maintained. The terms 'community' and 'foundation' schools will assist the latter to trade on their traditionalist image even if their current advantages in terms of funding and control over admissions are removed. Although this was not identified as a key issue for consultation, it probably received more adverse comment than any other aspect of the White Paper. The government has recently bowed to pressure, but only in response to the specific concerns of the churches about voluntary controlled schools, and its new proposals could actually make the distinction between community and foundation schools even starker.

The successful fostering of specialisation and diversity within a broader commitment to comprehensive secondary education demands that serious attention be given to ways of preventing differences becoming inequalities. This will require much stronger national guidelines and local procedures on admissions than are currently being considered as the "fairer ways of offering school places" promised in the White Paper.

Part Three

Social care

SIX

How providers are chosen in the mixed economy of community care

Russell Mannion and Peter Smith

Introduction

A new system of providing the social care services and support required by people affected by problems associated with ageing, mental illness, learning difficulties or physical disability was implemented in the UK in April 1993. Known as community care the system gave local authorities (LAs) the responsibility to assess the requirements of those in need, to design a package of care, and to purchase that care from a range of providers, many in the voluntary or private sector. This chapter will explore the nature of the process whereby providers were chosen, and will identify the key influences on that choice. In so doing, the approach taken goes beyond the conventional neoclassical approach to choice adopted by many economists. Instead, it uses the concepts associated with the emerging disciplines of behavioural economics and the new economic sociology. These perspectives can offer important insights into the decision-making processes used when choosing providers in quasi-markets. The empirical element of this chapter is based on fieldwork in six LAs.

The chapter begins by describing the background to the study, including a description of the community care reforms. This is followed by some theoretical background to the analysis of provider choice, and a description of the study methodology. Next, it identifies two broad sets of influences on the choice of provider: the 'macro' environment, which determines the broad framework within which any decision is made, and the 'micro' environment pertaining to a particular user. These are considered in turn. Finally, some inferences to be drawn from the study are discussed.

Background

Before the introduction of community care in 1993, social care services had been provided and funded by a range of agencies, including the NHS, local government and the Department of Health and Social Security (DHSS), and later the Benefits Agency. As noted above, the new arrangements gave LAs the lead responsibility for arranging a package of care. In general, those receiving residential care before the new arrangements came into force, predominantly those in private homes supported by the Benefits Agency and those in LA homes, continued to receive care from the same source (those users receiving Benefits Agency support before April 1993 have what are know as 'preserved rights'). Referrals since April 1993 have been assessed under the new system, and it is these users on whom this chapter concentrates. Attention has been focused on the issues raised by community care for older people, by far the largest group affected by the reforms of the Conservative administrations.

Central to the new arrangements was the establishment of a market in social care, in which the LA purchases services on behalf of its clients, and a range of providers compete to deliver the required services. A 'quasi-market' in community care has been established, along the lines of those already operating in health and education in the UK (Le Grand and Bartlett, 1993; Bartlett et al, 1994). The principal features of community care which distinguishes it from these other publicly-funded quasi-markets is that it is an *external* market, in which providers are drawn predominantly from the independent sector, and that many of the providers are likely to be profit-seeking.

The duties placed on LAs in relation to community care are set out in the 1990 National Health Service and Community Care Act. The practice guidance issued by the Social Services Inspectorate (SSI) (DoH, 1991) sets out the general framework within which LAs are to purchase social care services. The document recommends that social services departments obtain the information required to assess whether potential suppliers are reliable, commercially viable and share the values of the purchasing authority (Hudson, 1994). Part II of the 1988 Local Government Act (LGA) prevents LAs from specifying non-commercial considerations in contracts, for example, terms and conditions of employment, staff promotion and training. However, matters such as staff qualifications, ability to recruit and retain staff as well as likely ability to meet the terms of the contract can be taken in to account when selecting providers.

As with most procurement in the state sector in the reformed quasi-market, the principal mechanism for allocating resources and controlling activity was the contract between purchaser and provider. The SSI guidance identified three ways in which LAs could select providers: open tendering, in which all providers were invited to tender; select list tendering, in which providers were short-listed on certain criteria, thereafter competing mainly on price; and direct negotiation with suppliers, whereby service specifications were developed jointly between purchasers and providers.

In discussing the purchase of community care it was important to bear in mind the distinguishing features of the services being bought (Mannion and Smith, 1997a). First, the requirements of individual users were likely to be diverse. A key objective of the reforms was to match services more closely to needs, and for this to be achieved it was not possible to rely on standard packages of care. Second, the needs of users were likely to be unpredictable, and to change over time, so the system of care must be flexible and responsive. Third, at the same time, continuity of care was vital, with changes in provider potentially very damaging to the individual. Fourth, many users were vulnerable individuals who need to be protected from exploitation. Fifth, there was an intrinsic difficulty in specifying and monitoring quality standards in community care, particularly relating to eventual outcomes. With these issues in mind, the next section examines the theoretical framework within which this study was undertaken.

Models of provider choice

The standard model of choice used by economists was based on the neoclassical critique. In its crudest form, this entails choosing the amounts of each good to be purchased on the basis of the marginal utility it confers on the purchaser. Neoclassical analysis has been the dominant mode of analysis in the academic economics community, and its models have been developed to a high degree of refinement (Laffont and Tirole, 1993). In the context of community care, it is likely that the perceived bundle of 'characteristics' inherent in the products being offered matter more than the products themselves (Lancaster, 1966). A neoclassicist might view the choice of provider as a problem when assessing the performance of each bidder along a number of criteria, including price, and finding the bidder with the highest 'score' according to some concept of utility. The neoclassical paradigm therefore offers a compensatory model of choice, in which various criteria are traded off against each other.

The neoclassical analysis has great strengths - in particular its rigour and internal consistency. However, it has been frequently criticised for the unrealistic axioms on which it is based (Earl, 1983). Most especially, the neoclassical model assumes that the chooser has immense capabilities in collecting and processing the information necessary to make a choice. When the product is as complex as social care, all the requirements of the purchaser cannot be built into the contract; feedback on the provider's performance is needed throughout the term of the contract. The internal market in community care was likely to have large transaction costs, both ex ante and ex post facto. Although still conducted within a neoclassical framework, the literature on markets and hierarchies offers a useful critique of the transaction costs problem (Williamson, 1975).

A more radical response to the perceived shortcomings of the neoclassical analysis has been the development of the 'new economic sociology' (Granovetter and Swedberg, 1992). This approach emphasises that economic decisions are taken by individuals or groups of people within a social setting so economic choices cannot be viewed in isolation from the situation in which they are taken. In particular, social relations between the actors involved in the decision – or in the social networks – are likely to be important (Powell, 1990).

A recurrent theme within sociological approaches to the market is the notion that traditional neoclassical economic theory overstates the role of price in regulating patterns of exchange (Bradach and Eccles, 1991). Purchasing decisions, at both an individual and organisational level, are assumed to be determined less by costs and demand, than by social construction through a process of bargaining within networks of social actors. From this perspective, informal information transmitted through social networks concerning issues such as quality, trust, reputation and status are viewed as possibly more important determinants of competition than price, particularly in complex markets.

The increased interest in social network analysis represents a radical departure from the unrealistic axioms underlying neoclassical economic theory and has developed in parallel with the advances in behavioural economic theory. As Earl (1983) explains, although behavioural theories of choice have been commonly used by marketing specialists, they have yet to be integrated into a coherent framework capable of challenging the hegemony of the neoclassical view. However, it is considered that behavioural choice models are likely to be of great value when trying to understand the purchasing process in community care.

A common theme running through behavioural approaches is the notion that choices are made between alternative goods or services conceived as bundles of characteristics or attributes rather than goods as wholes, along the lines of Lancaster's model. However, in many behavioural models choices are also assumed to be non-compensatory, in the sense that purchasers do not necessarily maximise utility by trading off the (weighted) attributes of price and quality when making decisions to buy a good or service. Consumers are assumed to suffer from 'bounded rationality', in the sense that they are incapable of processing the vast amounts of information necessary to come to a rational decision.

For example, in the behavioural 'lexicographic' model, it is assumed that choosers consider alternative schemes of action in terms of a single attribute at a time. The choice process is assumed to be sequential rather then conforming to the neoclassical notion of simultaneous optimisation. Priority ranking of the various attributes acts as a filtering tool and schemes are chosen only if each attribute meets a required target. If two or more schemes are under consideration the scheme chosen is the one that satisfies the most attributes. Trade-offs in line with the neoclassical model occur only after higher attribute levels have been met. These models will be returned to later in the chapter to show how they can be used to model purchasing choices in the community care market.

In many ways the quasi-market in community care is about as complex a market as can be envisaged. The product is multidimensional and evolves over a period of time. It is impossible to specify complete contracts. An intermediary is purchasing on behalf of the beneficiary. As a prelude to any modelling work, careful empirical observation of the system at work was imperative. This study seeks to provide some evidence to that end.

Fieldwork was undertaken in six social services departments, chosen to reflect a wide range of circumstances. The authorities involved included two London boroughs, two metropolitan districts and two non-metropolitan counties. About five managers in each department were interviewed using qualitative, semi-structured interviews. The interviewees were chosen so as to elicit perceptions at all levels in the managerial hierarchy at which some element of discretion regarding resource allocation existed. In all areas, this included the Assistant Director of Social Services responsible for community care at the top of the hierarchy. The lowest level in most LAs was team manager, directly responsible for care managers, the front-line staff who arrange assessments and manage care packages. (Because anonymity of respondents was guaranteed, it is not possible to give details of staff interviewed.)

Macro-purchasing environment

In seeking to gain an understanding of purchaser choices, it is important to have a clear idea of the organisational, financial and legal environment in which decisions are made. This section introduces the 'macro environment', the framework within which all purchases within an LA must be made. Given the legal framework for community care set out above, five aspects of the macro environment relevant to the choice of providers will be examined: the profile of needs in the population; the financial constraints; the state of the market in providers of care services; local political considerations, and the organisational structure of local services.

Population needs

Underlying all of the macro considerations to be discussed below is the pattern of needs in the local population. The concept of 'needs' is in itself problematic (Doyal and Gough, 1991). In this study, needs might be interpreted as the personal circumstances that society considers qualify the individual for inclusion in the community care programme. In practice, needs criteria are likely to be based on national guidelines, interpreted at the local level in the light of resource constraints.

Few independent direct measures of needs exist. Social and economic considerations, as reported in the 1991 Census of Population, formed the basis for the government's allocation of funds to the LA. The local political priority attached to community care is then likely to reflect local perceptions of the need for social care, bearing in mind competing demands on the LA budget. Also, local needs and preferences are likely to have played a major role in determining the existing configuration of services for social care. There may be cultural and geographical considerations which affect the design of organisational form for delivering community care. Where those in need and their carers represent a potent electoral force, or are able to mount effective political campaigns, the authority may be more likely to give a high priority to the service.

The links between population characteristics, need for community care and programme budgets are immensely important, and deserve a study in themselves. In this chapter it will only be possible to note the central importance of population characteristics in shaping the nature of the local community care programme.

Financial issues

LAs are funded from three major sources: central government grants, including business property taxes; the local residential tax, called the Council Tax, and user charges. LAs are not allowed to borrow to fund current expenditure. The level of central government grant to an LA is determined principally by its standard spending assessment (SSA), which is the central government's estimate of how much an LA should spend if it were to deliver a standard level of services. Central government also specifies an upper limit on total expenditure, an expenditure cap for each LA. Most of the LAs responsible for personal social services spend at their caps, so the central government cap effectively determines the total budget for an authority. The authority's budgeting decision is therefore principally one of allocating expenditure between services, which for all of the authorities considered in this study include education, highway maintenance, and a range of other services, in addition to personal social services. The first significant determinant of the amount of resources available for the community care budget is the allocation secured in the authority's budgeting process.

Every social services department receives an annual budget for community care which determines the global financial constraint within which the system must operate. The budget must fund existing commitments, users already receiving care, and new commitments. To ease transition to the new system, central government distributes a special transitionary grant (STG), which must be spent on new referrals to community care. In the first year (1993/94) an authority's entitlement to STG was based partly on its social services SSA (50%) and partly on the number of people already being supported by social security benefits in independent homes in the area (50%). In the second year the formula for allocating the STG was abruptly changed so that it was based totally on the SSA.

The size of the local community care budget was ultimately determined by local political preferences, which are discussed further below. However, an authority's choice was in practice severely circumscribed by its existing community care commitments, by its global expenditure cap, and by the size of the STG. The evidence from our qualitative interviews was that the level of and conditions attached to STG had a profound affect on both the level of activity and the nature of purchasing decisions in community care. All authorities used the STG as a guideline for the community care budget. However, the government's expenditure caps sometimes compromised the ability of the social services department to win the full budget implied by government figures. Many authorities, in seeking to conform to the expenditure cap, applied a rule of equal pain for all, resulting in community care budgets below government figures.

A further fundamental financial consideration was the nature of the charges that the authority was prepared to impose on users. Budgets were prepared net of user charges, and so every £1 that an authority could earn in charges enables it to purchase an extra £1 of services. The charges an authority imposes often affect the demand for community care.

Market in providers

One of the central concerns of interviewees taking part in this study was the nature of the local market in providers of community care. The system was specifically intended to change the nature of social care, by shifting the emphasis from residential to domiciliary and respite care. The need to spend 85% of STG on the private sector ruled out the easy option of large-scale in-house provision to fill gaps in the market. It was hardly surprising that most respondents considered local markets to be seriously incomplete, in the sense that there were difficulties in finding providers for some services. In most cases the concern was with shortcomings in the domiciliary sector. However, in London, there was a major concern with the lack of affordable residential services within easy reach of a user's current home.

On deeper probing it became clear that the concern was not just with the absence of providers, but also with the quality of those providers offering services. (The issue of quality will be discussed below in the section on the micro-purchasing environment.) In the initial context the concern with quality was tied up with purchasers' lack of knowledge about the reliability and probity of fledgling providers.

This research found a high degree of information asymmetry existing between purchasers and providers. A particular cause of concern was the lack of reliable information concerning the quality of services delivered by providers in the unregulated domiciliary care market. A common response to the shortcomings in the information was for the LA to contract with independent providers mainly for social care, such as help with shopping and cleaning, rather than personal care, such as bathing. In this way purchasers felt they were minimising the opportunity for abuse or serious neglect of users. So in some ways the problem of quality was really one of trust in a situation where quality could be neither monitored or enforced.

Further crucial considerations relating to local supply were the nature of complementary services, as provided by other statutory and voluntary organisations. Most importantly, the links with local health services were perceived as crucial. For example, joint finance with health services may have important consequences for community care. The willingness and ability of local GPs to collaborate in social care may affect purchasing decisions. The attitude of local health services towards the difficult interface between healthcare and social care was universally perceived to be an area of prime importance. The following response was typical of many:

> **"The legislation does not clarify the important areas, like what are the circumstances in which someone can continue to use NHS facilities? It would help us if parameters were defined as to what constitutes 'continuing care'. The health services are always given the rider 'subject to local resources permitting'. [LAs] are subject to judicial review if [they] do not provide, which is a considerable inequality. Health service managers can say 'well we are not budgeting for that this year'. If we find an assessed need we are legally obliged to provide for it."** (area manager)

It was expected that information would be given on the important influence that local GP services, housing agencies and the voluntary sector have on the operation of community care. However, at this stage these were perceived to be far less problematic than the interface with hospital and community health services (HCHS).

Political constraints

As noted above, the size of the community care budget was in part determined by political processes within the LA. There was considerable concern in two authorities that social services fared badly in the budgeting process, in particular because, as a group, the elderly were not considered a political priority. Conversely, there were two authorities in which community care had become a political priority, and so the managers perceived that their services had relatively generous provision.

It was found that political attitudes towards private sector provision were also considered to be important in determining charging policies and the range of choices available to purchasers. However, explicit political constraints did not appear to be a major consideration so far as most respondents were concerned.

Organisational issues

The fieldwork showed that LAs were adopting a range of organisational forms to deliver community care. Organisational structure was crucial, as it was the mechanism the LA chose to ensure that the 'high level' constraints described above were adhered to in practice. All departments had given much thought to organisational issues, and two were in the process of reorganisation at the time of the fieldwork. Although all the social services departments were organised hierarchically, there were a range of possible ways in which functions, responsibilities and budgets could be devolved.

There are three aspects of organisational structure relevant to purchasing services: geographical organisation; the purchaser–provider split; financial devolution. The first consideration was whether social services departments were divided on an area basis, to a delimited population, or on a functional basis of the domiciliary, residential and support services and finance. Under the area model, senior managers were responsible for all functions in a defined area. Under the functional model, senior managers were responsible for specific functions over the whole LA area. In this study four authorities were organised on an area basis and two by function.

The second consideration was the level in the authority to which the purchaser–provider split occurs: that is, the extent to which in-house services were treated as an autonomous provider. At one extreme, LA services might have been floated off as separate entities. At the other, in-house services might continue to be integrated into the existing social services structure. The choice is clearly of importance to purchasing decisions. It determines the extent to which care managers feel constrained to make use of in-house providers in the design of their care packages. Only two of the LAs had a clear purchaser–provider split, at deputy or assistant director level. However, the other four were either planning, or in the early stages of implementing, a purchaser–provider split.

Thirdly, the level of financial devolution has important implications for purchasing decisions. In theory at least, care packages can be organised in a more flexible and responsive manner if budgetary discretion is moved closer to users and carers. However, in order to retain budgetary and policy control, it is likely that a high level of devolution will be associated with tighter bureaucratic controls, in the form of limiting the range of options open to purchasers and imposing strict reporting requirements. None of the LAs in this study had devolved financial responsibility to care managers, although one was piloting such a scheme. In most of the areas budget control was devolved down to team leader level. Generally, staff from all the authorities agreed that devolved budgeting would result in more timely and sensitively designed care packages.

A survey by the Audit Commission (1994) found that LAs were increasingly devolving budgets from the centre. It is now common for LAs to devolve budgets to area-, team- or even care-manager level.

The front-line care manager was central to the purchasing decision making in all authorities, subject to the constraints imposed by the authority. The major organisational issue was whether LA constraints should be imposed ex ante or ex post facto. In the former case the care manager was usually free to recommend the provider without further upward referral: because the constraints were set in advance of assessment, the purchasing decision could be devolved to the lowest level in the hierarchy. In the ex post facto case the decision was in the hands of a committee attended by the care manager after the potential user had been assessed. This was unwieldy and time-consuming, but obviated the need for firm guidelines to be issued to care managers. The committee was able to make flexible decisions in the light of up-to-date information about overall community care needs and resources. Whatever system was chosen, it was clear that the key individual was the care manager, who would usually have a fairly clear view about the provider an individual should be offered.

A final crucial organisational consideration was the choice of contractual form with providers that the authority was prepared to make. In some authorities, there was a considerable emphasis on 'block' contracts with large providers, which meant that, implicitly or explicitly, care managers were encouraged to refer users to those providers. At the other extreme, some authorities relied exclusively on 'spot' contracts for individual users, which afforded a greater degree of freedom in choice of providers.

Micro-purchasing environment

The macro environment sets constraints within which any purchasing decision must be made. In the context of this chapter, the micro environment comprises the considerations which, given the macro environment, determine the choice of provider for a given user. A package of care for a new applicant is designed on the basis of a formal assessment of his or her care needs. In principle, the assessment and the recommended package should be independent of the macro constraints outlined above, or of the financial circumstances of the applicant. In practice, it is likely that packages were recommended in the knowledge of local constraints. However, an assessment of the extent of this influence was beyond the scope of this study. The recommended package of care was treated as given, and the study concentrated instead on the influences on the choice of provider once that recommendation had been made.

The micro influences on the choice of provider are now considered, first in the situation in which the users (or their carers or relatives) make the choice, and then when the LA makes the choice.

User preferences

The White Paper *Caring for people* (DoH, 1989) made much of 'consumer sovereignty' in the new arrangements for community care, which were intended to match services to preferences very much more closely than hitherto. The team managers, those closest to users among the interviewees, all agreed that the new arrangements had given a much greater voice to users and their carers. A detailed examination of the decision-making process among individual users was beyond the scope of this study. Ideally, this issue should be addressed by a user survey. However, the interviews were used to explore the possible sources of information on which users might base their preferences. These fall into four categories: personal circumstances; provider publicity; LA advice; and other users.

The personal circumstances of the user were central to many user choices. Among the most important influences were the level of charges and the preferences of relatives and carers.

There was a great deal of evidence to suggest that providers were losing no time in developing a range of marketing strategies among potential users, as comments from two of the interviewees illustrate:

> **"The main marketing is still to the clients. It is more effective as they have free choice. All the hospitals have close circuit television and homes advertise on these."** (senior finance officer)

> **"One example in our [area] is that one home gives free day care if you arrive there in the afternoon and want company or a bath. They will do this free of charge as a loss leader. When a person needs permanent residential care there is no doubt which home they are going to choose."** (finance director)

LA advice might often be sought by a user who is asked to express a preference (the formation of preferences among LA staff is treated more fully in the next section). Respondents suggest that the usual role of staff at this stage of the purchasing decision was to advise only if a clearly inappropriate choice was being contemplated.

Interviewees suggested that users were becoming informed about the range of facilities available through a number of networks, ranging from word of mouth with other users and their families or carers, to the more formal advice offered by user groups and voluntary organisations.

The typical process through which potential users go was: the assessment was carried out and a package designed; a maximum acceptable price was determined, and the associated user charges calculated; the user was free to select the provider of their choice, subject to the price constraint and any quality standards imposed by the LA. Users may in principle be able to select packages costing more than the price limits by using their own funds to top up the LA contribution. However, this phenomenon was unlikely, as most LAs sought to capture any extra resources in the original user charge.

Given the importance of user preferences, there was some support for a system of direct payments to users, with which they would be free to purchase care without the mediation of the LA. Such an arrangement would transfer the role of purchasing and monitoring care to the individual, and would limit the role of the LA to that of needs assessor and financier. At the time of the study direct payments schemes to users were illegal (although some small payments under the Independent Living Fund were permitted). However, some authorities circumvented this restriction by providing voluntary organisations with funds to allocate to suitable applicants on the same basis as direct payments. Most respondents thought that there would be inherent problems with an indiscriminate direct payment scheme, given the vulnerability of many users but that direct payments could be beneficial among younger disabled people. Many respondents raised the problem that direct payments might not be spent on the care for which they were intended. An intermediate scheme would be to offer users vouchers which *must* be spent on community care.

There were some staff who thought that the new arrangements had not increased choice for those who required residential accommodation. For these users, the previous arrangements, financed by the Department of Social Security (DSS), had operated as a voucher system under which those who qualified for residential care could take their custom where they wanted.

Local authority preferences

Many users did not express a preference as to provider. There was also a clear acknowledgement that many users were, for various reasons, vulnerable individuals to whom it would be unreasonable and inappropriate to devolve the purchasing responsibility. There will always be a significant role for an agency such as the LA to act on behalf of such individuals.

LA officers often had a view as to the appropriate provider for a particular user, and would often be asked to express that view, either as an input to or as a replacement for the user's own choice. To varying extents, the macro constraints described above will play an important part in forming that view. The key officer to recommend a provider was the front-line care manager. The tendency was to use the macro constraints effectively to screen potential providers. When a provider satisfied all the qualification criteria, the two crucial issues that appeared to determine whether they were awarded the contract were price and quality, and purchasers were clearly encountering difficulties in balancing these issues.

Price is generally unambiguous. Quality is an elusive concept, beyond any simple and universal definition. It is put to different uses, to achieve different purposes to serve different interests. Nevertheless, colloquial and common sense notions of quality were frequently invoked by respondents and used as criteria to select providers. These 'street level' interpretations of quality can often differ from stated organisational policy objectives (Lipsky, 1980).

In practice, virtually all notions of quality in community care defy definition, measurement or monitoring. Consequently, whatever notion of quality in which they are interested, purchasers have to rely on informal information, status, trust and reputation as a basis of assessing the quality of providers.

> **"Trust is very important and increasingly so, particularly in the non-residential sector as you've no back up of the residential unit. It is also much more difficult to monitor, although this is crucial. Chances are that in a residential home there will be someone on duty every night, but with domiciliary services there is no back-up and someone could die in the night. So you can't afford the risks." (assistant director)**

Trust within this context serves as a lubricant of economic exchange by reducing the transaction costs associated with regulating the quasi-market. It operates as an intangible capital asset which "economises on the costs of bargaining, monitoring, insurance and dispute settlement" (Sako, 1991). Purchasers value trusted providers and are more likely to choose them when designing care packages. The challenge for both purchasers and providers is to establish relationships in which mutual trust and confidence flourishes. Trust is a reciprocal concept in which all parties – the LA, the user, the provider – must work together if services are to be provided in an efficient and appropriate manner. Evidence from this study suggests that many providers compete largely on the basis of perceived reputation and trust rather than price. It will be interesting to see whether this reflects a transitional stage, necessary until more formal mechanisms of quality assessment are put in place, or whether reliance on trust is intrinsic to the community care sector. Although dominant, the reliance on trust was not universal. A desire to test the market, or to stimulate competition, may encourage purchasers to seek out new providers.

However, the general rule was that providing the price was acceptable, status, trust and reputation were the most important elements of the purchasing decision. This raises the questions: How do purchasers assess potential providers on quality criteria? How do they form their views? Four possible ways in which information about the quality of providers could be transmitted to those with purchasing decisions were encountered in this study: inspection; feedback from users; informal networks and provider marketing.

Formal inspection is a statutory requirement for independent residential homes who wish to be registered as potential community care providers – they must be inspected twice a year. The system was generally felt to be inadequate, with a perceived lack of commitment to the formal inspection process. Formal inspection mechanisms may even have a deleterious effect on the flow of information:

> **"One of the things that changed under the community care legislation was that the registration and inspection reports had to be made public. Prior to that they were not. This resulted in a huge change in the type of report [inspectors] put out. The original ones which were confidential had lots of subjective opinion, gut feeling, anecdotes etc. As soon as they became public and there was a risk of a challenge it suddenly changed dramatically. So although the information now appears to be more formal, I suspect that over telephones, over lunch, a lot of what was written down before is now transmitted verbally and is not put in a report." (director of finance)**

The domiciliary sector was not regulated in the same way, but most authorities have already implemented or were in the process of implementing an approved registration scheme. However, there were difficulties in monitoring quality in terms of home-based services, and few resources available to do this.

User feedback was generally felt to be haphazard, partial, incomplete and difficult to record systematically. Some authorities had experimented with a limited range of user satisfaction surveys. However, the consensus was that this area merited much more vigorous development. In line with experience in the healthcare sector, there was some scepticism about the ability of user satisfaction surveys to capture the performance of providers (Carr-Hill, 1992), and some respondents suggested that the most desirable development in this area would be a responsive complaints procedure.

Informal networks among care managers were seen to be of vital importance. However, there were some misgivings about the value of the information:

> "Information gets passed round by word of mouth. It's richer information but I'm not sure that it's comprehensive and consistent, and it doesn't address the problem with the [provider]. The word of mouth may be not to use agency x, but agency x will wonder why no one is using them any more – they will not be told necessarily why." (team leader)

Perhaps the most obvious link of trust exists between purchasers and their former colleagues in LA providers. The most formal evidence of trust was embodied in the existence of a large block contract with a particular provider, which was often residential accommodation formerly run by the LA. The existence of such a contract would inevitably encourage the care manager to recommend use of that provider where appropriate.

Increasingly, the *marketing effort* by independent providers was being aimed at LA purchasers:

> "We get piles of stuff every week. I get a lot of phone calls. The most persistent ones will insist on coming here. We have no financial incentives to give business to specific agencies. I do know that [another area] were getting crates of beer and boxes of chocs, champagne etc." (team leader)

There was no evidence of any explicit trade-off occurring between price and quality at the micro level. All the LAs in the survey had broad guidelines determining how much to spend on specific types of service and in the residential sector there are nationally-prescribed guidelines. Purchasers generally consider only providers whose prices fall within the prescribed guidelines, and go outside these only in exceptional circumstances. Care managers appeared to enjoy a lot of discretion about whom to choose, within the prescribed limits for services. At the micro level, purchasers appeared to treat price as a constraint, and sought to find the maximum quality provider subject to that constraint.

Conclusion

Evidence uncovered in this study has shown that there exist four main types of macro constraints on the purchase of community care: financial, legal, political and organisational constraints. These constraints were transmitted to the care manager, the front-line employee, by means of guidelines and cash limits. The potential user was assessed and a package of care designed in accordance with those guidelines. On the basis of the assessment, a maximum acceptable price was identified. The user was notified of any charges that might have arisen. If the user then expressed a preference for a provider who satisfied all requirements, including quality standards, then that choice was usually respected. Where a user expressed no acceptable preference, the LA made the choice. The key actor in making that choice was the care manager. The process described is illustrated in schematic form in Figure 1.

At the micro level, there is not enough information from this study to allow an assessment of the decision–making model adopted by users. However, among LA purchasers, the tendency was to treat price as a constraint rather than a factor to be traded off against quality. This was particularly so where the purchasing decision has been delegated to the front-line care manager. The behaviour of the purchaser conforms to some of the lexicographic behavioural theories of choice set out above, in the sense that many of the variables relevant to a decision, including price, were used as *filters* rather than treated as arguments in a utility function. A mathematical formulation of the choice model might be that purchasers maximise $U_i = f_i(Q_j)$ subject to $P_j Q_j \pounds \leq B_i^*$, where U_i is an ordinal measure of welfare associated with a particular level of quality for user i, Q_j is a measure of the quality of provider j, P_j is a measure of price per unit of quality, and B_i^* is the maximum expenditure permitted for client i.

Figure 1: Decision process for applicants accepted into community care

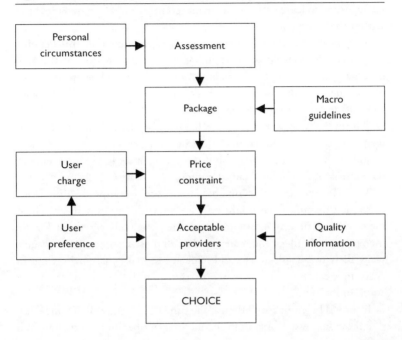

This contrasts with the standard neoclassical model, under which the LA would seek to trade off price and quality by maximising a weighted sum of individual welfare measures $W = f(U_1, U_2, ... U_n)$, subject to an overall budget constraint $\Sigma_i B_i \leq B$. The decision-making mechanisms which were less devolved, those in which care managers referred their cases to a committee, would appear to offer a closer approximation to this model, in that they permit managers to assess the relative merits of different claims on their budget. However, even among authorities adopting this model of decision making, very little evidence was found of price explicitly entering the decision-making process for individual users.

In many ways this finding was an inevitable consequence of the nature of the market being examined. Budgets were set annually. Referrals arose throughout the year, and each potential user was likely to have individual requirements which precluded the specification of standard packages. Under these circumstances, the only realistic means of securing budgetary control was to specify guide prices for particular aspects of packages and to leave users or care managers to seek out favoured providers within the price constraint.

The apparent lack of importance attached to price in the final choice should also be viewed in the light of the utility function of the care managers. They are predominantly social workers, whose professional ethos reflects values such as "respect, individualisation, confidentiality and self-determination" (Rojek et al, 1988). The managerial ethic on which the reforms were based was likely to be alien to the typical care manager. The utility function of the care manager would also inevitably include private goals, such as job preservation and career advancement, which may be in conflict with the interests of users (Smith and Wright, 1994). The service being purchased was often complex. Purchasers were then making what might be a long-term commitment, in which the costs of an unsatisfactory decision were potentially very high, for the user, for carers and for the manager. For all these reasons, care managers were likely to be risk-averse, and reluctant to make marginal savings in costs in exchange for increases in the quantity of users receiving community care.

It should be emphasised that, at the time of the study, the community care programme was only in its second year of operation, so the research could have been observing a transitional period. It may be, for example, that as authorities gained a better understanding of the 'going rate' for a particular level of quality they became more responsive to prices. However, all the evidence suggests that an increasing number of authorities were devolving decisions to the care manager, and that it could be judged from this that devolution would decrease still further the relevance of price.

A consequence of this analysis is that for the risk-averse front-line manager operating within hard cash limits, the incentive was to adopt strict criteria for accepting an applicant into community care. The available budget will then be spent on good quality services for high need users, even though this means being able to accept fewer low need individuals into care. In this way, purchasing managers can minimise the damaging consequences to their clients and to themselves of placements with unsatisfactory providers. Unsatisfied demand was likely to be distressing to these managers, but they can blame the inability to meet demand on higher level budget constraints. The pattern of care emerging under a strictly cash-limited budget was likely to be, as one manager put it, "a Rolls Royce for a few rather than a Metro for everyone".

Under this model, the process whereby 'quality' is assessed by the care manager is crucial. Four mechanisms were found to influence the care manager's assessment of the quality of a provider: formal inspection; feedback from users; informal networks; and provider marketing. It is unlikely that qualitative issues will ever be incorporated into formal contracts. These are replaced by the concept of trust, which can in many senses be considered synonymous with the purchaser's perception of quality. The central importance of trust identified in the interviews suggests that the new sociological view of market transactions is highly relevant to the community care quasi-market.

In rejecting the relevance of the neoclassical model at the micro level, it does not necessarily follow that its importance at the macro level is being rejected. For example, the LA budget-setting process may well conform to the neoclassical axioms, in which service budgets were set according to the principles of equalising marginal utility across each of the services. However, at the micro level – given the great importance of personal relations in the purchasing process – it is difficult to see how the neoclassical model will ever apply.

The findings relating to trust have important implications for the workings of the community care quasi-market which deserve further investigation (Mannion and Smith, 1997b). Trust is an intangible capital asset, analogous to brand names in more conventional markets. Providers might devote considerable energy to building up trust, in an effort to gain a dominant market position and to deter the entry of potential competitors into the market. Further work might examine the strategies that providers adopt in seeking to gain the trust of purchasers. Are their energies devoted to *marketing* or to pursuit of *excellence* in the delivery of services? How quickly does a provider's status depreciate in the eyes of purchasers? Most fundamentally, this study has raised the question of whether – given the inevitable reliance on trust – a market in community care can ever be truly competitive.

Acknowledgements

We should like to thank the interviewees, who without exception readily gave up their valuable time to answer our sometimes impertinent questions, and to the other members of the project team.

SEVEN

Markets, hierarchies and choices in social care

Irvine Lapsley and Sue Llewellyn

Introduction

In the past decade and a half, the UK's public sector has been subject to a series of dramatic changes: an increased visibility for accounting, an emphasis on managerialism, and the introduction of quasi-markets. This paper examines the implementation of quasi-markets within the area of social care. The major focus of this research is on how decision makers within local government use information on costs and quality of care, whether managers trade-off costs and quality when faced with a budget constraint and the extent to which detailed, disaggregated information on costs and quality of care shape decisions in the market environment of social services. This study reveals tensions and contradictions inherent in the operation of these markets, and, in particular, the extent to which substantive change in the underlying professional norms and value-oriented decision-making processes of social service workers has or has not resulted from their introduction.

The introduction of internal markets had the potential to bring about profound change in the public sector. It had implications for governance structures, for professional practices, and, thus ultimately for the delivery of services to clients. This study explores the impact of certain mechanisms associated with quasi-markets in a number of social services departments in local authorities (LAs). Market principles such as the purchaser–provider split, the use of contracts as a basis for service specification, and reliance on prices, rather than rule-based procedures, to mediate transactions are all associated with the operation of internal markets and would be expected to engender change in both structures and processes in the social services. However, the LAs still assume a close to monopsonistic role as *purchaser* of social services. It is they, rather than the consumers of services, agents, or intermediaries, who monitor service outcomes within the social services. Tensions and contradictions were inherent in the operation of these quasi-markets. Such tensions raise important questions concerning the extent of change in the LAs, in particular: did the introduction of an internal market in care result in change of a substantive kind, or was there merely an appearance of change with underlying professional norms and value-oriented decision-making processes remaining intact?

To assess whether decision making in the provision of the personal social services became more imbued with the formal rationality associated with markets and less permeated with a substantive rationality reflecting the public service ethic this study explored how purchasing decisions were made in social services departments. The specific focuses of the research were on how decision makers used cost and quality of care information, whether trade-offs occur between costs and quality when elderly people were placed in residential care under budget constraints, and the extent to which detailed, disaggregated cost and quality of care information was considered valuable when care packages were devised.

This paper explores these issues by a discussion of the markets and hierarchies perspective and how this might apply to social care, explaining the research methods used, and outlining the principal results of the investigation.

Markets and hierarchies perspective

The markets and hierarchies (M and H) perspective derives from the classic work of Coase (1937), in which he suggested that organisations supplanted markets for many products and services to minimise transaction costs. The shift from markets to hierarchies or bureaucracies has been documented by Chandler (1977; and Daems, 1979). This shift has aroused considerable interest in issues arising from the changing boundaries between organisations and the market and, consequently, theories of behaviour within organisations (see Stiglitz, 1991; Williamson, 1975; 1991; Williamson and Ouchi, 1981). Two behavioural assumptions are involved: bounded rationality – the recognition of the cognitive limits of rational individuals – and opportunism – the existence of the moral hazard in the pursuit of self-interest to the extent that sanctions or monitoring are necessary (see Table 2).

Table 2: Organisational implications of behavioural assumptions

Behavioural assumptions Implications	Bounded rationality	Opportunism
For contractual theory	Comprehensive contracting is infeasible	Contract as promise is naive
For economic organisation	Exchange will be facilitated by modes that support adoptive, sequential decision making	Trading requires the support of spontaneous or crafted safeguards

Note: The dashed vertical line denotes that the contractual implications and organisations' responses are joint responses to a combined condition of bounded rationality and opportunism.

Source: Williamson (1991b)

The implications of these assumptions for contract-setting are exacerbated, according to Williamson's theory, where there are frequent transactions, considerable uncertainty and asset specificity exists. The first two may be regarded as self-evident. However, the third, asset specificity, adds an additional dimension: where there is a transaction which entails significant investment in durable, highly specific assets the parties to the transaction are bilaterally dependent (Williamson, 1991b, p 94). A major response to such difficulties is to develop large organisations in which rule-based behaviour, penalties, incentives, and bureaucratic rules regarding approval and decision making constrain the likelihood of these imperfections in the contract-setting process in markets. It is a response to problems of incomplete contracts. The fragmentation of social services departments, found in large-scale LAs, into purchasers and providers, with contract-setting as the linchpin in such relationships, may introduce opportunities for moral hazard, heightened by uncertainties in the evolving quasi-markets.

The M and H perspective has been criticised. Granovetter (1985) argued that the M and H 'solution' to transaction costs – creating large bureaucracies instead of lots of smaller organisations – understates the role of social networks within the market setting, that is, forces for coordination exist because of the social interplay of key actors, even in different organisations in a competitive, market environment. A further attack (Perrow, 1981b) asserts that the M and H perspective concentrates on economic efficiency and does not adequately address issues of power and control within organisations. It has also been suggested (Simon, 1991) that the M and H perspective is itself incomplete because there are further dimensions of intraorganisational behaviour, for example, authority, coordination, and identification, which must be brought into play to understand processes within organisations. However, there have been attempts by M and H proponents to extend and develop the theory to take account of such criticisms, notably the contributions by Ouchi (1977; 1979; 1980); Ouchi and Price (1978); and Williamson and Ouchi (1981). They offer the concept of corporate or 'clan' culture as an important dimension in understanding modes of governance. This raises issues about motives. On the one hand, critics of the M and H approach (see, for example, Ezzamel and Wilmott, 1993, pp 120-1) equate this concept of the clan with modern management theories of exercising management control by engineering corporate cultures. A contrasting view is that the 'clan control' concept recognises the intrinsic values of key groups within organisations. This recognition facilitates the continuation of professional values rather than renders them to the domination of a corporate management ethos.

The concept of corporate culture has generated a wide literature which seeks to explain governance within organisations. The specific form of culture identified by M and H proponents is that of 'the clan' in which there is 'soft contracting' between parties within organisations based on incomplete contracts and a more elaborate informal governance apparatus (Williamson and Ouchi, 1981). The 'clan control' system relies on social controls rather than the legal or economic sanctions of the bureaucratic organisation. The emergence of such a regime is seen as being dependent on the "institutional infrastructure within which soft contracts are embedded" (Williamson and Ouchi, 1981, p 361). These observations may also apply to social services departments in which the traditional values of professional social workers may clash with those of market efficiency. Horne, for example, describes social work as:

> ... a value-laden activity. Despite the skills which it espouses as affording it 'technical' or 'scientific' validity, they do not remove within its practice the necessity of making evaluative judgements and decisions. (1987, p 1)

Many of these values which typify social work activity centre on the relationship between the social worker and their client. A typical schema of this set of values is:

1. **to respect the client**
2. **to accept him for himself**
3. **not to condemn him**
4. **to uphold his right to self-determination**
5. **to respect his confidence.** (see Timms, 1983, p 43)

The shift to more market–oriented behaviour has led to a reaffirmation of such values and scepticism about the role which markets can play in organising social care activities. Lewis (1994) expressed reservations about the ability of social workers to become purchasers in the new markets in social care, because professional judgements may be supplanted by 'a mechanical process' of checking boxes to reach decisions for commissioning care. She depicts a scenario of struggle and resistance as:

> ... the battle to separate social work from money was hard fought in twentieth century Britain and many social service departments may be expected to have a suspicion of 'cheque book social work', which in their view would serve to compromise social values. (Lewis, 1994, p 3)

This tension between values which place a primacy on client choice and the right of self-determination and drives for efficient, economical solutions to social care, may become more pronounced where a more proactive stance is taken with regard to client's rights. For example, Clark (with Asquith) advocates such an approach:

> ... social workers should stimulate and enhance the client's capacity for making his own decisions and living his own life by his own standards. Social workers should not deceive or propel the client into a course of action that runs contrary to his true wishes. (1985, p 31)

However, doubt has been cast over the extent to which such values permeate the social work service. The social work professionals have been depicted as powerful, not only because they aim to change and control behaviour but because of their role in structuring the social life of clients, by commanding definitions of reality with which the lives of clients are shaped; it is the social worker not the client who defines the problem (Abbott and Wallace, 1990). Perlman (1975) has described the principle of client self-determination "as nine-tenths illusion but one of the grand illusions". The outcomes of schemes of advocacy for clients whose frailties make the exercise of self-determination difficult, underline the problems of attachment to a value which may prove impractical (see, for example, Lansley and Whittaker, 1994). The M and H perspective suggests that, where 'clan' values are weakened by such problematic circumstances, opportunistic behaviour might occur.

In the present study, the focus is sharpened by examining referrals of elderly, sometimes confused persons, which may/may not lead to placements within residential care (with/without his/her consent) with circumstances under which the client may be judged incapable of caring for him/herself adequately and may even be at some physical risk from his/her own actions. This confronts the decision maker(s) with the need to address the primacy or otherwise of such values (see below).

Research methods

This study used the concept of real life constructs (see Lapsley and Llewellyn, 1995), in which researchers seek the views of members of organisations using contextualised information, which combines real qualitative and quantitative data to form a focal point of discussions. The research identified those involved in purchasing residential care for the elderly in each of nine Scottish regional authorities, usually a contracts or purchasing officer, a social worker and a finance officer. These personnel were asked to document and later discuss their purchasing decisions when confronted with cost and quality of care information from six different residential homes, two from each of the three sectors, private, voluntary and LA. The costs and quality of care data was drawn from a previous study of residential homes (Bland et al, 1992). This gathered data on the quality of residential care for the elderly and the costs of its provision in 100 such homes from the voluntary, private and LA sectors in Scotland. The project also incorporated six case histories of possible referrals for residential care to assess the criteria used in deciding whether a client can be adequately supported in the community or whether a residential or nursing care placement was desirable.

The research had two distinct stages. At the first stage decision makers were presented with a minimal data set, a single score for the quality of care delivered at each home and a single cost figure (it was assumed that charges are set at the level of total costs). The six homes were chosen to reflect a range of cost/quality possibilities: high cost/high quality; average cost/middle range quality; low cost/low quality. A budget constraint or fund was introduced at this stage. Decision makers were asked to record their choices, and reasons for such choices, for this data set within the funds available. Semi-structured interviews were then carried out by the researchers using mainly the following research questions:

- How are purchasing decisions currently made and on the basis of what information?
- To what extent would fundholders find a total composite quality of care score for a residential home helpful and would such a score have credibility for them?
- To what extent would fundholders use cost figures (expressed per resident day) when making purchasing decisions and how would cost/quality trade-offs be made?
- How would the provision of cost/quality information mesh with your current procedures and would the availability of such data enhance cost-effective decisions?

At the second stage decision makers were confronted with a greater degree of complexity in terms of both the quality of care data and the costings. The quality of care scores were broken down into separate scores for:

- buildings
- procedures
- regime
- medical care
- promotion of continence
- care of dementia sufferers
- general services.

Both running costs (wages, provisions and support costs) and capital costs were presented. At this stage, decision makers were given the six fictional case histories (taken from Bland et al, 1992) of possible referrals to residential care. These case histories listed medical and social conditions and, in some cases, brief details of the clients' financial position, where the clients concerned were able to fund, at least in part, their own care. Again, a budget limit, a fund, for placements was introduced to induce prioritisation of the options available. The exercise of asking fundholders to select homes was repeated and the following points were explored:

- how far the greater sophistication of the costing information was considered valuable by decision makers;
- whether or not the breakdown of quality of care scores into separate dimensions reflected current guidance within the social services departments;
- the pattern of responses to the case histories in terms of decisions between community and residential care and, if residential care is chosen, the homes considered suitable in matching client need with the resources the homes provide.

Fundholders' decisions were analysed to ascertain if detailed cost/quality information changed the perspectives, that is, 'markets' or 'hierarchies', from which fundholders made decisions. Focus was placed on the following facets of the contract-setting process:

- whether the *bounded rationality* (Williamson, 1975; 1981; 1991b) of fundholders inhibited the assimilation of more detailed financial information or whether greater sophistication in accounting numbers enabled fundholders to allocate resources more effectively;
- whether the 'culture of care' within the social services readily absorbed a new dimension in which cost concepts and efficiency assumed a dominant role – this question addressed the supplanting of a 'clan' culture (Ouchi, 1977; 1979; 1980) where social controls and rule-based behaviours predominate by a market-based system where economic sanctions prevail;
- whether a more market-orientated system increased the likelihood of fundholders engaging in more opportunistic strategies as they comply with *market-based norms* rather than *rule-based norms*.

Results and discussion

The responses to the Stage 1 minimal data set revealed the differing approaches that regional councils took to contract-setting: some regional councils had created the new post of 'contracts officer', usually a former social worker, but still sited within a social work department; some councils had moved closer to financing colleagues to appraise the implications of the contract-setting regime, and others had not. The responses also revealed distinct reactions to the limited information on: an overall quality of care score for each residential home, plus its sectoral location (LA, private, voluntary); the cost of making placements in these homes; and a budget constraint. In five of the regions, the view was expressed, strongly, that client self-determination was the overruling prerogative when making placements and, in the absence of information on clients' choices, no decision on possible placements could be made. In one of these authorities, a social worker stated that she, and her colleagues with whom she had shared the Stage 1 data, felt "challenged" by the inclusion of costing information in such decision making. Another social worker asserted that "the starting point is the individual ... and this [information] is the wrong way round...". However, one of the respondent's social work colleagues did consider that all placements could be made in the highest quality, but cheapest of all options, a private sector home, subject to suitable information on assessed needs and more information on what the overall quality of care score meant. In general, there was some scepticism within the five regions favouring self-determination on the merits of such scores, stressing the need for professional judgements.

While these responses reflect the dominance of traditional public service values in the face of 'markets' in care, the picture is more complicated. In two of the other regions, different patterns of response emerged. At the other extreme from the social workers cited above, there were two contract officers who favoured placements, on a sectoral basis, with two residents each being placed in a private, voluntary home and an LA home. This decision was based on an explicit desire to achieve a sectoral balance in provision across private, voluntary and LA homes, using the overall quality of care scores as indicators and using the cost information to remain within budget. Both of these contract officers stated that information on 'assessed need' would be useful, but, nevertheless, exhibited a willingness to reach conclusions in a manner which set them apart from their colleagues in other regions. The picture is further complicated by the responses of the remaining two regions. In both of these regions, notice was taken of the budget limit; there was also a willingness to take account of both costing information and the overall quality of care scores. In these regions, homes were deleted from the choice set, on the grounds of poor quality or being too small. Nevertheless, they still felt unable to make placements because the clients' views were not known.

The minimal data set was constructed in a manner which meant that bounded rationality could not appear. Bounded rationality was addressed by expanding the information available on both costs and quality of care. The issue of client self-determination was not explicit. Decision makers had to raise this as an issue, revealing their preferences. This suggests that the primacy of client self-determination is not a "grand illusion" (as asserted by Perlman, 1975). However, the discussion of client self-determination was made in the absence of the information which makes it such a thorny problem in practice – issues of advocacy, for example. This was examined by presenting the decision makers with six specific cases of frail elderly people for referral. What the decision makers did face at Stage 1 was the existence of major uncertainties (over the nature of the clients to be placed and their wishes and the detail of what the 'quality of care' score meant). The evidence of the Stage 1 results suggests that if opportunistic behaviour did emanate from such uncertainties, it was limited. By and large, the 'clan values' of the social workers held true, for those who were willing to work within the budget constraints and, more obviously, for those who were not. The placements made by contracts officers on a sectoral basis might be interpreted by the other groups as if not opportunistic certainly market-oriented behaviour. By relaxing the constraints imposed by the minimal data set, these issues were explored more fully by examining:

- how decision makers responded to costs;
- how decision makers handled the quality of care information;
- whether rule-based procedures were being supplanted by more market-oriented behaviour.

How decision makers responded to costs

There was limited interest and even indifference to being provided with more detailed information on costs (breaking these down into wages, provisions, other support costs, capital charges and showing these as a percentage of total costs). In part, this may have been influenced by considerations of uncertainty and bounded rationality, but overwhelmingly, it appeared to be because such information did not mesh well with the values, the procedures and the processes of decisions on placements for social care by social workers, and their LAs.

In general, decision makers did not find the costing information (with the exception of the wage costs, see below) relevant when they made placements. The principal finance officer of one regional authorities commented, "The cost analysis is immaterial to the interests of the region." The contracts officer and the finance officer of another region agreed that their department would not use detailed cost information. The contracts officer stated:

> **"The department is only concerned with the following cost information - homes' net charges to the local authority, any 'hidden' charges levied on clients by homes and the annual running costs of our own homes – they are cost centres."**

Where decision makers did scrutinise the cost analysis they focused almost exclusively on the wages category. In two regions there was a perception that wage costs were important since quality of care was thought to be directly related to the calibre and morale of staff which, in turn, was linked to wage rates. The contracts officer in one of these regions commented: "Homes which do not pay well and which don't provide adequate training are likely to provide a lower standard of care." In another region the principal finance officer would have liked more detailed information on wages. He remarked:

> **"As it stands information on wages is irrelevant – and open to differing interpretations; it could mean a lot of staff at a low wage rate or very few staff at a high wage rate."**

This respondent wanted information on staffing levels and details of training, or proposed training, in order to ascribe any meaning to the wages information. Such comments are an indication that the purchaser–provider split does not necessarily result in a separation of interests. This may be viewed as a strength or a weakness. If purchasers within social services departments continued to promote conditions of service for staff within provider units this may be beneficial, in terms of outcomes for clients, if wage rates are positively related to quality of care, as the decision makers in these regions believed. Alternatively, it may merely favour organisations where the service is run more for the benefit of provider staff than those for whom the service is designed. If purchasers are advocates for provider staff in this way, "Their agendas could focus more on the organisation of provision than on the needs to be met" (Stewart, 1993, p 8).

One or two respondents commented on the level of capital charges in the private sector homes. One contracts officer thought that the high capital charge, 42% of annual total cost, of one private home "cast doubt on the home's financial viability". The finance officer in the same region concurred, adding that, "If capital charges take up a large proportion of annual running costs client care will be compromised." In only one region was there a perception that the financial viability of the private sector was a concern to the LAs. In this region the finance officer had observed some private homes going bankrupt while others were "... kept afloat through assistance from the region". In contrast to this the finance officer in another region commented:

> "**We are not interested in the financial viability of independent residential homes. The commercial risk has been taken by independent providers – whether they make a profit or loss is of no interest to us – we pay up to defined rates. The market rates charged by independent providers – up to £700 (per week) in some nursing homes – [which] subsidise the rates paid by us (£290 per week for nursing care) should help the independents' financial viability.**"

No decision makers commented on or queried the level of food costs in the homes. This was curious in view of the variability of this element of running cost, from £391 per bed per annum in one LA home to £953 per bed per annum in one private home. You would expect that the quality and variety of food served would be a significant factor in ensuring residents' satisfaction with care and that variety and quality would be reflected in the homes' expenditure on provisions.

The regions varied in their responses to budget constraints. One finance officer reported that the region: "... does not want placements to be budget driven. Care managers are not constrained by budgets – any overspend/deficit is underwritten by the region." He also revealed that currently insufficient data existed to construct budgets. This was due to the region's inability to calculate or forecast demand for care in future periods and to predict service provision. However, somewhat surprisingly, this same respondent remarked at the end of the interview that although the region was not budget driven they ended up "spot on" last year. Another contracts manager added that budget constraints were not a consideration this year but would be next year.

How decision makers handled the quality of care information

Decision makers were more comfortable with the quality of care information, although not always accepting of its worth. One social worker expressed the view that she was:

> **"overwhelmed by the information and found it impossible to juggle with all these variables and reach the right conclusion and would therefore take account of other colleagues views ..."**

However, most of our decision makers were able to handle this high degree of detail by homing in on aspects of care delivery which they considered to be particularly important. These criteria reflected values relating to the client, expressed in terms of choice, dignity, needs and preference. For example, single rooms for privacy, the location of the residential facilities, such as being near shops.

The regions agreed that the dimensions of quality of care reflected their own current standards, albeit that the research information was, in some respects, more detailed. Several of the decision makers in the regions expressed the opinion that a weighting of the separate elements would have been helpful. Single rooms were considered essential in many regions: one contracts officer stated that he would "... only purchase single rooms for clients – unless they were a couple and specified a double room". The same officer also felt that the following items were particularly important: a written agreement between the home and the resident and a written care plan for each resident. He would also have appreciated further information about the following: en suite facilities, disabled toilets, complaints procedures, geographical location and group living. The last practice, in his view, promoted social interaction. Two regions mentioned as key dimensions those which empowered clients or reduced institutionalisation. In this respect clients were perceived as 'empowered' if they were able to replicate those decisions which they would take in their own homes, for example, holding their own drugs, having a choice of menu, receiving visits from friends and relatives at any time and being able to leave and return to the home at will. Choice of menu was also mentioned in connection with reducing institutionalisation, as was consumption of alcohol, for clients not staff.

Decision makers in one region considered that the dimensions of quality of care were too general. The information was not of sufficient detail to allow a matching between referrals' needs and placement with suitable homes. For example, in one case, a placement was not possible as the homes' policies on access to the home for visitors was lacking and, for another, who suffered from dementia, information on staffing ratios was missing – the region concerned indicated that they felt that 1:4 was a minimum level for homes which care for clients with dementia. In this region they commented that rather than assessing quality of care they would take a different approach – an assessment of the client's need was their starting point and this would be presented to the residential home's manager/office-in-charge. It would then be up to the home's management to decide if they could meet these needs. The decision makers in this region described this approach as "rebuilding wholeness – but the risk factor overlies this". In contrast to this position, which emphasised the importance of the case histories, one regional finance officer commented that, "If you set a very high standard of care, the case histories are meaningless as standards will be appropriate for all clients". She added that central government considered the standards in their region to be set far too high.

Although decision makers obviously considered quality of care to be very important they often lacked detailed information on the care provided in independent homes on a routine basis. In assessing their quality of care social workers may/may not have access to the inspection reports and registrations of social work departments and may have to rely on, for example, the homes' brochures. However, one region has constructed a catalogue of all homes in its area for reference purposes. Another operated a 'bed bureau' but the information on the homes listed in the bureau was very brief – mainly bed availability, the number of rooms with en suite facilities and whether the home allowed pets. The respondents in this region felt that the private homes were often reluctant to reveal figures on bed availability as owners considered that such information would be 'bad publicity'. In another region the comment was made that, "Independent homes often reserve their best rooms for self-funding clients". The quality of care for LA funded clients may then be compromised and class divisions may be perpetuated in such homes.

Whether rule-based procedures were being supplanted by more market-oriented behaviour

The majority of interviewees considered that the information contained in the case histories was sufficient to allow them to make a decision on whether or not a residential placement was desirable and which of the homes would be suitable. However, in one particular region, the information contained in the case histories was considered too vague and of little constructive use in assessing client need. The care managers in this region compiled needs assessments of "about 15 pages" and this length was judged necessary for a "full appreciation of a client's needs". Once again, the clan values of social work surfaced. Overwhelmingly, the language of the LAs in respect of the empowerment of consumers is dominated by the rhetoric choice. Discourses within the social services returned constantly to the theme of the overriding importance of client choice. However, when the notion of choice was explored with decision makers a 'hierarchy of choices' emerged. All regions emphasised client choice in respect of the decision to remain in the community or to enter residential care. In all departments there was also the view that client choice of residential home was important, albeit that many regions stressed that this choice was most usually directed towards a wish to enter a residential home within the client's immediate home area. The extent to which the decision makers were prepared to satisfy client choice was marked. For example, if the client had expressed the wish to remain in the community, extensive packages of care (daycare, outings, daily help, modification of buildings for security or to ease the access of disabled/frail persons) were considered, reaffirming the primacy of client self-determination.

The decisions on placements were also affected by implicit assumptions about the nature of some forms of residential care facilities and how this might explain both non–market-oriented behaviour and puzzles over what care costs mean. For example, one contracts officer disclosed that within the LA there exist "systems of excellence". The justification for the high cost/high quality LA facilities was that they provided models of best practice for other market participants. Given its high cost/high quality of care profile the officer concerned conjectured that one LA home was established as a "representation of best residential care practice". This provides further evidence that the values inherent within the LAs tended to support the notion that high cost and high quality of care were positively related, with particular emphasis being placed on high wage costs as indicative of high quality of care. The notion of value for money was much more weakly developed and was mentioned by only one contracts officer, so far, as a rationale for rejecting a voluntary home, where it was thought that its higher cost "contradicted" its lower quality of care. There is a tendency for costs and quality of care to be assessed 'in tandem' and high cost/low quality and lower cost/higher quality homes are viewed with some suspicion and thought to exhibit 'contradictions'.

The most fundamental factor which mitigated against the development of a more market-oriented behaviour was perhaps the composition of the clientele and what this meant for LAs in terms of price-setting. The most striking continuity in all the regional authorities was their adherence to a fixed rate of payment for residential care. One authority referred to their rates as "sealed figures". In the main, all homes received £185 per resident per week, or £215 as the higher need rate, regardless of the level of service provision or the quality of care provided. This continued adherence to standard rates reflected the tendency to have made as many placements as possible before 1 April 1993, before the new community care legislation was implemented, to ensure that those in residential accommodation had 'preserved rights' to DSS support. The high proportion of residents in this category means that reliance on DSS rates as a benchmark for rate-setting continued. LAs can and do move from these rates. This continuity is most probably a response to perceptions of the increased risks and uncertainties inherent in the functioning of quasi-markets, a fear that the private sector may, in the longer term, be able to hike up their charges and/or increase their power to direct future developments in the residential care sector. Referring to this concern, the opinion in one region was that the private sector may develop cartels and fix prices which were "not linked to real costs".

Rather than negotiate a lower price for homes, providing less in terms of facilities or quality of care, decision makers prefer to screen out such homes for residential care referrals. Several reasons were offered for those homes considered unsuitable:

- some decision makers identified a level of quality below which the home was considered unacceptable (75% and 60% were mentioned);
- some authorities rated the provision of a single room and private bathroom as minimum standards and would not contract with any home which failed to offer these;
- some private homes were considered too small to guarantee a consistent level of care;
- the level of capital charges borne by some private homes was viewed by some decision makers as raising unacceptable question marks over their long-term viability;
- some homes were excluded on the grounds that they failed to offer value for money when cost and quality of care information was assessed in conjunction.

Only one of the contracts and purchasing officers interviewed mentioned the possibility of negotiating lower rates. He felt that there was a distinct possibility that pressure could be applied to homes to achieve price reductions in an area where there was a surfeit of residential care: "... private homes will occasionally lower their weekly charges by about £5 in order to secure business."

The same contracts officer also felt that it may be possible to achieve cost reductions in LA homes by adopting models based on those LA homes demonstrating optimal cost/quality of care profiles. In contrast to this, the contracts officer in another region commented that they will pay up to £234 per week for a single room in either a private or a voluntary sector home but will admit referrals to any LA home as for these (their own) homes; "price does not matter".

There was limited evidence of decision makers contemplating premium payments for homes providing additional or specialist facilities. One region was beginning to develop its own fee structure for residential care. It adopted the same base rates as other regions but was willing to pay additional premiums to homes that provided single rooms, and en suite facilities. This region was also considering grading homes 1 to 5 according to their level of service provision and quality of care and paying higher fees to homes achieving higher gradings. The stimulus for this scheme came from specialist homes as they considered charges to be too low to sustain the higher level of care provided by specialist units.

Conclusion

This study has explored the implications of the new quasi-markets in social care by examining its effects on one client group - frail elderly people. The process by which this was undertaken was a two-stage simulation of choices made by key decision makers, social workers, contract officers and finance officers. A major aim of the study was to scrutinise the extent to which the formal rationalities of the marketplace, of prices, costs and trade-offs between costs and quality, might supplant the traditional public service ethic of social work. In particular, the issue of client self-determination was scrutinised as a critical indication of the primacy of the, to use Ouchi's terms, 'clan values' of the social workers.

There was an uneven response among the different social work departments. A dominant theme was the way in which the social workers adhered to prime values such as respect for the person, client self-determination and related attributes of the preservation of dignity and privacy. However, the beginnings of a new way of thinking emerged, characterised by a commitment to the idea of a balanced provision of care across all sectors (LA, private and voluntary), a willingness to consider the costing dimension, and a sensitivity to the concept of the budget constraint. However, these changes should not be overstated.

'Bounded rationality' did not surface as a major consideration in this study. When confronted with voluminous data, decision makers drew on their prime values to categorise residential homes as suitable for placement or not. This process was also assisted by 'due procedure' in which many of these values were captured in codes of practice used by social work departments – minimum standards for inclusion as a registered home in their area, which should then be demonstrated on inspection visits. However, uncertainties did appear to shape decisions, at least at the margin. A sub-group of decision makers, the contract officers, did address the issue and make recommendations on referrals in the absence of detailed information which the majority of social workers refused to do. Other institutional influences in the face of uncertainties also impinged on behaviour. For example, there was: a reluctance to delegate budgets down to field officers; the reliance on DSS rates as signals in the marketplace, trading on the high proportion of clients with preserved rights; the underwriting of expenditure if it exceeded the budget. All of this militated, if not confounded, against the operation of the market.

The concept of a quasi-market for social care was imperfectly aligned with the world of social care.

The research indicated the merits of retaining forms of 'soft contracting' in which the values of key professionals shaped the contracting process. Major considerations need to be made relating to the boundaries or restrictions to be placed on such activities. The tension between such an approach and the rationale of devolved budgets in quasi-markets is recognised. While these observations may appear to run counter to the moves towards more market-oriented behaviour, they may more accurately capture the best modes of governance for this distinctive type of activity. It became clear that what was described previously as the 'linchpin' of the quasi-market – the contract – was itself not uniform in its application and, appeared to sit with existing procedures for inspection and registration of homes. The reservations of Williamson (1985) on market behaviour were not being realised. There were uncertainties, but the clan values 'softened' the likelihood of opportunistic behaviour and there were existing monitoring procedures which were aligned with the new contracts. This quasi-market was evolving – but was it doing so in a different way to what M and H proponents had predicted, and policy-makers intended?

Postscript

This chapter has explored the interplay between accounting information, devolved budgets and social work values in the context of quasi-markets in the social services. Since this work was carried out the political context has evolved further and the government has signalled the demise of the quasi-market in health and social care. Prima facie, contracting – the key mechanism of the market – will now assume less relevance in the public services. However, the evidence from this study suggests that the market did not operate as intended and that resource-holders (social services departments) had to make placement decisions in areas of mixed provision by charitable, local government and private organisations even before these arrangements were formalised as a 'market'. However, the abandonment of market ideas will not eliminate issues relating to the efficacy of devolved budgets and accounting information for resource allocation in the social services, which are still very much a live issue for social workers. This view is supported by recent research in the social services (Llewellyn, 1998) which has shown that budgets are now delegated to team manager level (personnel who are one level away from the front line of service delivery). However, traditional social work values of client advocacy and close professional relationships with clients have been implicated in decisions not to devolve budgets right down to care managers (front-line workers). It was felt that holding a budget would be 'intrusive' in terms of professional relationships with clients. Particularly in the present situation of resource constraints, front-line workers felt that their professional counselling relationship with their clients would be compromised if they were put in the position of having to refuse certain services on the grounds of cost. They also felt that if they were responsible for the budget they would be focusing on the availability of resources rather than the needs of their clients. All of this demonstrates that issues of cost, quality of care and budget constraints continue to be implicated in the value-oriented decision-making processes of social services workers.

Acknowledgements

The authors wish to acknowledge the financial support of the ESRC (Research grant number R000221128). Earlier versions of this paper were presented at the ESRC Quasi-Markets Seminar at the London School of Economics, September, 1994, at the University of Canterbury, Christchurch in March, 1995, at the Graduate School of Business, Sydney University, March, 1995 and at the European Accounting Association, Birmingham, May, 1995. The authors gratefully acknowledge the helpful comments of participants at these seminars, particularly Gerald Wistow (Leeds).

Part Four

Healthcare

EIGHT

Healthcare quasi-markets in a decentralised system of government

George France

Introduction

This chapter addresses the question of the institutional setting in which healthcare quasi-markets operate. Bartlett and Le Grand (1993) argue that quasi-markets in social policy are ultimately to be judged in terms of whether they produce superior results compared to the systems which they are intended to replace. They suggest four criteria for establishing this: efficiency, equity, choice and responsiveness. Recognising that it is still too early to evaluate in any detail how quasi-markets are *actually* performing, Bartlett and Le Grand propose conditions which must hold for quasi-markets to be considered a priori capable of achieving their desired results. These relate to market structures, information, motivation of purchasers and providers, transaction costs and uncertainty and cream skimming.

Hardly any attention is paid in the literature on quasi-markets to what may be called the 'institutional environment', defined as "the set of fundamental political, social and legal ground rules that establishes the basis for production, exchange and distribution" (Davis and North, 1971, p 6). The aspect of the institutional environment which is of interest here is the distribution of power among different tiers of government. Following the Davis and North terminology, quasi-markets may be considered as an 'institutional arrangement', that is,

> **an arrangement between economic units that governs the ways in which these units can cooperate and/or compete ...**

> or it (can) provide a mechanism that can effect a change in
> laws or property rights. (Davis and North, 1971, p 7)[1]

It is probably correct to say that the bulk of theoretical and empirical research on quasi-markets has been done with reference to the UK which is a unitary state, that is, one in which sub-central government is formally subordinate to the central government. If this study of quasi-markets were to be limited to the UK, the institutional environment can perhaps be treated as a constant, at least in the short to medium run, and so may be ignored. This is not the case if considering adopting quasi-markets in a different institutional environment, which this chapter will be doing. For example, Italy, which is currently introducing a type of quasi-market into its health system, has a much more decentralised form of government than the UK. With the health reforms, introduced with national legislation approved in 1992 and 1993, virtually total responsibility for the organisation and administration of the health service will rest with the regions. Hence it will be the regions which set up and run the new healthcare quasi-markets. It is obvious that *institutions matter*; what will be of interest to this study is gaining a better understanding of the way in which they matter.

Quasi-markets in a decentralised country

The institutional environment in which Bartlett and Le Grand (1993) lay down the conditions necessary for quasi-markets to obtain their desired results seems to be that of a unitary state. Their analysis shows just how problematic predicting the performance of quasi-markets can be and how difficult it may be to meet the criteria (listed above) for them to be superior to the system being replaced. A leitmotiv of their discussion is the need for extensive and intensive monitoring and, on occasions, for direct regulatory action to ensure that the conditions are met or to compensate for failure to meet any one of the conditions, that is, to allow for second-best considerations.

Let us now assume that this unitary state divides into two federated entities, regions A and B. It is not necessary to specify the precise distribution of powers between the federal government and the regions; it suffices to accept that the regions hold considerable powers. Regions A and B are assumed to be very similar in the following ways: population size and key demographic and epidemiological characteristics and hence healthcare needs; gross domestic product and hence the levels of total healthcare capacity, types of services and geographical distribution of services which they can afford to finance; mix of public and private providers; political ideology and hence attitudes regarding the 'proper' roles of the public and private sectors and, in consequence, the type of quasi-market model adopted, and administrative capacity.

In such a world, quasi-markets can be expected to produce effects broadly like those (albeit difficult to predict) which they would produce in a unitary state. That is, satisfaction of the criteria for judging whether quasi-markets are superior to the integrated model will depend on the Bartlett and Le Grand conditions being met. This is because the above assumptions tend to neutralise the influence of the institutional environment. What cannot be assumed away is the fact of separate jurisdictions, the essence of federalism. This means that transaction costs will almost certainly be higher than in a unitary state.[2] Since regions A and B will each have their own arrangements for setting up and running quasi-markets within their jurisdictions, there will be duplication and diseconomies in information collection and processing and in administration and monitoring. However, other transaction costs should remain unchanged because the quasi-market models adopted are assumed to be virtually identical and administered with equal efficiency. Both purchasers and providers will be indifferent whether they deal with providers or purchasers in their own region or in other regions and they can use standard forms of contracts, confident that these are enforceable. (For analytical simplicity, zero financial and non-financial distance costs are assumed.)

Let us now remove the assumption that the two regions share the same vision of the proper public role. In this case, each region will probably adopt a quasi-market model with different specifications. These will regard, for example: the extent of the separation between purchasing and provision; the basis of the purchaser–provider relationship (contracts between provider and third party payer or GP fundholder or, alternatively, patient vouchers); how providers are financed, for example, fee for service or prospective funding on basis of a block contract; the role assigned to private providers, and the extent and detail of regulatory arrangements. This heterogeneity could have a number of effects. Some of these are suggested here, with the criteria for which an effect could have implications being indicated in brackets.

A lesser degree of separation between purchasers and providers in one of the two regions could permit hidden subsidisation of providers located there, creating unfair competition for providers in the other region (*efficiency*). If one region gives greater freedom to the private sector to compete with public providers, this could cause problems if public, non-profit providers are less motivated than their private, for-profit, counterparts or if they have less flexible decision-making processes or if regulation of market behaviour is less rigorous (*efficiency*). In the analysis, differences in the extent and detail of regulation may be the most significant dimension of inter-regional diversity. This could suggest monitoring for market imperfections, abuse of market power or collusion between public providers and purchasers (*efficiency, choice, responsiveness*). Regulations may differ regarding cream-skimming by providers or queue-jumping by patients (*equity*). There may be differences in the legal status of contracts between purchasers and providers where patient vouchers are not used and in procedures for their enforcement (*efficiency, choice, responsiveness*).

Purchasers (providers) may not be indifferent about whether the providers (purchasers) were in- or out-of-region. Where less regulation means lower prices, purchasers will prefer trading with the less regulated regions and providers will prefer the contrary, other things being equal. However, in the likely event that things are not equal, purchasers and providers may feel it advisable to take additional precautions, compared to when regulation is equal, against opportunistic behaviour by out-of-region trading partners. An example of such behaviour is acquiring more information on potential trading partners or writing detailed contracts and requiring legally binding contracts and/or security bonds. This increases transaction costs (*efficiency*). If there is a problem of extra-regional contract enforcement, the transaction costs involved and the risk of opportunistic behaviour may be perceived as unacceptably high, inducing purchasers and providers to trade wherever possible within their home region. This would have the effect of reducing market size for specific services, creating local monopolies and eroding economies of scale (*efficiency, choice, responsiveness*).

The situation is further complicated if the assumption of equal administrative capacity is removed. This means that, even if the regions apply the same quasi-market model including regulatory provisions, this model will not necessarily be implemented in the same way. Monitoring of market structures or of trading behaviour may be laxer or more haphazard in the region with the weaker administrative capacity. This region may consciously opt for a quasi-market model with a lower regulatory content which is then simpler to administer.

The implications for the performance of quasi-markets, compared with that of the system being replaced, of relaxing the assumption of homogeneity of quasi-market models and of administrative capacity will be more or less serious depending on the scale of inter-regional trade in health services. A corollary of the assumptions of similar population size, demography and epidemiology and similar per capita GDP is that the overall healthcare capacity of the two regions will be similar, as will be the mix of services and their territorial distribution. This would imply low patient mobility between the two regions, limited mainly to border areas and to very high level specialties. If these assumptions are relaxed, it is realistic to suppose that the regions will differ in the overall size of their health systems, in the types of services available, for example, advanced technologies, and in the geographical distribution of services. There is now a greater likelihood of patient mobility or, better, of a desire by patients to move between regions for care – mobility which, as seen above, may be constrained. Relaxing the equal income assumption also means that differences in administrative capacity could be even greater: the poorer region has less resources to dedicate to regulatory activities.

A typical federal state consists of more than two regions. This complicates matters further. Administration and other transaction costs attributable to setting up and running quasi-markets will be greater in a state with numerous regions simply because of greater fragmentation of the administrative machine. Diversity is the raison d'être of federalism. The more numerous the regions, the greater the likelihood of heterogeneity and, therefore, of differences in the quasi-market models adopted and in the efficiency with which they are administered. The more regions there are, the higher the probability of differences in the size and characteristics of regional health systems; potential inter-regional mobility of patients could be considerable.

To sum up the analysis so far, if quasi-markets are problematical in a unitary state, the effect of their introduction in a federal setting may be even more uncertain. The principal reason for this is inter-regional diversity. Poor performance by quasi-markets in a given region, compared with the system being replaced, will have negative implications for the national health system as a whole: lower efficiency or reduced equity in that region means lower efficiency or reduced equity overall. The choice of quasi-market model and how it is administered in one region may have negative repercussions on the performance of quasi-markets in other regions.

There seems to be a natural role for central government to harmonise, or compensate for, differences in quasi-market arrangements. However, this will not be without cost because of administration expenditure and will in any case depend on the powers given to central government under the federal constitution. The remainder of the chapter is devoted to examining the implications of differences in the institutional environment for the performance of healthcare quasi-markets by looking at the case of Italy.

Healthcare in Italy

Italian institutional setting

Italy has three tiers of sub-central government: 20 regions, 103 provinces and 8,100 communes. This three-tier system is contained in the Constitution and can only be modified by constitutional amendment, a complicated procedure. The regions enjoy considerable independence in matters of internal administration and organisation and have legislative power for the areas of responsibility assigned to them by the Constitution. Conflict between national and regional legislation is common and in the last instance is resolved by the Constitutional Court.

A perennial problem for central-regional government relations in Italy has been the question of finance. Over time, there was a transfer of functions from the State to the regions, including healthcare, but this was not accompanied by cession of revenue-raising powers. Until recently, the principal source of regional funding was from central government, mainly specific grants. This imbalance between spending and revenue-raising responsibilities weakened the accountability chain between, on the one hand, the regions and central government and, on the other, between the regions and their electorate, creating serious problems for public expenditure control and value for money (France, 1996). Healthcare has been at the centre of the debate on this question since it is by far the single most important function of the regions, representing on average more than 50% of their total budget.

Background to the health reforms

Until 1978, Italy had a health system along the lines of the continental or *public contract* model (OECD, 1992a). This was replaced by a hybrid *public integrated/public contract* model: the bulk of publicly-financed healthcare was provided in publicly-owned and operated facilities, but a non-marginal share of care was delivered by contracted non-profit and for-profit hospitals and ambulatory facilities and by GPs and specialist doctors staffing public ambulatory care clinics with contractual rather than employee status.[3] The reformed Italian healthcare system was, like the UK health system, a national health service (Servizio Sanitario Nazionale [SSN]). Perhaps the most important difference between the two services prior to the reforms in both countries in the early 1990s was that the government of the SSN was considerably less vertically integrated.[4]

In the NHS, a strong line of command extended directly from the DoH, through the regional and district HAs down to individual providers. Sub-central governments in UK healthcare were little more than peripheral offices of the central government, delegated substantial decision-making authority but only because it suited the centre. The SSN also had a three-tier system of government: Ministry of Health, region and local health authority (Unità Sanitaria Locale [USL]), but the line of command was far less clear. Was the USL responsible to the centre or to the region (an elected body), or to both? The 1980s saw a contest between the central authorities and regions for control over the USL. The evolution of jurisprudence of the Constitutional Court tended in favour of the regions. This created a serious accountability problem: the regions (and USLs) had significant discretion in how resources were used but bore scarcely any revenue-raising responsibility; this fell almost entirely on the shoulders of central government which, however, had limited control over resource utilisation once the funds left Rome. This was not an ideal governance system for what was, despite its considerable use of external suppliers, nevertheless a highly vertically integrated organisation with a strong potential for generating high 'internal' transaction costs (Bariletti and France, 1994; France, 1996).

When the SSN was created in 1978, the Italian public finances were already beginning to show signs of strain. The situation deteriorated throughout the 1980s and early 1990s[5] and healthcare was a major target of expenditure containment strategies. Given its limited powers of intervention at the micro level of resource utilisation, central government had to rely on crude across-the-board capital expenditure cuts, hiring and pay freezes, deliberate underfinancing of the SSN and other macro tools (OECD, 1992b; Di Biase and Citoni, 1994; Mapelli, 1995a). It did succeed in keeping aggregate spending fairly well under control but with possibly quite negative effects for important dimensions of the performance of the SSN.

Reforms

The health reforms, still in the process of being implemented, were two-pronged: they modified the intergovernmental distribution of powers and responsibilities in healthcare to make the arrangements for the governance of the SSN internally more consistent, and they 'de-integrated' the SSN organisation with the aim of improving efficiency, quality, choice and responsiveness.

Modification of intergovernmental distribution of powers and responsibilities

The new arrangements explicitly recognised the constitutional reality that the region was an elected tier of government and that the USL was accountable to it. The new health legislation confirmed and codified the discretionary power on the expenditure side of the budget accumulated by the regions over the years since 1978 and matched this with an extension of powers and responsibilities of the regions on the revenue side, for example, compulsory health contributions are now returned to the region of residence. The State contribution to funding healthcare is fixed prospectively. The Ministry of Health sets a per capita allowance, the *quota capitaria,* supposedly sufficient to guarantee a citizen in any part of the country access to so-called 'uniform levels of care'. Any care provided but not covered by the *quota capitaria* has to be paid for by the regions and the same is true for the additional costs attributable to efficiency levels being lower than those assumed by the Ministry of Health in calculating the financial resources necessary to provide the uniform levels. Regions are given the power to increase contribution rates within limits contained in national legislation. They can apply higher patient co-payments rates, again within specified limits, and can introduce co-payments for services so far exempt. Finally, they can spend untied revenues on healthcare.

The hope was that, with responsibility for deciding how much was to be spent on health in their territory placed squarely on the shoulders of the regions, they would undertake explicit priority setting and rationing in allocating resources among competing health needs. It was also hoped that they would take steps to ensure that healthcare resources were used more efficiently, so tightening their grip on the USLs.[6]

Introduction of quasi-markets

The modification of the intergovernmental distribution of powers and responsibilities meant that the task of implementing and administrating quasi-markets lay unambiguously with the regions. This situation contrasted markedly with that of the UK. There, healthcare quasi-markets have been introduced under tight central control, perhaps even tighter than with the pre-1990 arrangements (Paton, 1993, p 105; Hughes, 1991, p 5). "The overall effect of these changes will be to introduce, for the first time, a clear and effective chain of management command running from districts ... to the Minister of Health" (DoH, 1989, p 13).

While the intention of the UK authorities was to introduce a standard model uniformly throughout the country, in Italy the national reform legislation was limited to defining a broad framework of reference within which each region was free to adopt the form of administered competition consonant with its particular situation and, presumably, with the preferences of its residents as expressed through their elected representatives. Key aspects of this reference framework are: the bulk of funding received by the USL is population based and set by central government, providers are reimbursed on the basis of fee for service set by the region and money is presumed to follow patients; providers must be accredited by the region; important changes to the organisational, management and accounting arrangements of USLs with public healthcare facilities aimed at enabling them to operate on a more business-like basis.[7] The reference framework gives the regions the possibility to adopt one of a variety of quasi-market models. These fall into three main categories.[8] These are the: USL third party payer model; USL sponsor model; USL planner model.

USL third party payer model: the patient-consumer is virtually sovereign, together with his or her doctor-agent, and is free to use any accredited provider. Providers, both public and private, are reimbursed on the basis of services rendered to clients. The USL has the passive role of third party payer, financing decisions taken by patients or their agents with little or no power to plan health expenditure or set priorities. It is difficult to see how under such arrangements a USL can live within its budget constraint determined by the quota capitaria. Judging by other countries' experience, supply – financed as it is on a fee-for-service basis – will have a built-in tendency to rise and/or shift to more remunerative services. The USL third party payer model's chief merit is that it gives patients wide freedom of choice. It is also relatively simple to administer. This model can be classed as being a very mild version of administered competition. It will incur considerable costs for billing and reimbursement[9] and for monitoring for illicit behaviour. In the short to medium term, private providers might have an advantage over public providers, being less constrained in investment decisions or by accountability rules and bureaucracy. They also have clear-cut monetary incentives to compete.

USL sponsor model: under this model the USL, as the sponsor of patients, makes contracts with 'preferred' providers selected from among those accredited with the SSN and chosen because they are considered able to supply the best cost-quality combination. These contracts include negotiated tariffs and specify the services to be delivered, provisions regarding quality of both clinical and non-clinical services, limits on volume, delivery features, complaints procedures and sanctions. Patients are free to choose between different preferred providers and care is free, except for co-payments at the point of consumption. They can opt to go to other accredited, but not 'preferred', providers; in this case patients pay the provider in the first instance and are then reimbursed by the USL up to the level of the tariffs set by the region or perhaps only up to those negotiated by the USL with its preferred providers. This model allows the USL and region a much more active role in planning, priority-setting and expenditure control than under the third party payer model and is a much stronger version of administered competition. The principle of patient freedom of choice is formally respected but de facto constrained. The USL sponsor model requires greater administrative capacity on the part of the USL and region, compared with the third party payer model, with regard, for example, to the search for, and comparison of, potential preferred providers and for writing and enforcing contracts.

USL planner model: under the third model, the USL negotiates a form of annual 'business plan' with its own hospitals and ambulatorial facilities and possibly also with private providers. The activity rate projections for the coming year contained in the plan are monetarised using the regional tariffs to calculate the global budget the facilities will receive. The activity rates actually recorded are used to adjust the funding levels upwards or downwards during and at the end of the fiscal year. The business plan could contain many of the conditions included in the contracts described for the USL sponsor model. Patients are free to choose among providers with approved business plans. The providers should have an incentive to minimise costs and maximise quality in order to live within their budgets. This model exalts the planning role of the USL. This model exalts the planning role of the USL and calls for close collaboration between purchasers and providers. It may prove to be the least disruptive of the three models compared with previous arrangements. However, without appropriate regulation there may be purchaser–provider collusion with the aim of maintaining as far as possible the status quo.

Prospects for quasi-markets in Italy

The new arrangements were supposed to be fully operational by the end of 1997. Instead implementation has been slow, particularly in setting up accreditation procedures, and the regions vary considerably in their progress. It is too early to predict the type of quasi-market models the individual regions will opt for. This section uses data on key characteristics of the regions, selected on the basis of the analysis of quasi-markets discussed above, to suggest what *may* happen. It then examines regional legislation for the reforms to look for indications of where the regions may be headed.

Implications of inter-regional diversity

Table 3 presents 12 indicators of regional diversity. These are intended to illustrate, no more, the considerable heterogeneity of the 20 Italian regions in the respects that the above analysis concluded might influence the character and operation of healthcare quasi-markets. Administration costs are almost bound to be higher than under the old arrangements as the 20 regions set up and operate quasi-markets, in particular given that they start off with a very meagre database. The regions vary regarding the political ideology. This difference has become more evident with the adoption of a new electoral system at the regional level based on proportional representation with a strong majority bonus used for the first time in the spring 1995 regional elections (Desideri and Santantonio, 1996). This suggests that between them the regions may adopt quite different quasi-market models, especially perhaps in terms of regulatory content.

Differences in the vision held of the public role are accompanied by diversity in administrative capacity, with north–central regions tending to be more efficient than southern regions. This could create tensions. Some northern regions, for example, are perhaps now more politically inclined to the USL third party payer model, but their recent administrative history may make them instead partial to the USL planner model, which they are capable of administering. The virtual monopoly of the public hospital sector in these regions might reinforce this tendency. Instead, the southern regions might be politically and culturally predisposed to the USL planner model, which represents the least break with the past, but are less able to administer it. They are perhaps also under pressure from the private sector, so might end up by adopting the USL third party payer model. In any case, even if southern regions were to adopt a 'strong' form of administered competition, its actual implementation probably would be 'weaker' than elsewhere.

Table 3 shows there to be big differences in population, demography and income[10] as well as in the size of regional health services. As might be expected there is considerable inter-regional mobility, particularly from southern to north-central regions.[11] Measures of concentration in markets for hospital services are not available, but the size of inter-regional flows may suggest the existence of considerable market power in certain high level specialties and a consequent need for regulation of pricing policies of providers. Increased information will be necessary to administer this inter-regional trade, hence there will be higher transaction costs. The need for regulation is made greater by the quite substantial size of the private sector in a number of regions.

In short, the new SSN will have to guard against the effects predicted by the theories discussed above. It is not clear what role the central authorities can play in harmonising quasi-market models. With a view to obtaining a degree of uniformity, the Ministry of Health has tried, via the Standing State-Region Conference, to involve the regions in the preparation of the statutory instruments. These include ministerial decrees relating to tariff-setting and the accreditation necessary to implement the new health legislation. Under the new arrangements the centre has limited regulatory powers and some form of inter-regional authority may emerge to fill this regulatory vacuum.

Traces of quasi-market models[12]

All the regions have approved legislation setting tariffs, based on diagnosis related groups (DRGs) for reimbursing hospital providers, and tariffs for ambulatory care. Most still have to take action on accreditation procedures. Traces of quasi-market models are detectable.

Some regions have simply adopted the national reference tariffs published by the Ministry of Health, in general adjusting these downwards by between 5-40%. Other regions have used the DRGs weighting system contained in the national guidelines and costed the DRGs using, generally very limited, sample data on hospital costs. In a few regions, tariffs are the same for public and private providers in the same hospital category but in most regions public and private providers are being treated differently. Some regions are still funding public hospitals on the basis of historic expenditure. Regional legislation is generally vague on the precise relationship between purchasers and providers and on whether that relationship is to have a contractual basis. Only a few laws explicitly envisage negotiation between public (and private) providers and the USL which concludes in a contractual agreement. Almost all regional laws imply that there will be agreement between the USL (and/or region) and hospital providers on the volume and types of services to be delivered or at least on maximum permitted billing levels. One regional law explicitly allows patients to use accredited non-preferred providers, but limits reimbursement to 50% of the tariff negotiated with preferred providers. What is interesting is that all regional laws contain mechanisms against opportunistic volume expansion by providers, demonstrating awareness of the risks for cost containment of using tariffs to fund providers. This suggests that the regions may be wary of adopting the USL third party payer model described above. All regions fix penalties for over-shooting agreed volume or billing levels. A few regions apply these to private providers only, but the majority cover all hospital providers, often though with steeper penalties for private providers. For most regions, the penalty involves reducing reimbursement rates for the excess in agreed volume or billing, with this becoming progressively greater the larger the overshoot. Two regions halve the tariff paid if there is *any* overshoot and some regions apply a 90% penalty for as little as 10% overshoot. One region – after only three months of tariff-based financing – found evidence of a reduction in average stay, increases in short stays, increased transfers of patients from private to public hospitals and increased frequency of complex DRGs. Its reaction was to reduce tariff levels and increase the progression rate of the scale of penalties, but only for private providers.

Table 3: Indicators of regional diversity

	Population (1,000s)	Population 65 and older (%)	GDP per head (Italy=100)	Number hospital beds	Beds per 1,000 inhabitants
	(1992)*	(1992)†	(1992)‡	(1992)§	(1992)§
Piemonte	4,304	18.2	115	26,167	6.1
Valle d'Aosta	117	16.8	126	555	4.7
Lombardia	8,882	15.3	127	63,578	7.1
Trentino A A	897	15.4	124	6,910	7.7
Veneto	4,395	16.1	116	34,457	7.9
Fruili VG	1,195	20.0	118	9,574	8.0
Liguria	1,669	22.5	116	13,135	7.9
Emilia Romagna	3,920	20.5	123	28,469	7.3
Toscana	3,529	20.3	107	23,083	6.5
Umbria	815	20.2	94	5,158	6.4
Marche	1,434	19.4	105	10,865	7.5
Lazio	5,162	14.9	116	42,276	8.2
Abruzzo	1,256	17.6	88	10,229	7.2
Molise	331	18.2	72	1,796	5.5
Campania	5,669	11.6	67	29,819	5.3
Puglia	4,050	13.0	72	29,521	7.3
Basilicata	611	15.0	61	3,865	6.3
Calabria	2,075	13.9	58	12,101	5.9
Sicilia	4,998	14.2	68	27,378	5.5
Sardegna	1,652	13.1	77	10,521	6.4
Italy	**56,960**	**16.0**	**100**	**389,457**	**6.8**

Notes: * Istituto Nazionale di Statistica (1994a, pp 27-8)
† Istituto Nazionale di Statistica (1995, p 43)
‡ Istituto Nazionale di Statistica (1994b)
§ Istituto Nazionale di Statistica (1995, p 52)
¶ Ministero della Sanità (1994b, pp 43-4)

Public–private mix				Administrative capacity		
Private bed stock/ total bed stock (%)	Private amb facilities/ total amb facilities (%)	Attraction rate for hospital care (%)	Political colour of majority coalition	Score for implement- active capacity	Score for overall institutional performance	Average no days to pay invoices (Italy=100)
(1992)§	(1992)¶	(1991)‖	(1995)**	(1984)††	(1984)‡‡	(1994)§§
25.8	27.2	1.03	C-R	11	9	44
0.0	14.3	0.71	C-R	na	na	30
27.1	51.1	2.23	C-R	12	41	47
20.5	19.7	1.10	E	na	na	31
10.9	64.4	2.48	C-R	9	27	55
10.0	40.0	2.30	C-R	na	na	55
12.2	55.6	2.50	C-L	7	15	90
20.4	56.0	3.31	C-L	15	45	82
14.0	48.3	1.91	C-L	13	29	87
8.8	63.0	2.02	C-L	12	31	95
21.5	37.6	1.04	C-L	9	21	112
43.5	66.8	1.15	C-L	9	12	168
21.7	62.6	0.72	C-L	10	11	104
12.1	61.9	0.89	C-L	3	4	133
32.0	80.0	0.19	C-R	6	6	173
20.3	71.9	0.46	C-R	6	7	171
23.8	47.7	0.30	C-L	7	10	68
30.6	67.5	0.18	C-R	3	3	205
16.7	85.1	0.11	C-R	na	na	135
18.2	52.1	0.27	C-L	na	na	114
23.4	**66.5**					**100**

‖ Ratio of interregional emigration and immigration of patients adjusted for distance between region of residence and region of hospitalisation; Geddes (1994, p 8)
** C-R: Centre-right; C-L: Centre-left; E: mainly ethnic parties
†† From 0 to 15; Putnam et al (1985, p 274)
‡‡ From 0 to 45; Putnam et al (1985, pp 146-7)
§§ Assobiomedica (1995)

A clearer idea of where the regions are headed with quasi-markets in health will emerge from assessing how they behave with accreditation. The way in which accreditation criteria are set and applied will have an important influence on the degree and character of competition between public providers and especially perhaps between public and private providers. In any case, Ministry of Health provisional accreditation guidelines (Agenzia Sanitaria Italiana, 1996) seem oriented against the acquisition of accredited status by a provider which would give it an automatic right to serve SSN patients. The guidelines propose that purchaser-provider contracts be made which specify typology and volume of services to be delivered, tariff levels, quality, billing and payment procedures and sanctions. Central government seems to be trying to sell the regions the USL sponsor model.

The terminology used for the different quasi-market models attributes a key role to the USL in the negotiating, contracting and regulatory functions. However, it is not a foregone conclusion that regions will assign their USLs such functions rather than exercising them themselves. Quite different quasi-markets may emerge, depending on the degree to which regions are willing to delegate power downwards to the USL. A recent study of regional legislation and other official regional sources indicates that a number of regions are opting, at least for the present, for the USL planner model; only one has unambiguously chosen the USL third payer model. Several regions are still undecided (France, 1997). One probable reason for the caution in introducing quasi-markets is concern about the implications for expenditure control. In any case, central government may be having second thoughts about quasi-markets in healthcare; the Ministry of Health recently announced a review of the 1992-93 reforms.

Final considerations

This chapter may seem to suggest that a decentralised system is per se less favourable an environment for quasi-markets than a unitary state. However, this assumes that the unitary system of government guarantees the 'best' choice of quasi-market model. If this is not the case, its ability to enforce a standard quasi-market model uniformly throughout the country is a dubious merit. Decentralised government may perhaps be less efficient than a unitary system of government if judged in terms of capacity to economise in the use of scarce political and financial resources for policy implementation. It does permit, and may even encourage, diversity in institutional arrangements. This could lead to 'natural' experimentation and, in turn, to convergence by sub-central governments on the more successful innovations. This is all the more likely if, as some students of federalism argue, sub-central governments compete in satisfying the demands and preferences of citizens for services (Breton, 1987) and are ready to imitate successful innovation in institutional arrangements (Salmon, 1987). The UK is an exceptionally centralised case of unitary state; in some other unitary systems, such as Sweden, Denmark and Norway, there is an enduring tradition of strong local autonomy (Batley and Stoker, 1991). This is reflected in Sweden, for example, in considerable diversity in the approaches adopted by the counties in the introduction of pro-competitive health reforms (World Health Organisation, 1996). This is not to deny that diversity does not emerge even in highly centralised settings, as is evidenced in the UK by the wide variety of ways developed for involving GPs in resource allocation (Mays and Dixon, 1996).

Notes

[1] This distinction is useful for the analysis here although institutional environments and institutional arrangements may not be intrinsically different in nature but part of a continuum. This could be especially the case in some continental European countries where many decisions, which in an Anglo-Saxon context would be purely administrative, require legislative action.

[2] The question of who bears these additional transaction costs is ignored. This could be an important factor in determining the particular type of quasi-market model a region (or country) adopts (see Bariletti and France, 1996).

[3] In 1993, in expenditure terms around 10% of total SSN hospital care was delivered in contracted hospitals while roughly 30% of all SSN ambulatory diagnostic and specialist care was delivered by contracted providers (Ministero della Sanità, 1994a).

[4] Pierson (1994, p 32) defines *vertical integration* in government as "the degree that power is concentrated nationally or devolved to more local government authorities".

[5] By 1993, the public debt/GDP and debt costs/GDP ratios had risen to almost 120% and 12% respectively. These ratios and that of the public sector borrowing requirement to GDP were all around twice the EU average (Bosi et al, 1994, p 21).

[6] The new financing arrangements could have potentially serious implications for geographical equity due to large inter-regional differences in revenue bases (Artoni and Saraceno, 1995; Dirindin, 1995; Mapelli, 1995b). The central contribution to financing the SSN will almost certainly decline over time and with it the leverage the central authorities have over the regions to ensure broadly similar standards throughout the country. This seems to be what is happening in Canada with the federal government's gradual withdrawal from healthcare financing (Banting, 1995)

[7] The national legislation contains provisions for clinical and performance budgeting and for protection of patient rights. It makes no mention of procedures for the treatment of capital assets or against cream-skimming. GP fundholding is not envisaged but only a mild form of GP indicative budgets.

[8] Unlike with the UK quasi-market health reform, there was no White Paper or other official document describing the overall design of the Italian reform. The reference framework and three categories of models offered here are based on a reading of the following sources: Law 502/1992 with amendments contained in Law 517/1993; Law 724/1994 (Finance Act for 1995), Article 6; National Health Plan, 1994-96 (Atto di Intesa tra lo Stato e Regioni per la Definizione del Piano Sanitario Nazionale Relativo al Triennio 1994-96, *Gazzetta Ufficiale*, no 8 [supplemento ordinario], 12 January 1994); Ministerial Decree 14 December 1994 ('Tariffe delle prestazioni di assistenza ospedaliera'); Guidelines on Application of Ministerial Decree 14 December 1994 (Linee di Guida no 1/95); Law 549/1995 (Finance Act for 1996), Article 2; Decree of the President of the Republic 14 January 1997.

[9] For hospital care alone, in 1992 there were almost 10 million SSN admissions, that is, transactions (Ministero della Sanità, 1994b).

[10] It is difficult to find a synthetic epidemiological indicator that is meaningful for this purpose.

[11]   In 1993, 214,000 patients moved out of the southern regions for hospital care, which represented 6.6% of total admissions for southern residents (Ministero della Sanità, 1995).

[12]   An important source for this section is the systematic analysis of the regional legislation on hospital tariffs by Arcangeli et al (1996).

NINE

Purchaser plurality in UK healthcare: is a consensus emerging and is it the right one?

Nicholas Mays and Jennifer Dixon

Trends in NHS purchasing at local level

The NHS White Paper of 1989 (DoH, 1989a) introduced a purchaser–provider split into UK publicly-funded healthcare with two seemingly incompatible models of purchasing. In one model, health authorities (HAs) were to be transformed into purchasing organisations responsible for purchasing rather than providing *all* the hospital and community health services (HCHS) for populations in excess of 250,000 people. In the other model, single practice GP fundholding was introduced in which individual GP practices volunteered to hold a budget withdrawn from the overall allocation of their local HA to enable them to manage their prescribing costs and to purchase a selected range of mainly *elective* health services for the patients on their practice lists. Fundholders were allowed to make and keep a negotiated share of any savings which they were able to accrue through more resource-conscious decision making.

Fundholding was to be an essentially 'bottom-up' style of purchasing built up from the GPs' clinical experience and their interaction with many patients. In this sense, it was more consistent with a market-type system than HA purchasing. By contrast, the HA model stressed an epidemiological, strategic approach which had much in common with past models of 'top-down' NHS planning. In the early period of the NHS reforms following the White Paper *Working for patients*, the two models were frequently viewed both by analysts and those implementing the NHS reforms as being in competition with one another. In retrospect,

Table 4: Profiles of purchasing models in the NHS (1997/98)

Model type	Population size	Practice or locality/ geographical basis	Involvement of FHs	Budgetary control over funds to purchase services	Payments to participants for management	Range of services purchased/ commissioned	Management structure/ organisation	Degree of autonomy from HA/ influence over HA
Conventional HA purchasing	250,000 plus	Geographical boundaries	Not directly	Own capitation-based budget	Professional managers paid by HA	All HCHS (minus that of SFHs)	Bureaucratic hierarchy with GP advice on purchasing	na
Locality commissioning	40-60,000	Usually geographical though sometimes practice-based (volunteer)	Primarily non-FHs but FHs involved sometimes	Not generally any devolved budgets (ie commissioning rather than purchasing)	Often paid coordinator/ locality manager (paid by HA)	Varies, emphasis on needs assessment/ locality profiles	Locality groups/GP fora and GP representatives	Modest – usually orchestrated by HA
Practice-sensitive commissioning/ GP commissioning	Wide range	Usually (volunteer) practice-based; based on groups of practices	Primarily but not exclusively non-FHs	Sometimes indicative or devolved budgets from HA (mixed capitation/activity basis)	Sometimes GP sessional fees from HA to take part	Varies, can be wider than locality schemes	Sometimes paid GP committee to advise HA	Greater than locality schemes
GP total purchasing pilots	15-100,000	Practice-based (volunteer); usually groups of SFHs	Almost exclusively SFHs	Delegated budget from HA	Variety of management fees/support from HA and regions	Potentially all HCHS but normally a sub-set in practice	Usually formal sub-committee of HA with specific powers	Similar to SFH but HA input to decisions

Extended FH pilots	6-15,000 (as for SFH)	Practice-based (volunteer)	SFHs only	Delegated budget for extensions of SFH	Variety of management fees/support from HA and regions	As for SFH, plus one of a range of specified services (eg maternity, mental health)	As for SFH – practice-based	Similar to SFH
FH multifunds	50-250,000	Practice-based (volunteer)	SFHs and CFHs only	Own budget top-sliced from HA (capitation with activity element)	Variety of management fees/support from HA and regions	As for SFH; specified elective inpatient care, most outpatients, CHS, diagnostic tests, direct access, drugs, practice staff	Practice-based and joint managers appointed across all practices in the multifund; GP representation on board of multifund	Large degree of autonomy and some influence over HA
Standard fundholding	6-15,000	Individual practices (volunteer)	SFHs only	Own budget top-sliced from HA (capitation with activity element)	Variety of management fees/support from HA and regions	Specified elective inpatient care, most outpatients, CHS, diagnostic tests, direct access, drugs, practice staff	Practice-based through FH manager	Large degree of autonomy and some influence over HA
Community FH	Less than 6,000	Individual practices (volunteer)	CFHs only	Own budget top-sliced from HA (capitation with activity element)	Variety of management fees/support from HA and regions	Most CHS, drugs, diagnostic tests and practice staff	Practice-based through FH manager	Large degree of autonomy; relatively little influence over HA

this seems unhelpful since the two models are in crucial respects not fully comparable. However, the two models of purchasing were regarded as *independent* of one another and operating largely separately.

In practice, as the contrasting fundholding and HA models have come face-to-face with the pervasive problems of purchasing healthcare – particularly the difficulty facing large purchasers in understanding the needs of individual patients and the difficulty for small purchasers of influencing providers' behaviour – a wide range of other approaches to purchasing below the level of the HA area has developed (see Table 4 for details). Whereas before 1991, the principal source of organisational variation in the NHS lay on the supply side, increasingly this came to be echoed by local heterogeneity on the demand side as the NHS tried to relate purchasing decisions more closely to the needs of patients by taking into account the views of GPs, and sometimes others, as agents for the patient. Each district now has its near unique blend of purchasing carried out by:

- the HA at a district level;
- standard fundholders (SFHs) and community fundholders (FHs);
- multifunds and other constellations of fundholding practices;
- locality commissioning organisations and GP commissioning on behalf of non-fundholders and sometimes SFH patients;
- increasingly, the pilot extensions of SFH and total purchasing pilots (TPPs).

Figure 2 attempts to summarise the range of models which may be present within the boundaries of HAs. Compared with the situation at the beginning of the period of the so called 'NHS reforms', there was far more emphasis by 1996 on forms of purchasing involving both GP practices and HAs working together and those which comprised groups of practices and larger populations.

From the features of the schemes in Table 4 and Figure 2, it may be observed that the differences between the approaches are blurring. The developments such as the GP TPPs amount to a hybrid of SFH and HA approaches to purchasing (Mays et al, 1997). In practice, the differences between GP commissioning and GP total purchasing may turn out to be more in terms of their ideological origins and terminology than the way in which they operate. GP commissioning has largely emerged spontaneously among practices opposed to fundholding whereas the national TPP projects became aligned far more with the Conservative government's policy of extending the SFH model (DoH, 1994a).

Figure 2: A typology of current purchasing organisations in the NHS (1997/98)

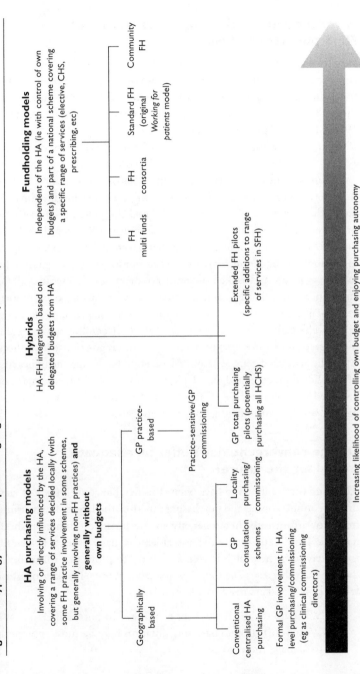

A convergence of thinking on the future of NHS purchasing of HCHS

Despite a paucity of evidence on the comparative merits of the different approaches to purchasing, there was a growing convergence of thinking from the three main political parties as to the broad features which should be adopted in NHS healthcare purchasing in the future (DoH, 1994a; Labour Party, 1995; Liberal Democrat Party, 1995). In March 1996, the Conservative Secretary of State for Health, Stephen Dorrell, agreed to consider the possibility that GP commissioning might be put on a similar footing to GP fundholding, that is, to reimburse GPs for time devoted to commissioning in the same way as in fundholding. He stated that, "there is no single blueprint and the government has never suggested there should be" (*Health Service Journal*, 1996). Similarly, before the 1997 General Election, the Labour Party softened its original antipathy to fundholding by hinting that it would accept some form of fundholding so long as it was undertaken by groups of practices representing all GPs and patients in a locality and the practices were made to be properly accountable for the decisions they took (*The Guardian*, 1996; Smith, 1996). The principal difference of *emphasis* between the parties became the degree and nature of external scrutiny and regulation which should affect the actions of general practice-based purchasers and the importance of individual practice budgets. Labour and the Liberal Democrats both favoured a greater degree of regulation; Labour, unlike the other two parties, was against individual practice budgets.

Do the convergent views offer an adequate model for the future?

Although there appears to have been considerable convergence of views on the commissioning and purchasing function, the largely unscrutinised trend towards greater heterogeneity in the forms the function should take (see Table 4 and Figure 2) raises at least as many issues as it solves. It is unlikely to be helpful, if it ever was, to try to prove that one model is 'better' than the rest (*The Guardian [Society]*, 1996). The key questions which policy makers need to ask are:

- What are the goals we want to achieve in purchasing?
- Which sorts of purchaser organisation may be most appropriate to achieve these goals?

Since there is little evidence available to assist the development of policy, much of the discussion on these key questions, which follows, has to be hypothetical.

Which goals do we want to achieve?

The aim of NHS purchasing is to achieve high quality, effective, acceptable and equitable healthcare at minimum cost. For this to be achieved, the *purchasing process* should comprise:

- assessing the needs of the population for care;
- having adequate information about services to be purchased;
- having the ability to influence providers regarding the efficiency and quality of services;
- involving patients and offering them choice in decisions affecting their care;
- setting appropriate priorities;
- monitoring and maintaining equity;
- managing financial risk adequately;
- minimising transaction costs.

Additional goals relate to the *qualities of purchaser organisations* themselves rather than the purchasing process. Organisations should be sustainable, accountable, have an appropriate mix of skills, and there should be minimal or no conflict of interests operating. To what extent are the current models of purchasing likely to achieve these goals?

Processes required to meet the goals of purchasing

Assessing patients' needs

Since patients who demand care do not always need it, and vice versa, rational and efficient purchasing requires at least an acknowledgement of the importance of assessing need. However, so far, needs assessment has been an activity almost exclusively carried out by HAs, for HA or locality populations, largely because staff with the necessary epidemiological skills are located there. In contrast, GP fundholding practices have been more preoccupied with demand, and needs assessment has been rare. This is likely to be so because of:

- a lack of understanding in general practice of the rationale for needs assessment;

- a lack of data in general practice to conduct practice-level needs assessment – many GPs distrust the accuracy of routine hospital and HA data;
- the fact that the practice population is based on enrolment rather than geography;
- a lack of understanding of how to incorporate meaningfully the results of a needs assessment into purchasing decisions.

Although there are examples where public health physicians have lent their needs assessment skills to fundholding practices, or to the new TPPs (DoH, 1994a), the results and benefits of this effort have not yet been clearly demonstrated (Mays et al, 1997). Without a clear impact, it is likely to remain a peripheral activity in practice-based purchasing/commissioning.

On this basis it could be argued that, without further action, geographically-based forms of purchasing which have a heavy input from the HA (such as locality commissioning) are more likely to incorporate needs assessment into purchasing decisions than other models of purchasing.

Obtaining adequate information about services

The policy of devolving budgets to practice or locality level relies on staff in these organisations having the information to secure appropriate services. There are two types of information involved:

- '*descriptive*', which is about local services; for example, the type of care offered, by whom, where and when, and the experiences of patients;
- '*evaluative*', which is about, for example, the costs and effectiveness of a treatment or a service.

GPs are likely to have detailed *descriptive* information about local services for common, straightforward and predictable conditions; for example, elective surgery included in the fundholding scheme. These services are likely to be provided by the majority of acute (general) hospitals, giving GPs both a choice of provider and adequate knowledge with which to make an informed choice. GPs are less likely to have descriptive information on services for rarer conditions which are not offered locally, such as paediatric cardiology or organ transplantation. To keep up with recent developments will be too time-consuming to be feasible.

GPs are less likely to have *evaluative* information on services from a variety of published sources (*The Guardian [Society]*, 1996; Long and Sheldon, 1992). It may also be unclear to busy GPs how to incorporate this information into decision-making. In contrast, the HA is less likely to have detailed descriptive information on local services, but more access to descriptive information about less common services and evaluative information in general.

It appears that there are merits in both the HA and GP purchasers/commissioners having access to each other's information when purchasing. Unless information technology, linking general practices to the information held by HAs, improves, it may be appropriate to have three levels of purchasing in order to maximise the availability of information. These levels could be:

- specialised services funded and purchased centrally or regionally, outside the internal market;
- common, elective, treatments purchased at practice or locality level or by patients directly (see below);
- other services purchased through an organisation covering at least the size of a current HA.

Influencing providers

The features of purchasing or purchasing organisations which most influence providers are likely to include:

- holding a budget;
- size of budget;
- local personal or professional networks, the power of 'voice' (Hirschman, 1970);
- capacity and willingness (incentives) to move contracts between providers, the power of 'exit' (Hirschman, 1970);
- knowledge of services offered and alternatives;
- other features of the local environment such as the power of the local provider.

There has been little or no systematic research to compare the influence of various models of purchasing in this respect. Surveys of fundholders show that they report being able to produce change through holding a budget, typically altering the *processes* of care, such as speedier discharge letters, rather than its clinical content (Dixon and Glennerster, 1995). Similar process changes have also been reported by commissioning GPs who are non-fundholders and by HAs (Ham and Shapiro, 1995; Office for Public Management, 1994; Graffy and Williams, 1994). However, anecdotal reports by fundholders also involved in locality commissioning claim that holding a budget, coupled with detailed local knowledge of services, has wrought more changes than working through the HA. The greater impact of direct purchasing by GPs has been confirmed elsewhere (Mason and Morgan, 1995). The only UK study which has attempted to compare fundholding with locality commissioning via the HA suggested that they each do different things well, with fundholders improving micro-efficiency and locality schemes improving equity of access (Glennerster et al, 1996). The study also suggested that the two models tend to attract different types of GPs. The most effective alternatives to fundholding looked most like fundholding!

Increasing patient involvement and choice

Giving patients the power to purchase care directly

One of the reasons for introducing fundholding was to encourage providers to be more responsive to GPs and, through them, to their patients. So far, the evidence suggests that providers have been more responsive to GP fundholders than to HAs (Glennerster et al, 1996; Glennerster et al, 1994), but how *patients* can themselves exert meaningful influence over their fundholding practices remains unclear. One option might be to consider giving patients direct purchasing power, for example, using a voucher. For many services, this may not be appropriate because of the information imbalance between the patient and doctor. However, it may be feasible for some uncomplicated elective procedures. This may encourage purchasers of all types to take more account of patients' wishes before setting contracts or making referrals, and to provide more patient information.

However, there are likely to be significant drawbacks from such action which would have to be guarded against. These include the problems of:

- moral hazard;
- making information accessible for the patients to make an informed choice;
- setting an appropriate value for the voucher;

- ensuring that less demanding and less knowledgeable patients receive appropriate care.

These drawbacks may be too difficult and costly to overcome compared with the potential benefits.

Giving patients more power to choose an appropriate purchaser

It is likely to become increasingly necessary to provide patients with more information about who purchases their services. With HA and locality purchasing, patients have had no choice of purchaser for most of their care and very little information to make a judgement about the competence of their purchaser. Purchasing at practice level involves purchasing for an enrolled, not a geographically-defined, population and this does offer the opportunity for patients to enrol with a different practice if desired. However, even at practice level, patients have had scanty information about the: extent of involvement of their practice, or others locally, in purchasing; portfolio of services bought; competence of the practice as a purchaser; purchasing priorities made. With the trend towards larger conglomerates of practices in purchasing, such as multifunds or TPPs (Mays et al, 1997; Little, 1995), there will be less opportunity for patients to have a choice of purchaser. None of the current purchasing models offers patients a great deal of involvement or choice.

Setting appropriate priorities

Purchasing organisations set priorities in broadly two dimensions: between services and between patients. At HA level, broad priorities are set using a combination of information including: historical activity; needs assessment; effectiveness of treatments; local and national policies; public preferences. Responsibility for setting priorities between patients is left largely to healthcare professionals, except in the case of extra contractual referrals (ECRs), where a decision is made usually between the patient's doctor and public health physicians at the HA.

Devolving budgets to GPs has implications for setting priorities in both dimensions. First, for the reasons outlined earlier, GPs may not have access to, or the willingness to use, information on population needs or the effectiveness of treatments. HA purchasers are held to account through the mechanism of the corporate contract for implementing national or local policies. This includes the requirement to consult patients on purchasing decisions. This structure of accountability is weak or non-existent for GP purchasing organisations despite recent efforts to strengthen it (DoH, 1994b).

It could be argued that GP purchasers may be better placed to judge the merits of extra contractual referrals (ECRs). Unlike HAs, GPs know the individual patients concerned and are technically available 24 hours a day to give authorisation for the ECR. On the other hand, GPs are not in a position to judge the priority of their patients relative to patients from another practice and may not be fully aware of the opportunity costs of ECRs. This is important if the aim of a HA is to maximise benefit from the resources available to it and other local purchasers.

Monitoring and maintaining equity

While providing equity of access for equal need is a basic principle of the NHS, in recent years far more attention has been paid by HAs to other priorities such as efficiency. HAs have access to routine data across a large population on, for example, use of hospital care and patients on waiting lists, and are more likely to have the capacity to analyse this information. GPs, especially fundholders, may also have this information and other data, for example, on consultations and referrals, albeit for a smaller population, but they are unlikely to have the time, skills and computing capacity required to use it.

There are similar issues in relation to maintaining equity. Having more purchasers covering smaller populations of patients, each with different contracts with providers and different priorities, may lead to a more uneven service than having a single purchaser purchasing for a large population. If ensuring equity is a goal for purchasing, there needs to be a greater incentive for all the current forms of purchasing organisations to treat this issue as a priority.

Minimising transaction costs

A greater number and variety of purchasing organisations is likely to increase the volume and complexity of contracting and all the activity which goes with it. This includes drawing up purchasing intentions, negotiating contracts, monitoring activity and finance, invoicing and payment. In this sense, the existence of more organisations having direct responsibility for holding a budget must lead to higher transaction costs.

The National Association of Commissioning GPs claims that the transaction costs of practices involved in commissioning are lower than those involved in purchasing through SFH (Black et al, 1994). An NHS with a diverse range of purchasing models, a lot of small purchasers, more sophisticated cost-per-case contracts and greater freedoms for purchasers is likely to face higher transaction costs and costs of monitoring compared to models where HA purchasing and GP commissioning predominate.

Managing financial risk

Organisations purchasing care for large populations are likely to be less vulnerable to random fluctuations in the demand for care than organisations covering smaller populations. The question is, how large must the population covered by a purchaser be to manage financial risk comfortably for which range of services? The range of purchasing models currently in the NHS (Table 4) is not based on any systematic analysis of this question. The following possible division of responsibilities is put forward to stimulate debate in the absence of empirical data. A population base of at least:

- 250,000 (the approximate size of a HA) for purchasing expensive and unpredictable treatments; for example, organ transplantation, neonatal care, neurosurgical services, secure beds, major trauma care, and screening programmes where investment in expensive equipment is required;
- 50,000 (the approximate median size of a locality or a TPP) for purchasing more 'routine' emergency care;
- 10,000-50,000 (the size of a large practice or group of practices) for purchasing elective treatments, most mental healthcare and care for people with learning difficulties;
- 3,000-10,000 (the size of a small practice) for purchasing community health services and perhaps, in future, social care.

It may not be feasible for each of these types of purchaser to manage a separate budget and financial risk for its own range of services, as much of the recent evolution of purchasing presumes. If the budgets for each purchaser are not integrated, then the larger purchasers, buying costly and unpredictable treatments, will not have access to the elective budget, managed by the smaller purchasers, to cushion the financial risk when necessary. Without this ability, services bought by the large purchaser may be prohibitively expensive to insure on the private market. Instead, it may be preferable for the larger purchasers bearing more financial risk to have the ability to influence expenditure from the budgets of the smaller purchaser. To stop abuse by the larger purchaser, it may be necessary for the smaller purchasers to be involved in the management of the larger purchaser as is the case to an extent with the new TPPs which are 'hybrids' of fundholder and HA organisations (Mays et al, 1997).

Qualities required of purchasing organisations

Sustainability

Although many practices involved in purchasing have been given support to help manage their purchasing, this still represents a significant workload. Typically, the workload is the responsibility of one or two GPs and a practice manager. However, there are likely to be workload implications for the rest of the practice staff, who may have to cover for absent GPs involved in purchasing. Sustainability also depends on the continued willingness of GPs to take time away from their clinical work and be involved in managerial tasks – this is more likely if the GPs are supported through appropriate training and adequate resources. The costs to the practice are likely to be a significant factor in the sustainability of its purchasing activity.

Similarly the actual or potential for benefit is also likely to be a factor. If there is less opportunity to make savings on the budget or to influence providers as may be the case with locality purchasing, then this may be a disincentive for GP purchasers to sustain their purchasing role in future.

Appropriate mix of skills

In devolved purchasing models such as locality commissioning, where GPs' opinions about local services are sought, the skills required of GPs are mainly to have a good knowledge of local services and a flair for problem-solving. However, where budgets are devolved from HAs a whole range of extra skills is required. These include:

* financial management;
* knowledge of demands and needs of the population;

- awareness of current evidence on the effectiveness and cost-effectiveness of alternative treatments;
- management, teamworking skills and an ability to delegate;
- ideally, a knowledge of the ethical principles of priority-setting.

Some of these skills are in short supply in HAs and it is likely they will be even harder to find at locality and practice levels. In addition, the extent to which general practices are developed in organisational terms is very variable (Audit Commission, 1996). In this respect, individual practices may not be an appropriate building block for purchasing services directly. All this points towards the need for significant investment in many practices or groups of practices to increase organisational capacity if the purchasing system is to be driven by GPs.

Accountability

Developing effective means of making GPs accountable for purchasing decisions appears to be a problem in other countries which like the UK are experimenting with some form of quasi-market (Mason and Morgan, 1995). Three years after the introduction of the fundholding scheme, the DoH issued guidelines designed to strengthen accountability in the fundholding scheme in four main areas: practice management; relations with patients and the wider public; financial management; and relations to professional peers (DoH, 1994b). However, the extent to which HAs and GP purchasers followed the guidance is unclear. Unlike for fundholders, there are formal mechanisms by which the HA is held accountable to the NHS Executive, for example, through the corporate contract system and yearly review, at which progress against agreed objectives is monitored. This level of scrutiny has not been in evidence for GP purchasing. For example, the National Association of Community Health Councils (CHCs) in England and Wales found that CHCs had difficulty obtaining basic information about fundholders' purchasing plans, and public consultation on these plans was rare (National Association of Community Health Councils, 1995).

Professional accountability for the provision of health services occurs through a variety of means, for example, clinical audit and routine performance indicators of the process of care, such as waiting times. There is no such formal peer review of the purchasing of health services by any purchaser, with the exception of HAs through the corporate contract system. This is a gap which should be filled, possibly by an independent organisation.

New models of devolved purchasing, particularly where GPs actually hold a budget for care, may stimulate greater peer review *within* the purchasing organisation. On the other hand, where the HA holds the budget for purchasing and GPs have influence but are not given any rewards through 'savings' made, there may be less incentive for peer review by GPs. In these cases, the HA may need to take a more active role in peer review, although past efforts by HAs to influence referrals and GP prescribing met with considerable resistance. Fundholding was introduced to tackle this long-standing perceived problem.

Minimising conflicts of interest

When the GP primary care provider is also a purchaser there could be conflicts of interest, for example, skimping on specialist care in order to protect fundholding 'savings' which could then be invested in the practice. This could still be the case even if budgetary arrangements for general medical services (GMS) and HCHS resources remain separate. Although there is little evidence suggesting that conflicts of interest have been a problem to date, a number of the TPP projects are planning to pay their own GP colleagues to provide specialist services, paid for out of their HCHS total purchasing budgets (DoH, 1996). In other health systems, serious problems have arisen in facilities in which doctors have a proprietary interest or where they provide a large range of ancillary services in their offices, such as dispensing drugs (Rodwin, 1993).

There are more far-reaching implications if the budget for GMS is integrated with the budget for HCHS and held by GPs, one of the options likely to be piloted following the October 1996 White Paper on primary care (DoH, 1996). A conflict of interest may arise where a GP has a choice to invest in a service which could be provided by the hospital or by the practice in which the GP has a direct financial interest. The purchasing and providing activities of GPs would have to be carefully monitored (see above, discussion on accountability). However, policing this area is likely to be difficult and expensive and there may be resistance from GPs who see themselves as professionally accountable to the General Medical Council rather than to an organisation such as a HA or other local regulatory body.

Assessing the current models

There are two main conclusions from the discussion so far. Firstly, each of the different models of purchasing currently in existence has a different combination of merits and drawbacks in the selected dimensions discussed. The models which are permitted to develop in the NHS will depend on the choices made about the most appropriate dimensions on which to judge purchasing decisions and purchasing organisations and the weight to be given to each. Secondly, further developments in purchasing can only sensibly proceed with careful monitoring and regulation. The next section describes some options for future purchasing models, highlights their potential merits and disadvantages and outlines areas where regulation or monitoring may be required.

Policy options for the future development of NHS purchasing

The seven options

Each of the following seven options attempts in different ways to respond to the limitations inherent in current models. The options can be divided into the less radical ones which largely accept the location of the current purchaser–provider split in the NHS, and the more radical ones which address more directly some of the issues and concerns identified earlier in this chapter. In contrast, the less radical options accept the partial erosion of the purchaser–provider split through fundholding, the existing national GP contract, the budgetary separation of HCHS, GMS and the resources of the LA social services and current notions of patient choice of general practice.

Less radical options

1 *Modified status quo:* the current trend towards a plurality of purchasers would continue, but with a more explicit recognition of the likelihood that different forms of purchaser organisation and budgetary devolution will work better in different circumstances. As a result, the extension of the various models currently in existence (see Figure 2) to new sites would be more closely regulated and research would be carried out systematically comparing them with one another in different contexts to ensure a more appropriate mix of models.

The strengths and weaknesses of this option would be largely the same as currently exist until evidence suggested that one or more models appeared to work particularly well in specific circumstances.

2 *Purchaser specialisation:* this option involves purchasing responsibility for different services being divided between a number of different purchasing models based on acquiring knowledge as to which purchaser purchases which services best in which circumstances from the type of research suggested in option 1 above. Table 5 gives one possible division of NHS responsibilities.

In addition, care for the mentally ill and those with learning difficulties might be purchased jointly by the HA and the LA social services based on their relative expertise and a willingness to manage the budget. Each purchasing organisation would be allocated its own budget, ideally based on some form of weighted capitation. It would be worth considering the scope for linkage or virement between the budgets of the different levels involved (see above, for discussion of this).

While this approach might ensure that services were purchased by organisations with appropriate expertise and access to relevant information on needs and cost-effective responses, the system would be administratively complex, not least for providers who would have to deal with a number of different types of purchaser as they do at present.

3 *Building on the GP total purchasing experiment:* this involves introducing primary care-based purchasing organisations directly holding their own capitation budgets for all HCHS, either based on groups of existing general practices as in the current TPPs (Mays et al, 1997), or in the form of new organisations, not necessarily led by GPs. The HA would cease to purchase any services, but would instead be required to monitor and, if necessary, regulate the purchasing behaviour of a number of primary care-based purchasing organisations. The HA would also set the local health strategy within which the purchasers operate and might market the services of specialist staff, for example in finance and public health, to the purchasers.

4 *GP commissioning:* this would consist of GP commissioning groups working within shadow or indicative budgets from the HA and including most or all general practices in an area, as proposed by the Labour Party (Smith, 1996). A notional capitation budget would be calculated for all practices in the area against which their use of resources would be

**Table 5:A possible division of purchasing responsibilities
for different types of health services**

Processes required to meet the goals of purchasing	Main types of services to be purchased		
	Common and elective	Less common and emergency	Rare or needing tertiary care
Needs assessment	HA	HA	HA
Obtaining information about services	P, L	HA	HA
Influencing providers	P, L	P/HA	HA/R
Patient involvement and choice	P, L	HA	HA
Setting appropriate priorities	P, L	HA	HA/R
Monitoring and maintaining equity	HA	HA	HA
Minimising transaction costs	HA	HA	HA
Managing financial risk	P, L	P, L, HA	HA

Key: R = purchasing at regional level
HA = purchasing at current health authority level
L = purchasing at locality or general practice group level
P = purchasing at individual practice level

monitored to ensure equity. Practices would not be compelled to take part in commissioning. Those which did not would rely on the HA to purchase services on their behalf.

More radical options

5 *Integrated primary care-based purchasing organisations:* this option would be similar to 3, above, but with the important addition of integrated budgets covering both HCHS and general medical services (GMS), that is, a total health services budget for enrolled patients. The purchasing organisation could either be based on existing general practices in which case the local HA would negotiate a contract with it for the *provision* of primary care and the organisation would purchase the rest, or it could be separate from general practice in which case it could, in turn, contract with local GPs and others to provide primary care services and could also purchase other services. Alternatively, the organisation could employ its own salaried GPs to act as primary care providers and purchasers of other parts of healthcare. In whichever form, the purchaser organisation would have the freedom, at least in theory, to choose how it obtained primary, secondary and tertiary care for its population, that is, how vertically integrated it wished to be. It would be particularly important to set a budget which minimised the risk of adverse selection. Patients would be free to change their registration, say annually, if they were dissatisfied with the performance of the organisation.

The version which is not based on existing general practices reduces the scope for perverse incentives for the primary care provider and conceptually would be closer to a US Health Maintenance Organisation (HMO) than anything seen hitherto in the NHS (Robinson and Casalino, 1996). It would involve ending the national GP contract in favour of local contracts held either by the HA or by the healthcare organisation, perhaps embodying 'core' national standards, for example, a periodic requirement to demonstrate competence to practice (Starey et al, 1993).

6 Integrated health and social care purchasing organisations: this would be like option 5, but the organisation responsible for a total health service budget would also be responsible for deploying the social care element in the LA social services budget. A number of the TPPs have plans to experiment with local, informal mergers of health and social care budgets in this way (Mays et al, 1997).

Although this option has a strong logic, it would require either shifting a significant amount of local government finance into the NHS, which would be resisted by the LAs, or it would require the local purchasing organisation to be accountable both to the HA and to the LA for different aspects of their purchasing.

7 'Mixed economy' of NHS purchasing: this option would be similar to 5 and 6, but based on allowing NHS and non–NHS bodies to contract to hold NHS funds in order to form a series of potentially competing healthcare organisations offering different healthcare packages to patients based on a risk–adjusted capitation fee or voucher received from the NHS. There were hints of a move towards some organisations of this type following the Conservative government's White Paper *Choice and opportunity* (DoH, 1996). Drug companies have already expressed an interest in providing managed care services to SFHs and this role could be extended. Private insurers might also consider entering this market. The system would either allow patients to 'top up' their NHS capitation fee using private insurance, or not, depending on the ideological slant of the prevailing government. These competing organisations would not necessarily have to be in the private, for-profit sector. For example, they could be developed as a 'community health agency', that is, non-profit-making, democratically self-governing organisations (Ham, 1996). Some of the current GP TPPs could develop in this way, with an emphasis on user involvement.

This model would require considerable monitoring and regulation, for example, to prevent non-NHS healthcare purchasers refusing to accept high cost patients. There would need to be regulation to prevent or mitigate potential conflicts of interest, for example, where purchasers developed a financial stake in local providers. It would also threaten the notion of a 'national service', in favour of competing local networks of purchasers and providers. For all the potential problems which such a system would bring, such as loss of equity, it would introduce a degree of demand-side choice and potential for competition into the NHS quasi-market which does not currently exist. This may become increasingly important if unaccountable GPs and others are given freedom to make more and more purchasing decisions on behalf of groups of patients as current trends indicate.

Assessing the options

Each of the options can be assessed against the requirements for a cost-effective model of NHS purchasing set out earlier in this chapter. None of the options appears to have the potential to meet all the requirements without considerable monitoring, regulation or external support from third parties. Broadly, the more radical options may have the potential to increase patient involvement and choice and, thereby, improve accountability to individual patients. These are the weakest features of the less radical options. The more radical options may also reduce some of the perverse incentives which may occur when GP service providers are put in dominant positions as purchasers. They would tend to replace purchasing based on the current pattern of general practices with more highly managed organisations dependent for their income on their ability to attract patients (Goldsmith and Willetts, 1988). However, these would require considerable external scrutiny to prevent discrimination against potentially high cost patients or to ensure that purchasers in areas with populations with high requirements for services would not be disadvantaged. There would still be a need for organisations such as HAs to act on behalf of the NHS to ensure that the purchasing organisations were capable of delivering acceptable services to desired standards. For example, it cannot be assumed that private and voluntary sector providers are necessarily more flexible and responsive than public providers as evidence from contracted healthcare markets in the United States shows (Smith and Lipsky, 1993). The transaction costs of the more radical options might also be higher. On the other hand, the less radical options might perform relatively well on activities such as needs assessment, managing financial risk and maintaining equity, without doing a great deal to improve public or patient accountability or reduce potential conflicts of interest faced by GPs.

Not all of these requirements are of equal importance for cost-effective purchasing. For example, option 4, GP commissioning, looks promising according to many of the requirements for *adequate* purchasing. However, perhaps the biggest concern about GP commissioning is whether or not it will be able to bring about desired changes since it still relies on the HA to purchase services.

Conclusion

The rapid and unplanned development of a plurality of purchasers of HCHS in the NHS has, perhaps inadvertently, established the pre-conditions for further far more radical changes on the demand side of the internal market. This is not to say that all or any of the purchasing options discussed in the previous section would necessarily be desirable or an improvement on the current situation. Each in its different way offers a possible response to certain of the limitations in current trends to give GPs greater influence over HCHS purchasing. The more radical ones, especially, offer a response to the problems of public accountability, patient choice and appropriate incentives for GPs to act in the public interest both as purchasers and providers.

However, some of the more radical responses could fundamentally alter the nature of the NHS since demand-side contestability may increase transaction costs still further, make integrated care more difficult to achieve and threaten the equitable basis of the service. The challenge for defenders of 'core' NHS values is to adapt to changing circumstances and put together an attractive package of demand-side changes which will pre-empt the need for further potentially destabilising and inequitable experiments.

Whichever direction the next stage of NHS purchaser development goes, it is to be hoped that the service will be given sufficient time to learn from the plurality of organisations which it has produced since 1991. The likelihood is that different purchasing approaches might work best in specific places with the right leadership, since experience suggests that there is rarely or never a single 'optimal' organisational response to complex policy problems.

Postscript

Since discussing the pros and cons of likely options for future models of healthcare purchasing in the UK in this chapter, a new Labour government has been elected and the White Paper for England, *The new NHS* (DoH, 1997), has been published. The White Paper outlines a phased process at the end of which the main responsibility for purchasing healthcare will move throughout the country from the current 100 HAs, 3,600 fundholders, 90 TPP sites, and an unknown number of locality, and practice-based, commissioning groups to 500 primary care groups (PCGs) each covering a 'natural community' of approximately 100,000 people. PCGs are to consist of groups of GPs (around 50) and community nurses (an innovation) and will, when fully developed, hold a budget for virtually all HCHS for their area. The groups will also be responsible for the cash-limited part of the GMS budget which covers, for example, prescriptions and practice staffing. HAs are likely to continue to purchase only selected specialist services and individual practice fundholding will be scrapped from April 1999.

PCGs are expected to develop in four stages: from stage 1, where groups of practices essentially behave as locality commissioning groups (essentially option 4 in this chapter), to stage 4, where groups of practices form primary care trusts to purchase secondary care and provide all primary and community healthcare in one organisation (option 5 in this chapter). In option 2 it was predicted that there would be some degree of purchaser specialisation. This is implied in *The new NHS* – the responsibility for purchasing a small and specified range of services such as mental health will remain with the HA, although the justification for doing so is not discussed explicitly in the White Paper. For example, questions of the appropriate size of purchaser to minimise financial risk, to minimise transaction costs, to obtain adequate information about services, or to promote equity, are not discussed. All other services will be purchased by the new PCGs.

There is an implication in the White Paper that all purchasers, whatever their size and adequacy of knowledge relevant to purchasing services, need better information to support purchasing decisions. *The new NHS* combines proposals for devolving purchasing more fully to primary care organisations, with greater central guidance on which treatments and service configurations are likely to improve effectiveness and equity of access to care for patients. This will be done through the work of the new Commission for Health Improvement, which will also be responsible, with the HAs and regional offices of the NHS Executive, for monitoring adherence to the guidance. Depending on how this aspiration is implemented, these proposals are likely to lessen the degree of autonomy of the new PCGs and increase their accountability, compared with their predecessors such as the TPP projects. The HAs will also be expected to support the purchasing function of the PCGs.

The White Paper is based on the view that it is less inequitable, in terms of access to services, to have larger purchasers (PCGs) than smaller ones (such as fundholders). PCGs will cover larger populations than the current GP fundholders (including many multi-funds) and larger than almost all total purchasers. While the definition of 'natural communities' of 100,000 was not made explicit in the White Paper, the implication is that PCGs will cover a geographical population. This means that there will be a requirement for GPs within the area to work with each other, rather than a voluntary arrangement as in existing models. This has implications for patient choice, as discussed in this chapter. Unlike the current situation where a patient can choose to enlist with another GP purchaser (fundholder or total purchaser), there will be much less opportunity in future for a patient to choose an alternative purchaser of secondary care if each PCG covers a population of 100,000. There is a clear trade-off between the desire for patient choice and the desire to minimise 'two-tierism'; the latter is being seen as a higher priority than increasing patient choice.

In the White Paper, proposals for PCGs are also implicitly based on the hope that larger purchasers will incur lower transaction costs, although most of the references to reducing 'bureaucracy' relate to changing the contracting process from annual contracts to three-year service agreements rather than the direct costs of managing local purchaser organisations.

The White Paper stresses that the evolution of the PCGs from stage 1 to stage 4 will take place over a period of 5-10 years, and will not be an overnight revolution. This allows models to evolve at their own pace, and will mean that heterogeneity in purchasing models continues for some years to come.

While the Government has shown that it wishes purchasing to evolve in the new NHS, a large number of questions raised in this chapter – chiefly which type of purchasing works best for which services – remain unanswered.

Armed with these insights, the challenge is to specify the behaviours and outcomes which the NHS expects of its purchasers, identify factors which help and hinder these, devise an appropriate system of monitoring and evaluating the consequences and then allow the precise mechanisms to develop through local discretion. This chapter is a small contribution to this task. However, it *is* evident, even at this stage, that decentralised purchasing involving providers in primary care will require them to be externally supported and regulated in ways which are only just beginning to be considered.

Acknowledgements

The authors are very grateful to the following for taking the time to offer constructive criticism and encouragement in response to an earlier version of this chapter: Angela Coulter, Rudolf Klein, Tony Harrison and Julian Le Grand from the King's Fund, London, and George Maddox from Duke University, Durham, North Carolina. None of these people is responsible for the way in which the authors have responded to their help. A longer presentation of the material in this chapter is available as a short book published by King's Fund Publishing in 1996 with the same title.

TEN

Private agencies and public purposes: a quasi-market in the interwar years

Noel Whiteside

As it will be in the future, so it was at the birth of man,
There are only four things certain since earth and heaven began –
That the dog shall return to its vomit and the sow shall return to her mire
and the poor fool's bandaged finger goes wobbling back to the fire.
Rudyard Kipling

Introduction

The creation of quasi-market structures to deliver public services is not as novel as is sometimes supposed. Academic studies have pointed out similarities between the recent administrative transformation of the NHS and public healthcare in interwar Britain – between old voluntary hospitals and new trusts, between healthcare purchasing by LAs then and now (Powell, 1996). The object of this chapter is less to review the historiography of interwar performance than to set another aspect of the 1980s health reforms in historical perspective since private agencies, competing for customers, were also used in the delivery of public services in the interwar years. This form of public administration, in its turn, was also deemed wasteful and inefficient by reformers in the 1940s – reformers who were the architects of those centralised bureaucracies which have recently received such adverse publicity. Historically, it can be seen that during the past 50 years constructions of administrative 'efficiency' have shifted from a competitive, decentralised model to rationalised central control and back again. To avoid coming full circle, it is helpful to understand the apparent failings of the earlier period – to reveal the problems that undermined initial attempts to adapt private agencies to public purposes.

The focus here is on the National Health Insurance (NHI) scheme, from 1911 to 1948. By 1938, it covered 43% of the population (Gray, 1991, p 242), overwhelmingly manual workers, but not their dependants. Members registered with an 'approved society' of their choice; this offered GP care, sickness benefits and frequently purchased additional health services on its members' behalf. While this 'quasi-market' was not comprehensive, it offered subscriber choice of doctor and society, it embodied elements of competition and it separated purchaser from provider in medical services. All societies offered supplementary medical care under private insurance; most members subscribed to both public and private schemes – rendering the separation of public and private health funding impossible. Although only an estimated 10% of medical expenditure was apparently transmitted through NHI itself (Gray, 1991, pp 234-5), this figure does not include sickness benefits – again both public and private – administered by the societies. The NHI 'quasi-market' operated in two fields of welfare – social services and healthcare – which were subsequently separated by the Beveridge Report, making it an interesting precedent for more recent policy initiatives.

To avoid boring readers with too much detail, attention will be confined to issues concerning quasi-markets which have received recent attention, namely the cost of their operation and their ability to ensure efficiency and equity in service delivery. These were also the problems identified by social reformers in the 1920s and 1930s and specified in the Beveridge Report (HMSO, 1942), all of whom saw the rationalisation of administrative processes as the route to improvement. Beveridge was particularly scathing about the performance of the industrial assurance companies, the main commercial agencies involved in administering health insurance (Harris, 1977, pp 379-80). While the private voluntary societies registered under the system (chiefly friendly societies and trade unions) were viewed in a more benign light, even they were excluded in the drive to create a centralised, efficient administrative machine. With hindsight, these judgements might appear a little harsh. It is worth while analysing earlier experience to reveal the advantages and disadvantages of employing private agencies for public purposes.

Historical background

The interwar period, characterised by mass unemployment and strict constraints on public expenditure, bears some resemblance to our own. Then as now, industrial recession increased the incidence of social dependency (Whiteside, 1988). Then as now, governments tried to minimise existing responsibilities in providing social protection by fostering private thrift, by limiting exchequer subsidies and by containing public services (Webster, 1985). Then as now, access to state-funded benefits became increasingly difficult (Deacon, 1977; Whiteside, 1992, ch 4). All of these characteristics became more visible following the slump of the early 1930s, as numbers of claimants rose and official revenues fell. In this context, administrative efficiency and cost-effectiveness were at a premium. The Treasury sought to contain public liability by subsidising voluntary agencies and other organisations, to minimise official obligations. This was preferable to the expensive option of extending public provision unilaterally.

Official welfare obligations in the 1990s and the 1930s are not identical. The responsibilities of government in interwar Britain were essentially residual; those who could afford to pay were required to pay. Statutory social insurance was confined to lower income brackets; publicly-funded healthcare existed, but middle class consumers expected to pay for medical services. This pattern changed in the 1940s, with the development of universal welfare. From the earliest years of the war, in the views expressed to and by the Beveridge Committee (HMSO, 1942), the pre-war systems were condemned for fostering social injustice through unequal treatment. Rationalisation of central surveillance would promote fairness, cost-effectiveness and economies of scale. Competition between service providers caused duplication, waste and high administrative costs; eliminating these effects would secure greater efficiency and fair shares for all. Postwar reform conformed to this new vision, expanding direct provision by the State; the approved societies found no role within the new welfare state. Whether their condemnation was as fully justified as contemporaries supposed will be the theme addressed in the rest of this chapter.

National Health Insurance: the interwar quasi-market

The NHI scheme, the brain child of Lloyd George, survived the interwar years in largely unchanged form (Whiteside, 1983). In many respects similar to continental systems of health insurance – being modelled on the Bismarckean system introduced in Imperial Germany in 1883 – NHI provided access to GP medical care and sickness benefits to manual workers earning below a stipulated minimum income. Funded by tripartite contributions, involving employer, employee and the state, NHI operated on quite different principles from those of the better-known Unemployment Insurance Scheme. It was designed from its inception to promote consumer participation and choice and to minimise the contact between contributor and the state. The approved societies paid sickness benefits and – through the local insurance committees – employed 'panel' doctors who offered basic GP services to sick members in return for a per capita fee. This covered working contributors, not their dependants. Approved societies were non-profit-making; any surplus accruing to society accounts under the scheme could be spent only on the provision of centrally approved additional medical treatments (dental treatment, ophthalmic care, specialist hospital services) or extra cash benefits. The larger, richer approved societies used these 'additional benefits' to attract new members and to extend their business. Societies also sought (with official encouragement) to persuade their members to take out supplementary private policies; this private activity allowed the societies (notably the industrial insurance companies) to make their profits. Numbers covered expanded from 11.5 million (1912) to 20.264 million (1938) (HMSO, 1926, Evidence: Appendix I, s 8, p 10; Ministry of Health, 1939, pp 32-4). The expansion was due to population growth, to raising the ceiling for earnings to £250 per annum and to the growth of female employment (female membership rose from 3.68 million to 6.11 million in those years [HMSO, 1942, p 25, tables i and ii]).

NHI was centrally administered by the controller of health insurance in the Ministry of Health, who managed society accounts, held within the ministry, determined the panel doctors' salary and – with the government actuary – decided the proportion of society profits to be transformed into centrally approved 'additional' benefits and the proportion to be invested against the possibility of rising future claims. While day-to-day administrative decisions were supposedly left to the approved societies, the audit formed the foundations of central control. The controller and government actuary determined how NHI was allowed to develop. As mass unemployment reduced contributory income and raised the incidence of claim, the actuary and controller, making common cause with the Treasury, pushed the approved societies into meeting deficits from their own resources, thereby avoiding the expensive public subsidies needed to shore up the bankrupt Unemployment Insurance Fund. Central government was squeezed between two contradictory forces: political pressure to protect the rising numbers of the unemployed, and economic pressure to minimise public expenditure by securing actuarial solvency. The consequences were reflected in a mass of new regulations governing questions of access, levels of benefit and the policing of claimants and doctors, to ensure that the former were genuinely 'incapable of work', that is bedridden (this condition governed access to sickness benefit), and the latter were properly instructed as to what this meant. As regulations became increasingly complicated, so society autonomy tended to diminish. "There are very few people", wrote a senior civil servant in the summer of 1931, "who can claim to be familiar with all the provisions under which insurance can be kept alive" (Public Record Office, 1930). Those who understood the system, how particular changes would affect access and the vexed problem of society solvency were in a peculiarly influential position. The problem of information asymmetries in this area were heavily biased in favour of the central regulators of the scheme.

The system was, none the less, very elegant; it separated purchaser from provider and, ostensibly, the State from both. According to current criteria governing healthcare administration, NHI contained several desirable features. First, it was driven by consumer choice; new labour market entrants decided which society to join. Choice was heavily influenced by efficient management; the profitable society offered members better benefits for the same contribution than its less successful competitors. Second, as societies competed for new members by providing additional benefits from profits, society rivalry and competition fostered the extension of medical care at no additional cost to the taxpayer. Further, societies purchased medical services and appliances from other (charitable, commercial or publicly-owned) institutions and agencies, fostering market incentives among hospitals, opticians and dentists. Third, administrative efficiency was encouraged because the (small) exchequer subsidy for administrative costs was calculated by membership size; ultimately management costs and other overheads were the liability of societies themselves. This reduced the cost of administration to the taxpayer. Fourth, managerial authority resided largely at branch level; as there was no statutory protection against bankruptcy, both societies and their members had a vested interest in protecting their funds against fraud ('malingering', in contemporary terms). This did not mean that policing was particularly strict; the society that treated claimants badly lost members. In general, claimants approaching their approved society received better treatment than the unemployed did from the employment exchanges.

Finally, there was the issue of funding. All moneys accruing under the scheme ended up in the coffers of the Ministry of Health. Employers bought stamps at the General Post Office which were affixed to employees' cards, with appropriate deductions from the wage packet; these cards were returned to the member's approved society, which returned them to the ministry as proof of contributory income. The ministry credited society funds held within Whitehall; reimbursement of benefit paid and associated expenses was made retrospectively to the societies, following the quarterly submission of accounts. 'Improper' payments were not reimbursed; the Treasury insisted that taxpayers' money was used only as Parliament intended. The other point relating to the funding issue is that from its inception, the scheme was designed to foster self-help and voluntary provision; the approved societies cooperated because the state scheme offered the chance to recruit members who might purchase a private policy to supplement the public one.

These advantages, particularly the incentives to increase private provision at low administrative cost, were not lost on contemporaries. In the early 1920s, the approved society system was viewed as a potential administrative structure to unify all state insurance. Between 1923 and 1925, separate initiatives developed to unite unemployment insurance and the new contributory pensions with NHI under the aegis of the approved societies (Public Record Office, 1925b). This directly contradicted Beveridge's proposal to create a single, central insurance fund for the sick, widows, orphans, pensioners and unemployed (Beveridge, 1924). At this point, the debate came to nothing. When the situation was next reviewed, in 1942, the use of private agencies for public purposes was rejected. As there is a renewed interest in the operation of quasi-markets in the field of social welfare, it is as well to understand what went wrong.

Flaws in the market

The three main flaws in the operation of NHI impeded its smooth development and helped secure its abolition: the effects of central regulation; the impact of the market system on the distribution of resources; the issue of administrative costs (transaction costs in polycentric administrative structures).

NHI: the quasi-market and central regulation

The Treasury's contribution distinguished the British scheme from its German prototype, allowing Lloyd George to boast in the Commons in 1911 that his system offered better benefits for lower contributions than the German equivalent. However, public subsidy required public controls over expenditure, necessitating centralisation of approved society funds and the meticulous and expensive audit of society accounts. Although society members and their executives nominally controlled how profits were spent, central surveillance rendered this autonomy meaningless – particularly when industrial depression reduced income and raised the incidence of claim. As the exchequer contribution was attached to benefit paid, not contributions raised, it was in the Treasury's interest to minimise benefit expenditure.

However, this official interest remained hidden. Ministers and civil servants alike continued to claim that the scheme could not be extended or developed for fear of approved society opposition. This was a lie. Whenever society opinion was solicited, by the Royal Commission on National Health Insurance (RCNHI) in 1925, for example, their representatives claimed that the scheme should be extended, to incorporate extra medical treatments and cover for dependants (HMSO, 1926, Appendix XXVI, sub-appendices 1-4). These recommendations featured in the Commission's final report, but were never implemented. The 1925 Widows, Orphans and Old Age Pensions Act and the 1925 Economy Act both reduced the exchequer contribution to NHI and the Treasury refused to sanction new statutory and publicly-subsidised treatments (Public Record Office, 1925a). Approved society opposition was cited as the main obstacle to reform. When a Labour government re-opened the question in 1929, again the Treasury and government actuary rejected the option of 'pooling' profits to allow richer societies to subsidise poorer, to fund extensions. This policy would foster 'lax' (meaning more generous) administration; it would raise benefit expenditure and thus the cost to the exchequer. Tight administration accorded with Treasury policy. As the controller of health insurance minuted his minister in 1934: "... the Health Insurance Scheme is highly decentralised and the 'buffer' Approved Societies divert much criticism from the government" (Public Record Office, 1934). (Nearly every historian of National Insurance has accepted that approved society political influence prevented the expansion of healthcare.)

This type of chicanery undermined society independence and crippled the growth of state health insurance. The British experience stands in contrast to Germany in many ways. First, in Germany, contributions from employers (one third) and from the employed (two thirds) went direct to registered societies; administration (being vested in proportion to funds provided) was dominated by the members. Before the First World War, there can be seen an unexpected contrast between an autocratic regime supporting democratic participation in the administration of health benefits and a democratic one creating a system of centralised autarchy (Dreyfus et al, 1998). In the longer run, this tradition of self-governance helps explain why health insurance thrived in Germany. In Britain, public participation in the running of friendly societies dwindled (Harris, 1986), and they were removed in 1946 without popular protest. Second, in Germany, contributions were income related, allowing rising wages to be reflected automatically in rising resources for healthcare. Third, the rationalisation of German insurance administration by locality reduced competition between purchasers, permitting the rationalisation of provision; few accusations of 'duplication and waste' accompanied the development of health insurance in that country.[1]

In Britain, not all central controls operated against society wishes. In the interwar years, unemployment climbed and the incidence of claims rose (Whiteside, 1987). To counteract this threat to the scheme's funds, societies and the Ministry of Health tried to 'tighten up' access – in similar fashion to recent attempts to reduce claims to incapacity benefits. The Scottish DoH was exemplary: stipulating the maximum period of claim for specific medical complaints and referring all female claimants aged 16-35 to district medical officers for review (Public Record Office, 1933). In Scotland, the medical profession was subject to a marked degree of official bullying. Their case records were scrutinised, their practices of certification inspected. They were subject to lectures on diagnosis, treatment and the evils of over prescription and were occasionally sued if they failed to follow official advice. Nor did approved societies escape; their use of the referral system was tabulated and 'lax' societies were threatened with fines. In England and Wales, the message was similar, but the methods were gentler. The use of 'sickness visitors' for domestic surveillance, the referral of cases to the ministry's regional medical officers for reassessment and the lecturing of panel doctors on the meaning of 'incapacity of work' – all became more common.

Mass unemployment thus helped to undermine NHI. Throughout the interwar years, both the ministry and societies argued that tight controls over unemployment benefits were raising their costs. Throughout the interwar years, administrative expense was raised by the ensuing battles between government departments over the official status of numerous claimants – the partially disabled, the pregnant, the bronchial, the feeble minded – whose health status, while poor, did not render them 'incapable of work'. Again, during the past decade, we have witnessed history repeating itself. Recession encourages officials to indulge in expensive and pointless struggles to shift responsibility for some claimants elsewhere.

In terms of the interwar years – and arguably in the 1980s as well – it seems that the employment department won. The Unemployment Fund's debt in 1931 forced the introduction of the hated household means test – long associated with pauperism and stigma – for long-term claimants. Anyone who could do so reverted to their approved society. Although sickness benefit was lower than unemployment benefit, the member with a private policy to supplement the public one, or who belonged to a society offering additional cash benefits, could get more money with less fuss from that society than from the labour exchange. Political pressure required that the unemployed retain some rights to health benefits; this raised society liability to support non-contributing members – without any compensation from the exchequer. By 1937, the unemployed were entitled to two years 'free' health insurance and members of 10 years' standing could retain their rights to health benefits indefinitely. The extension in liability was only partly compensated by reduced benefits for women (condemned as 'benefit spongers' because of their high rates of claim) and cutting out 'additional' benefits for six million members. During the peak slump years (1931-34), these measures protected health insurance from financial crisis. However, the strain produced some approved society bankruptcies in the depressed areas, where doctors themselves became unemployed, leaving the most vulnerable without any medical protection at all (Davies, 1995). Hence, official parsimony exacerbated existing tendencies towards uneven treatment – the next criticism of this quasi-market system discussed below.

Equal contributions and unequal treatment

The object of a market system is to sell goods and services at a profit; society prosperity relied on an ability to attract 'good lives', or young male workers in regular employment. Some friendly societies instructed their panel doctors to reject applicants liable to prove a drain on the funds. Hence the most profitable societies – who offered the most attractive range of additional benefits – claimed the healthiest as members, leaving the more vulnerable to those agencies that could only afford minimum cover. Trade union societies suffered badly, picking up residualised contributors in heavy industries (coal, ironfounding, shipbuilding, textiles) where unemployment was high, disease and accidents rife. One exception was the print unions. The ex-London coordinator of the Co-operative Approved Society (itself able to provide only basic medical care) asserted that while the Co-op could not provide any specialist services at all, the London Compositors offered "gold-plated hospital beds" to their members (personal contribution from a DHSS record officer, May 1984). The experience of the trade union approved societies made them the foremost advocates of extensive pooling and the creation of a nationalised system of healthcare (although one whose services would be purchased by approved societies for their members).

The tendency for the market to provide the best care for those least in need formed a continuing criticism of the health insurance scheme from the Report of the Royal Commission in 1926 to the assessment by Political and Economic Planning more than a decade later (HMSO, 1926, Minority Report, para 17: Majority Report, pp 95-101; PEP, 1937). As the former noted, this type of inverted selectivity sprang directly from the incentive to good management based on values common to any commercial enterprise. This could be avoided, the report argued, if health insurance was rationalised in the hands of publicly-elected local authorities (LAs), who would act as approved societies for all resident in their area. As such agencies were responsible to their electorate, political factors would counterbalance economic ones, promoting equity. Public expenditure constraints guaranteed that such recommendations were ignored, and the imbalance became worse over time.

The price of efficiency?

The use of private agencies for public purposes offered public savings on administration. Under the health insurance scheme, the Treasury paid one sixth of total administrative costs; this was considerably less than the burden imposed by state pensions or unemployment insurance (PEP, 1937, pp 199 and 228). Administrative subsidy was calculated on a membership basis; additional costs were met by the societies themselves and this fostered good management. Further, the societies' interest in guaranteeing their income made them more efficient at chasing defaulting contributors than the employment exchanges. However, there are other administrative expenses not covered here, not least those involved in the audit of society accounts. Although the number of separate units fell from 15,000 to 5,700 between 1912 and 1938, the paperwork involved in audit remained considerable (HMSO, 1942, pp 23-4), thanks to increasingly complex regulations with which societies were obliged to conform. Beveridge calculated that, by 1939, NHI represented the worst value for money from the contributors' perspective; administrative costs absorbed 17% of income, while the corresponding figure for the unemployment scheme was 10% and for contributory pensions 3.5% (HMSO, 1942, Appendix E). These figures were as nothing compared with the costs of the societies' private business; the industrial assurance companies, the worst offenders, allowed administration to swallow 40% of premium income. Social insurance schemes under a state monopoly offered an administratively cheaper option than a commercially-based alternative.

These costs were imposed by several factors, which Beveridge identified as duplication and waste. In a manner reminiscent of present day building societies and high street banks, numerous societies touted for business in every town in the country. While the number of accounting units for auditing purposes fell, competition at local level remained high. Between 1926 and 1942, the number of societies recruiting in Liverpool and Bolton dropped from 488 to 437 and from 285 to 248 respectively, while numbers in Reading and in Brighton rose from 245 to 361 and from 304 to 325 respectively (HMSO, 1942, p 24). This reflects commercial responses to shifting locations of economic growth, not any local rationalisation of approved society distribution. When set in the context of falling audit units, the figures illustrate the trend away from small, local friendly societies with autonomous branches towards centralised friendly societies and industrial insurance companies. The creation of the NHS allowed the exchange of a centralised, private bureaucracy for a centralised public one, which, through the minister of health, was at least nominally accountable to the electorate.

Contemporary observers identified other costs. The existence of an independent health insurance scheme prevented the integration of state social insurance and the rationalisation of medical provision at regional level. Competition between service providers encouraged the duplication of expensive resources. For the local medical officer of health, the activities of the approved societies (which were outside their control) obstructed rationalisation within the locality and generated extra facilities in richer areas, where they were least needed. Reformers argued that public subsidies under the NHI scheme operated in direct contravention to the proper object of policy, namely the targeting of resources to the sick and the poor. While arguably the NHS failed to correct this imbalance, it is important to note how the quasi-market had helped to create it.

Conclusion

Julian Le Grand and Will Bartlett (1993) identified four criteria against which the performance of quasi-markets should be evaluated: efficiency, responsiveness, choice and equity. These will be used to assess the performance of the health insurance scheme, which displayed many features of a quasi-market during the 30-or-more years of its existence. Bartlett and Le Grand predict that equity is going to be the most problematic issue in market performance; this is fully supported by the interwar evidence. Most societies assiduously recruited young, healthy males, leaving the rest (those most in need of comprehensive healthcare) to the poorest agencies offering minimal cover, who could not be choosy about who they took on. As statistics cited in the previous section indicate, choice of purchaser remained wide for those whose health was good and who had steady employment; the scheme discriminated against those already disadvantaged on the labour market. On responsiveness, there is extensive evidence that societies responded to membership need. First, despite tighter central regulation, the rising incidence of health claims during the recession indicates that those unable to get unemployment benefit managed to claim from their approved society. This was particularly true of married women, virtually disqualified from the unemployment scheme by the early 1930s, whose health claims rose from 125% to 300% of the male rate between 1914 and 1932 (Public Record Office, 1932). Second, the structure of the NHI favoured generous assessment. Public profit could be used only for the benefit of members; it could not be diverted into the pockets of management or society directors. Even industrial insurance companies, indicted by Beveridge for selling life policies to households unable to afford the premiums (and pocketing the profits when policies lapsed), were benevolent administrators of statutory health benefits. The status of approved societies was valuable for recruiting private clients; a management responsive to claimant demand was attractive to new members.

On the question of efficiency, the evidence is more problematic. Leaving aside the question of whether an inequitable health system can be deemed 'efficient', did NHI represent good value for money? Was quality assured and were administrative overheads minimised? The competitive element in health insurance necessarily raised transaction costs. Central regulation also fostered other inefficiencies – partly by its sheer cost, partly by perpetuating information asymmetries – to the advantage of central administration, since the complexity of central regulation rendered consumers ignorant of their rights. The extension of health benefits to the long-term unemployed was not widely understood; local evidence indicates that neither doctors nor the unemployed themselves knew these rights and neither approved societies nor the ministry were eager to advertise them. Central control operated to the disadvantage of providers and hence their customers. While space has not permitted an exploration of the doctors' experience under NHI, the cut in exchequer subsidy to GP salaries in 1922 encouraged panel doctors to expand their lists to maintain their income, to the disadvantage of panel patients. This stimulated complaints that doctors spent more time with private than public clients. Further, competition failed to raise efficiency in hospital management. Voluntary hospitals continued to be run on traditional lines, dominated by medical interests and with nursing support staff managed like nuns in a convent – from which tradition their position was arguably derived. These factors combined to damn the system as inefficient, to promote its abolition and its replacement by the centralised, rationalised structures of social security and the NHS.

In a recent paper, Glennerster and Le Grand (1994) speculate on the reasons why quasi-markets have become so popular. After discussing possible explanations such as cost-cutting, reducing government bureaucracy, extending private provision and so on, they reach the broad conclusion that the primary motive is political: to allow the more articulate middle-class consumer greater choice in welfare provision. This is quite credible. Other political dimensions which have equal significance, should be considered. The involvement of private agencies in the administration of public policy allowed and allows criticisms of welfare services to be diverted away from Westminster and Whitehall towards the agencies themselves. It becomes more difficult to distinguish inadequacies consequent on public expenditure constraints from the results of poor management, especially when a poor performance by one agency can be measured against the 'best practice' target set by another. In interwar Britain, the approved society 'buffer agencies' served central government well. They were held responsible for the shortcomings of NHI by the press, politicians and bureaucrats – shortcomings properly attributable to tight public expenditure and tighter central control of their activities. With a freer rein, British approved societies could have operated like their continental cousins – attracting custom and extending services. In similar fashion, recent Conservative administrations in Britain proved adept at creating nominally independent agencies which are subsequently held responsible for the consequences of containing public expenditure in a period of rising social dependency. The attraction of a quasi-market for Whitehall lies in the ways it can divert responsibility for the consequences of political decisions over public finance. This aspect should not be forgotten when assessing the quasi-attractions of using private agencies for public purposes.

Postscript

The experience of interwar health insurance calls into question almost traditional assumptions about the difference between state and market – or state and quasi-market – as a system for distributing goods and services. In this early example, we witness how central government shaped and reshaped the nature of competition, redefining rights and apportioning costs. Some might argue such adjustments were necessary to prevent the scheme going bottom up; this chapter claims that most central intervention was stimulated by the desire to contain public expenditure. In short, this quasi-market structure did nothing to prevent Treasury raids on society funds (by cutting the taxpayer's contribution) when the occasion required. It was thus not immune to budgetary politics and it is hard to imagine that it could be. Quasi-markets are little more than alternative systems of public administration, as vulnerable to the effects of central meddling or changes in official regulation as any bureaucratised, centralised alternative. The main difference lies in their running costs, as Frank Dobson (Secretary of State for Health) has concluded in deciding to bring the NHS internal market to an end, in order to save money on administration and management. Beveridge – in promoting central rationalisation – had a point.

Does this mean that recent restructuring has been a waste of time, that the new Labour government will go back to square one and re-rationalise public administration? Such a reversal seems unlikely. In a recent Green Paper (HMSO, 1998), New Labour laid out – in very general terms – its future vision for the welfare state. While the language of competition and markets which so characterised the Thatcher and Major administrations is no longer prominent, the document does not signal a return to Beveridgean principles. On the contrary, it uses concepts like contracts, mutual obligation between citizen and state, private–public partnerships in welfare provision. New Labour's first reforms have centred on returning people to work, on transforming benefits into tax credits, on individualising welfare. 'Stakeholding' has emerged as one watchword, indicating that welfare rights are attached to responsibilities – and that the last entails making some contribution towards society before demanding its support. The means to ensure this will not lie directly in the hands of the state, but rather in its regulation of other agencies – voluntary, mutual, commercial – to ensure that citizens can provide for their own futures, can exercise personal responsibility. There is a subtle distinction with the Thatcherite past; this is a document stressing coordination and partnerships, not competition and markets, as the route to securing improvement. The furtherance of private interest in a war of all against all is no longer held as the means to secure collective prosperity and justice. The implicit hope seems to be that public and private can cooperate in securing the nation's future.

Although details on administrative structures are yet undeveloped, the new agenda still promises to separate the purchase of welfare from its provision, to involve consumer choice, to use central regulation of private agencies (rather than extensions in the public sector) as the main route to welfare reform. This does not indicate the wholesale abandonment of quasi-market systems, particularly in the provision of social services where they have always been prominent. Their apparent extension into social security, through proposed pensions reform, for example, also indicates that the boundaries between state and market will become increasingly blurred as government seeks to 'regulate in' the type of provision it wishes to encourage. The great lesson from the interwar quasi-market (and the approved societies were – through the provision of sickness benefits – involved in social security as well as healthcare) lies in its potential costs. On the surface, public regulation of private provision appears to be a cheap and effective way of securing comprehensive cover; in practice, it has proved anything but. Unless New Labour (and particularly New Labour's chancellor) is prepared to leave any new scheme alone, unless New Labour can persuade Whitehall, financial institutions and the public to adopt and accept European principles of subsidiarity (allowing new agencies to operate freely under the rule of law), unless, in short, New Labour abandons dubious distinctions between the state and market in promoting greater institutional integration – we may yet witness history repeating itself.

Note

[1] I am grateful to comments by Professor Hennock and Christian Toft for these points.

Part Five

Legal aid

ELEVEN

Legal aid: a case study in quasi-market failure

Gwyn Bevan

Introduction

The UK system of legal aid is (in the main) publicly financed but supplied privately in a market in which professionals compete for clients. It provides an interesting case study for three reasons. It was introduced in 1949, and hence appears to have anticipated the quasi-market reforms which are the subject of this book. It provided a model for other countries (Paterson, 1991). It offers a case study of quasi-market failure and is to be reformed (LCD, 1995; 1996).

The UK system of legal aid was set up to:

> establish a framework for the provision ... of legal advice, assistance and representation which is publicly funded with a view to helping persons who might otherwise be unable to obtain advice, assistance or representation on account of their means. (LCD, 1995, p 3)

Arrow (1963) remarked on the strong institutional similarities between the legal and medical care markets. The UK model is known as Judicare, after Medicare – the US publicly-financed quasi-market for healthcare (Paterson, 1991). UK Judicare is similar to US Medicare in both structure and poor outcomes (Bevan et al, 1996; Bevan, 1996). Klein's description of US healthcare, "spending more and feeling worse" (Klein, 1991), also offers a description of UK Judicare.

UK Judicare has produced a paradoxical combination of outcomes:

- total costs in real terms, numbers of people helped by the scheme, and sums paid to lawyers are all at record levels (see LCD, 1995; Bevan, 1996; Hope, 1997); yet

- eligibility is at a record low (Gray, 1994); those with low incomes who are eligible for legal aid can often not get the help they need in social welfare law, and lawyers are dissatisfied with their fee rates for legally-aided work (see Paterson, 1991; Goriely, 1992).

This chapter illustrates the characteristics of failure of the private market and quasi-market for legal services and subjects these to formal economic analysis. It discusses the developing system of legal aid and the programme of reforms outlined in the Green and White Papers (LCD, 1995; 1996). It considers other options for reform by looking at models in other countries and in healthcare. A final section draws conclusion from this review.

Markets which work and markets which fail

This section offers an illustrative economic analysis of Judicare. It begins with characteristics of a market which we know works, in which individuals pay for lunch. It then transforms this market by introducing characteristics and likely consequences of, first, the private market for legal services, and, second, the quasi-market for legal aid.

Consumer pays for lunch

The market for lunches works because it has many of the characteristics which create an effective market. The consumer decides and pays at the time. Typically consumers are likely to become repeat buyers if given good service. Although difficulties arise when the consumer buys a lunch in a strange place, the market has also developed to respond to this problem with guides, and franchises offering similar food at similar standards. The development of chain restaurants is one of the examples cited by Akerlof (1970) in his seminal examination of the problem of asymmetry of information between buyer and seller. He described chain restaurants which most often appear on inter-urban highways and are used by people from outside the local area. This is because the chain restaurant offers "a better hamburger than the *average* local restaurant; at the same time, the local customer, who knows his own area, can usually choose a place he prefers!" (Akerlof, 1970). The market offers a wide variety of providers who face no barriers to entry (apart from inspection of hygiene). Consumers are mostly able to buy the type of lunch they want and know where to go to get it.

Consumer pays in a professional market

However, suppose now, however, that the market for lunches is professionalised with structural changes on the supply and demand sides.[1]

On the supply side, barriers to entry are introduced so that lunches are available only from professionally qualified lunchers. To become a luncher, requires a degree, passing professional exams and an apprenticeship with a qualified luncher. Within the profession there are further restrictions on banquets. These can only be supplied in crown restaurants by banqueters who have been trained in registered inns where they have eaten a required number of lunches. From these, an élite of queen's banqueters (QBs) are selected who are able to charge much higher rates. The luncher can only say in advance what the hourly rate will be. He does not know how many hours will be involved as this depends on a complex sequence of assessments: thus initially, an individual might begin with a bowl of soup, but on examination might need many more lunches, culminating in a banquet prepared by QBs for many parties.

Under these circumstances we can predict what would be likely to happen. Lunches would become so expensive only the rich would be able to afford lunch. As lunches became rare events, consumers would become poor judges of the value and quality of what is supplied. This market is close in structure and outcomes to the current private market for legal services.

It is worth amplifying an important difference between the chain restaurant and this fictionalised professional luncher market. As Akerlof (1970) points out, the chain restaurant and professional licensing are intended to fulfil the same function, namely, countering asymmetry of information between buyer and seller. However, the way this is done is very different. The chain restaurant seeks uniformity in the commodity and the price, and the customer decides. In the professionalised luncher market the commodity is customised, the luncher decides what will be supplied and cannot say what the consumer will have to pay.

The remedy to the predictable failures of the professional luncher market is obvious: remove the distortions, namely, professional barriers to entry, and the profession deciding what is provided. The problem with law is that these distortions are a consequence of the nature of legal services: no Arcadian free market is available.[2]

Government pays in a professional quasi-market

Suppose further that a system in which only the rich can afford lunch is deemed to be an affront to a civilised society. This results in a sequence of three responses by government.

First, the government introduces Lunch Aid. Individuals who satisfy a test of hunger and are judged unable to pay for lunch are able to choose any luncher. The lunch-aided individual then receives the same services as for the rich, except that the government pays. This addresses the problem of lack of access to lunches. It does not address the cause of the problem which is the high costs of lunches. Unfortunately, it is designed to exacerbate this problem, because individuals now get 'free' lunches.

Under these circumstances we can again predict would be likely to happen. There would be increases in both the number of lunches, in costs per lunch and in total expenditure on Lunch Aid. This would result eventually in the government trying to contain costs, by reducing both the eligible population and the hourly rates paid to lunchers. One consequence is that only the rich and eligible poor are able to afford lunches, and what the lunchers provide reflects the tastes of the rich rather than what those who are eligible for Lunch Aid want. Another consequence follows from the accounting identity that every pound of government expenditure on Lunch Aid is also someone else's (mostly lunchers') income.[3] The significant body of lunchers whose income now depends on Lunch Aid naturally seeks to maintain its income. These lunchers discover that the eligible population, although reduced in size, has greater needs than before. They supply more lunches per capita, more courses per lunch, and take more time to prepare each course. The outcomes are that lunchers complain about rates of pay for Lunch Aided work and there is continued escalation in expenditure.

Subsequently, the government addresses the problem of inflation in costs per lunch by setting standard prices for different types of lunches. Unfortunately, banquets defy standardisation and account for much of total expenditure (although low in volume). Lunchers respond to standard prices in two ways: where standard prices apply, they only provide lunches that cost less than that price; they then expand volumes for types of lunches which fall outside these categories.

The first two responses and the introduction of standard prices are in essence the story of legal aid in the UK. Evidence for consequences of standard prices is from US Medicare (Schramm and Gabel, 1988). The next section gives a formal economic analysis of the private and quasi-markets for legal services. This is based on analyses of the principal/agent problem, moral hazard and transaction costs.

Economic analysis of market failure

Principal/agent problem

The problematic nature of the private market of legal services arises from the principal relying on an agent to deliver a service, with asymmetry of information and a difference in incentives. This constitutes a principal/agent problem (Milgrom and Roberts, 1992), but two caveats limit the relevance of conventional analysis of this problem (Rees, 1985). First, conventional analysis assumes the agent is driven solely by self-interest, but professional services are more complex (Evans, 1981). Second, there is likely to be a fundamental transformation to a monopoly which undermines the conventional remedy of contractual design (Williamson, 1975; 1985). Both these points are explored below.

Combination of moral hazard and the principal/agent problem

Legal aid is mainly paid for by a third party. The Legal Aid Board (LAB) pays for civil and criminal legal aid, except for criminal cases in the Crown court and higher courts, which are paid for by the Lord Chancellor's Department (LCD). LAB and LCD confront the common insurance problem of *moral hazard*: insured individuals lose interest in the costs of services being supplied (Milgrom and Roberts, 1992). The normal solution of requiring the client to pay part of the costs has limited efficacy when that individual also encounters a principal/agent problem.[4]

The consequence of moral hazard is that LAB/LCD encounter a more profound principal/agent problem than the private client. This is because each is even more weakly placed than a private client to assess whether lawyers are providing value for money.

Transaction costs

Paterson (1991) argued that salaried service ought in part to be introduced in legal aid for the UK. The White Paper announced that the government intends to take powers to allow the LAB to employ staff – see below. Williamson's analysis of transaction costs (1975; 1985; 1990) offers a framework for comparing a salaried and contracted legal service. This is based on two crucial behavioural assumptions and three key dimensions. What these mean and their relevance to legal aid are now discussed.

The two crucial behavioural assumptions are bounded rationality and opportunism. Rationality is bounded when a complete contract cannot be drawn which covers all possible outcomes. This obviously applies to litigation. More generally, complete contracts are inconsistent with the customised nature of legal services. Williamson (1975) characterises opportunism as "self interest seeking with guile". However, the concern about opportunism in professional services is rather different. What is at issue is not the unregulated pursuit of self-interest, as the whole justification of the profession is to address this. What matters is that what the agent defines as good professional standards may not offer the principal value for money: this is manifested in the problem of supplier-induced demand (McGuire et al, 1988; Matthews, 1991; Bevan, 1996).

Williamson observes that the two crucial behavioural assumptions, which will generate high transaction costs in a legal aid quasi-market, in combination have profound ramifications for economic organisation:

> **Given bounded rationality,** *all complex contracts are unavoidably incomplete.* **Given opportunism,** *contract-as-promise unsupported by credible commitments is hopelessly naïve.* **Taken together, the following organisational imperative obtains: organise transactions so as to economise on bounded rationality while simultaneously safeguarding transactions against the hazards of opportunism. (Williamson, 1990, p 12, emphases in original)**

Williamson's three key dimensions are asset specificity, uncertainty, and frequency. Asset specificity means that the agent has assets, which include professional expertise, specific to the principal. This obviously applies for criminal legal aid as the Crown finances both prosecution and virtually all defence. There is uncertainty over what services each case may need. The government proposes to reduce this by contracting a greater number of cases (which is explored further below). Hence, of Williamson's three dimensions, only the specificity of assets for criminal legal aid poses intrinsic difficulties.

Williamson (1985) highlights the common *fundamental transformation* in contractual markets characterised by high transaction costs. Ex ante when contracts are first let, there may be many competitors. However, ex post, when contracts are up for renewal, the winners in the first round may enjoy such considerable advantages in later rounds (known as 'first mover' advantage) so that what appears to be a competitive market is in effect transformed into a monopoly. This has been found to be a common problem with attempts to introduce competitive markets in the US in publicly-financed social and healthcare (Propper, 1992).

Williamson argues that first mover advantage in markets with high transaction costs means that the dominant firms are able to sustain their monopolies without having to resort to anti-competitive practices (and hence these monopolies cannot be broken with reference to traditional legislation). He points out that the fundamental transformation to a monopoly means that any solution developed by formal analysis of the principal/agent problem based on clever contractual design becomes irrelevant.

Analysis of transaction costs points to the potential advantages of a salaried service. There are also costs: Will a public bureaucracy be more efficient? Will there be conflicts of interest in a state run legal service? Other countries' experiences of a salaried service will be considered below.

Changing UK quasi-market for legal aid

Traditional system

The traditional basis of legal aid has been grafted on to the private system of legal advice and representation. Individuals are allowed free choice of lawyer who is then paid a fee determined after the event on the basis of a separate assessment of the work done in each particular case (LCD, 1995). The fee rate per hour for different types of work is determined by the Lord Chancellor. However, there is poor choice in welfare law which is typically an area of little interest to lawyers (Paterson, 1991; Cousins, 1994; LCD, 1995).

Legal aid is granted subject to various tests of eligibility and merit according to the type of legal aid sought. Associated with tests of eligibility are rules requiring payment of user charges. The merit test for civil legal aid, for example, is that "the applicant can show reasonable grounds for bringing defending or being party to a case before the civil courts in England and Wales" (LCD, 1995). In the current system, costs cannot be awarded against a legally-aided individual (LCD, 1996).

There is no limit on spending for each financial year: the actual spend is determined by the volumes of work billed at the determined rates. In

1993-94 expenditure in real terms[5] on legal aid was *five* times the level of 1979-80. Comparative analyses by Cousins (1993) and Blankenberg (1992; 1995) of different countries' expenditure on legal aid highlighted the high level of spend by the UK (Blankenberg, 1995), with estimates that spend per capita on legal aid in 1989-90 in England and Wales was nearly four times that of what was West Germany (for North Rhine Westphalia) and more than twice that of The Netherlands. Blankenberg (1995) observes that changes since 1990 make this comparison even more remarkable: "While the relatively high expenditures of the Legal Aid Board have more than doubled since 1990,[6] expenditures in The Netherlands and West Germany have been decreasing slightly." (p 182).

The explosive increase in spend on legal aid after 1990-91 was caused neither by increases in the volumes of criminal cases, which declined, nor by welfare law in the recession, which accounted for less than 0.4% of spend on legal aid in 1993-94. Nor does it seem likely that changes in the regulation and efficiency of courts would have had a significant impact (Hope, 1997). The explanation appears to be that in the late 1980s the number of lawyers increased at a time when income from private work fell. Lawyers helped make up some of the shortfall by increasing legal aid work (Bevan, 1996). These excessive expenditures led to reductions in eligibility for legal aid and pressure on fee rates paid.

Standard fees

The Conservative government changed the traditional system by introducing standard fees, which were fixed and predetermined, for various types of cases (LCD, 1995):

- in 1986 for barristers in Crown Court cases covering junior counsel only in less serious cases lasting up to three days; in 1993/4 the scheme covered 61% of barristers' claims in the Crown Court, but only 14.5% of expenditure;
- in 1988 for solicitors in Crown Court cases covering cases lasting up to two days; in 1993/4 the scheme covered 65% of claims, but only 25% of expenditure;
- in 1993 for criminal cases in magistrates' courts designed to cover approximately 90% of magistrates' court cases;
- in 1995/96 the intention was to introduce new standard fee schemes for advocates and litigators: on the criminal side in the

Crown Court and on the civil side in the Family Proceedings Courts, the County Courts and the High Court.

The purposes of standard fees are to reduce both costs of transaction, by removing the need for detailed bills and production, and the number of hours worked. To set standard fees fairly requires a premium to be paid over the average expected payment for each case, as the lawyer now bears the risk of the number of hours worked on a case. Variation between cases will mean that some cases will be more profitable than others and on some the lawyer may make a loss.

If lawyers can recognise cases which are and are not likely to be profitable, they can counter the system by 'cream-skimming', that is, taking the profitable cases only. This would mean that clients with cases on which lawyers would make a loss would have difficult finding a lawyer and lawyers would get more than fair remuneration for the cases they did take. If lawyers cannot identify and refuse difficult cases in advance, then there will be pressure to skimp on these cases after they have taken them on.[7] It is difficult to monitor quality in terms of outcomes of individual cases.

Contracts

The policy of the White Paper (LCD, 1996) is that firms will bid for, and be paid through, contracts. Two basic approaches to contracts are outlined: a block of cases at an agreed price per case, such as representation in civil and Crown Court proceedings, which may be seen as an extension of standard fees; a specified service over a particular period of time, such as being available for advice at police stations.

A contract addresses uncertainty by offering the successful firm a guaranteed income stream. Block contracts spread risk associated with standard fee for one case across a number of cases. However, contracts do require regulation to safeguard against cream-skimming, unbundling services, such as splitting one case into a number, and reducing quality.[8]

Rationing

In future the White Paper proposed cash limits to spending on legal aid and to ration resources through:

- separate budgets for the three categories of criminal, family and civil, non-family, legal aid;
- the Lord Chancellor giving directions about priorities to LAB;
- LAB allocating budgets to regions for each category based on estimated relative needs;
- LAB being responsible for rationing spend on litigation.

The White Paper implies that rationing spend on litigation will largely be done by applying criteria of the current merit test.[9] This includes assessments of the: chances of winning the case; importance of the case; likely cost compared to the likely benefit. However, the current merit test is based largely on applying professional criteria of 'reasonableness' and has failed to control spend. Hence, if expenditure control is to be secured, the interpretation of these criteria will have to change. The organisation of rationing is explored below.

Choice of provider

The current system of legal aid allows eligible individuals free choice of lawyer. Enthoven (1987) identified free choice of provider as a fundamental structural problem of US healthcare and one which insurers have sought to change. Restrictions on choice of lawyer may also be applied on legal expenses insurance.

The policy of the White Paper (1996) is that LAB rather than individuals will choose firms of lawyers and improve quality through becoming frequent purchasers. Stephen et al (1994), argued that the deregulation of conveyancing, has not been as beneficial as what could be achieved by building societies becoming skilled buying agents through repeat buying. However, for legal aid there are potential difficulties posed by monopolies and asset specificity of criminal cases.

The White Paper also intended to increase choice for advice in welfare law by encouraging new entrants: LAB would seek contracts with organisations other than traditional legal firms (LCD, 1995; 1996).

User charges and inter partes' costs

The White Paper outlined a complex reform of user charges based on greater certainty in costs. Although it does not see cost control being achieved simply by increasing user charges, it does see these as a deterrent to use of litigation, particularly in civil cases "for which all, including those on income support, would have to pay something" (LCD, 1996). The objective here was to try to place legally-aided individuals on the same basis as those not eligible for legal aid by taking account of ability to pay. This also extends to the important change that legally-aided parties would be liable for inter partes' costs and be treated by the court "in much the same way as other litigants" (LCD, 1996).

Options for organisational reform

Models of legal aid

Paterson (1991) reviewed four models of paying legal aid. These are the:

- *charitable* model which relies on lawyers doing pro bono publico work, which still exists in the US;
- *Judicare* model in which the State funds the private profession to provide legal services to individuals, as in the UK; this succeeded the charitable model in most western countries, in the second half of the 20th century;
- *salaried* model in which lawyers are salaried and independent of the profession and funders of the service; this predominates in few jurisdictions outside the US and Quebec, but is also found alongside the Judicare model;
- *mixed* model which combines the Judicare and salaried models.

Of these models, Paterson rightly dismisses the charitable model as offering a sticking plaster to people in need of surgery. The following sections consider the relevance of the other three models by drawing on experience in other countries of publicly-funded legal services and of health services. The three models are of rationing within Judicare; the salaried model as compared with Judicare; and a mixed model.

Rationing Judicare

The proposal to cash limit spend on legal aid looks radical in the UK, but has been applied in New Zealand (Rowann, 1993). Districts with defined populations are funded on the basis of past patterns of expenditure and the National Legal Services Board maintains a contingency reserve. Each district has a legal services committee which acts as gatekeeper and assesses each case for its likely costs and benefits. Any case costing more than $100,000 (about £40,000) has to be approved by a sub-committee. Each legal services committee:

- identifies needs of districts;
- monitors the provision of legal services;
- establishes, funds and monitors community law centres;
- administers and funds the duty solicitor scheme, for advising those facing criminal charges;
- funds the criminal and civil legal aid schemes;
- allocates cases to lawyers on a rotating basis to avoid cream-skimming.

The White Paper states that LAB will be responsible for rationing but will have the power gradually to delegate this to suppliers. It emphasises that this option will be exercised cautiously. One way of extending this option would be to develop contracts with lawyers for defined populations as in healthcare: GPs and fundholders in the UK, and HMOs in the US (Mooney, 1994; Glennerster et al, 1994). However, it would leave the management of all risk to lawyers. It obviously changes the incentives from contracting by volume, either hours or cases: in a capitation system the more work a lawyer does, the less profitable the contract will be.

Regulation can rule out gross abuses in capitation-based payment such as doing no work. Allowing individuals to use the market to register with different suppliers will only offer a safeguard against 'underservice' if individuals can detect this. Their capacity to do so is likely to depend on the frequency of their use of services: it is thus likely to be identified in, for example, use of GPs, but not in use of lawyers. If 'underservice' cannot be detected, it is the population rather than the lawyer who bears the risk. Introducing competition by allowing choice of provider requires regulation to avoid 'cream-skimming' by suppliers who wish to discourage high risk individuals. For these reasons, paying lawyers by capitation does not look to be a promising option for legal aid.

A salaried service?

The White Paper briefly states that a salaried service will become an option for LAB. Paterson (1991) summarises findings of studies comparing the cost-effectiveness of the salaried and Judicare models as follows:

- in Australia, the cost of delivering legal aid by salaried lawyers rather than through referrals to private practice was up to twice as cheap in civil cases and three times as cheap in criminal cases;
- in Quebec, Judicare lawyers received on average 50% more for each case than the salaried lawyers;

- in British Columbia, there was little difference in cost;
- in the US, some studies found the salaried model to be cheaper, but a recent study found no significant difference.

Paterson (1991) points out that while there is dispute between experts over the cost-effectiveness of the Judicare and salaried models, there is consensus that a mixed model offers the best way forward for western countries. He argues that there is a strong case for developing a genuinely mixed model in the UK, given that:

- the Australian Federal Government, the Ministry of Justice in The Netherlands and the State authorities in Ontario are increasing the share of resources being allocated to the salaried sector;
- the salaried model accounted for only 0.25% of public funds in the UK but 20% in Australia.

A mixed model?

The Netherlands offers an example of a mixed model. Goriely (1992) described how the system worked in 1991. Total spend on legal aid in The Netherlands was divided with 15% on Buros voor Rechtshulp (funded by the Ministry of Justice) in The Netherlands and 85% on private practice. The buros:

- referred clients to private practice particularly in the fields of family and criminal law (but clients can also go directly to private lawyers – there was no requirement to go to Buros before going to private lawyers);
- provided advice and assistance for appeals through administrative processes for disputes over social security, housing, employment, immigration, and as consumers;
- acted as legal aid offices granting the equivalent of legal aid certificates;
- organised the purely administrative aspects of duty solicitor schemes for those held under police custody.

The buros were staffed by full-time salaried law graduates. In 1991, there were 20 main buros with 57 offices employing 214 legal staff and 157 administrative staff. If England and Wales were to have the same ratio of offices to population, there would be 190; a substantial increase on the current 50 law centres financed by LAs and by LAB. The

Netherlands also has an equivalent to Citizens' Advice Bureaux in the form of Raadslieden.

Paterson (1991) criticised The Netherlands model because the salaried and Judicare services are not designed to be integrated with each other, but are to an extent in competition. He sees the UK model with law centres as more appropriate because it emphasises their complementary nature, although this has largely been unplanned. However, in terms of performance in 1989 the citizens of The Netherlands were offered higher coverage at lower cost: 70% of its population was eligible at a cost of about £6 per capita; in England and Wales about 37% of the population was eligible for legal advice and assistance, and 50-60% for legal aid at a cost of about £9.80 per capita, and that cost has approximately doubled since then. As Goriely (1992) pointed out, the implied threat of competition by the buros may be part of the explanation of these differences: if private practice refuses to do legally-aided work, then the buros may be expanded to do so.

Buros in The Netherlands might offer a model for the UK. This could be developed into a legal aid equivalent of the GP: a legal aid practitioner (LAP). The LAP would be someone with a defined population who would offer advice and act as gatekeeper to contracted firms they would choose themself. The sanction for poor service would be to expand the salaried service. The mix of the salaried/contracted service could vary across areas according to cost and quality of these elements. This is the 'make or buy decision' for which the guiding principle of the economics of transaction costs was identified by Coase (1937).

Conclusion

In this chapter it has been argued that the failure of the original quasi-market for legal aid is a consequence of its design. Legal aid was introduced to address the problem of lack of private access to law caused by its high cost. In retrospect it can be seen that the quasi-market for legal aid was designed to result in escalation of costs. The surprise is not that the system was in such serious problems because of cost escalation in the late 1980s, but that these took 40 years to emerge.

After the legal aid quasi-market had been established, over time the livelihoods of a significant number of lawyers came to depend on it.

Legal aid also offered income when supply exceeded demand for private work. Various attempts to control costs failed as lawyers' responses maintained their incomes: every pound of expenditure on legal aid is someone's, mostly lawyers, income. Nevertheless, without such measures, it is likely that the spend on legal aid would have been even higher (Bevan, 1996).

This chapter began with a story of a market for lunches which was transformed into a professional private market and then a professional quasi-market. There are simple solutions to problems of those fictional transformations: remove barriers to entry and require individuals to pay the full costs themselves. These are inappropriate for the private market for legal services, where professional barriers to entry reflect the weakness of consumers to know how their best interests may be served. They are also inappropriate for legal aid because we do not want people to be denied access to justice because they cannot afford it.

The economic focus of reform of legal aid has rightly been to transform the role of government from being a passive third party payer and to take advantage of its position as a significant buyer; individuals have free choice of lawyer, who was traditionally paid by the hour at a standard fee for each case. The change in which the LAB/LCD will choose lawyers and other types of advisers and introduce contracts is likely to increase quality and reduce costs. However, there are two problems. One is that it is unclear how demand will be rationed. A second is that if there is a fundamental transformation to local monopolies, although prices may be controlled, quality may suffer.

The Green Paper did not discuss a salaried service. The White Paper briefly mentioned that legislation will enable this to be introduced. In those jurisdictions where a salaried service has been introduced, it seems to have proved more cost-effective and has been extended. This looks to be a promising option which might be developed into a mixed market for legal aid.

For the purposes of this book on quasi-markets, legal aid shows that quasi-markets can fail, and that there is scope for a mixed market. We cannot simply import quasi-markets from other services, for example, Health Maintenance Organisations (HMOs) as in US healthcare. What is required is ingenuity in market design to address the intrinsic complexities of each service.

Postscript

After the May 1997 General Election, the Lord Chancellor asked Sir Peter Middleton to conduct a review of the reforms of legal aid as proposed by the White Paper and of Civil Justice proposed by Lord Woolf. Sir Peter reported in September 1997 and broadly supported the White Paper's proposals for the reform of legal aid through block contracts and cash limits. In October 1997, the Lord Chancellor laid out the government's policies for legal aid and a consultation paper in March discussed changes to be made in the short term. This government's policies are for the most part a continuation of the policies of the previous administration with, however, an even more radical innovation in which legal aid will no longer be available for most personal injury claims except for those involving medical negligence. Personal Injury (PI) claims are the biggest category of money claims. It is proposed that PI cases will be financed through Conditional Fee Agreements (Bevan et al, 1998). In these agreements, clients obtain the services of a lawyer without paying his or her fees unless or until the client receives an award of damages. The principle is that of no win, no fee. Under a conditional fee agreement if the lawyer wins, the lawyer receives the full fee with a percentage. Such arrangements reflect the principal/agent problem.

Acknowledgement

The research on which this paper is based has been financed by the LCD. The author is grateful for comments and criticism of working papers produced as part of that research to: officials in that department, the LAB, and members of the Advisory Group on the Fundamental review of Publicly Funded Legal Services. He is also grateful to: Michael Rodney for his review of legal aid in other countries, to Frank Stephen as discussant for comments on an earlier draft of this paper presented in the seminar of March 1995, and to officials of LCD on subsequent drafts. However, the views expressed in this chapter are the author's own. They ought not to be attributed to the LCD, nor to the LAB, nor to members of the advisory group.

Notes

[1] For more general recent formal analyses of the implications of markets for professional services see, for example, Dingwall and Fenn (1987) and Matthews (1991).

[2] As Evans (1981) observed for healthcare.

[3] As Evans (1987a) observed for healthcare.

[4] As Evans (1987b) pointed out for healthcare.

[5] As deflated by the Treasury GDP deflator.

[6] The increase in real terms of public expenditure on legal aid in the four years from 1990-91 to 1993-94 was 55%.

[7] This was recognised to be a problem with the introduction of a similar system of Medicare in the US in which hospitals were paid standard charges by type of inpatient admission classed into Diagnosis-Related Groups (Worthman and Cretin, 1986; Bevan and Price, 1990).

[8] When the US introduced standard payment by DRG they accompanied this by a regulatory scheme (of Peer Review Organisations) to monitor appropriateness of care, unbundling and case-splitting.

[9] It also suggests introducing other criteria such as excluding people who use the courts simply to take advantage of the legal system.

Part Six

Careers guidance

Applying market principles to the delivery of careers guidance services: a critical review

A. G. Watts

Introduction

In Britain, as in most other countries, it has conventionally been assumed that careers guidance services are public services provided by the State. There has been a small private sector of independent guidance agencies, but it has been restricted to limited market niches. Most guidance services have been funded, directly or indirectly, by governments, and have operated within structures which have been bureaucratic rather than market-driven.

However, in the last few years the British government has sought to explore the extent to which market principles can be applied to the delivery of guidance services. This has been part of a major review of all public services. This chapter will explore the rationale for this review, and the forms which its application in the guidance field has taken.

Rationale

The argument for applying market principles to public services is in part pragmatic and in part ideological. Pragmatically, it is argued that market forces are preferable to bureaucratic procedures because they are more cost-effective. Ideologically, it is argued that they are preferable because they respect principles of individual liberty and serve the needs of consumers rather than the needs of providers. Both sets of benefits, it is contended, are achieved through the effects of competition and financial incentive.

These benefits are contrasted to the operations of public services administered bureaucratically by the welfare state. Goodin (1982) identified six respects in which the welfare state is alleged to reduce freedom, by:

- infringing the freedom of taxpayers to dispose of their property as they please;
- limiting the range of services;
- paternalistically directing citizens towards defined choices;
- imposing bureaucratic and/or legal restrictions on individuals;
- producing dependency among welfare recipients;
- creating its own supporting interest groups among bureaucrats and beneficiaries, who then oppose alternative social and political arrangements.

The latter point has been developed by public-choice theorists such as Niskanen (1971), who argue that the welfare state induces its bureaucrats to be self-interested budget maximisers, and that this – allied with the absence of profit criteria, and with pressures on politicians to promise goods and services to voters in order to get elected – encourages the public sector to expand in a reckless and economically inefficient manner.

It is accordingly argued that goods and services should, wherever possible, be transacted through the market. This suggests that existing public services should be privatised, and paid for directly by the consumer rather than indirectly by the taxpayer. Extreme versions of this argument contend that all taxation represents a violation of individual rights and that even such functions as the police, the courts, the bureaucracy and the military should be privatised (Rothbard, 1977).

However, most people recognise that there are some goods and services which offer widespread benefits but for which the individual is unlikely to pay. Savas (1987) identifies a range of 'collective goods' which are used by people jointly and which, once provided, it is impossible or impracticable to exclude people from using: this means that people will not pay for them without a coercive framework such as the taxation system. He also notes that there has been a growing range of 'worthy goods', such as education, which society has moved into the class of public goods by deciding that they are so worthy that their consumption should be encouraged or even stipulated regardless of the consumer's ability or willingness to pay. This may be on the grounds that they are so intrinsically desirable that individuals have a right of access to them regardless of the resources at their disposal; and/or on the grounds that their consumption offers public as well as private benefits.

Some advocates of market principles recognise the legitimacy of such public goods, and the role of the State in securing and funding their supply, but argue that market principles should still be applied to their delivery. In other words, they do not question the State's role in *paying* for such goods through the taxation system, but they contend that it should apply market principles wherever possible to the administrative mechanisms through which the goods are *delivered* to their consumers. Osborne and Gaebler (1992), in their influential text on *Reinventing government*, declare unequivocally at the outset that "we believe deeply in government", but add that "to make our governments effective again we must *reinvent* them", by applying entrepreneurial principles to their operations (pp xviii–xvix).

The result of this line of thought is the concept of 'quasi-markets' (Le Grand, 1991) or 'social markets' (Davies, 1992). These can take a variety of forms, including contracts and vouchers (Savas, 1987). Le Grand (1991) suggests that quasi-markets differ from conventional markets in one or more of three ways: not-for-profit organisations competing for public contracts, sometimes in competition with for-profit organisations; consumer purchasing power in the form of vouchers rather than cash; and in some cases, consumers represented in the market by agents instead of operating for themselves.

The emergence of such concepts reconfigures the politics of the market. Instead of being exclusively viewed as a right-wing notion, it can have attraction to the Left. Le Grand and Estrin (1989), for example, promote the concept of market socialism, in which market means are applied to socialist ends: preventing exploitation of the weak by the powerful, securing greater equality of income, wealth, status and power, and assuring the satisfaction of basic needs. They point out that vouchers can be used for redistributive purposes, and that the fact that the idea of vouchers has in recent years been colonised almost exclusively by the New Right does not mean that there is anything inherently right-wing in what is perhaps their principal merit – that they empower the welfare client. Conversely, Gray (1993) has argued that the Right has become too influenced by neoliberalism and that it should return to its traditional conservative recognition of the imperfectability of all human institutions, including the market.

Applicability to careers guidance provision

The application of market concepts to careers guidance has taken two main forms (Watts, 1991). The first is the concept of 'guidance as market-maker': a means of making the labour market, and the training market, work more effectively by ensuring that supply-side actors within these markets have access to market information and are able to read market signals. The second is the concept of a 'market in guidance': seeking to improve the quality of guidance services by applying market principles to their delivery. The main proponent of both concepts has been the Confederation of British Industry (CBI), in a series of reports (1989a; 1989b; 1993a; 1993b; 1994) which had a considerable influence on the policy of the Conservative government.

The notion of guidance as market-marker was advanced clearly and strongly in the CBI's seminal report *Towards a skills revolution* (1989b). The CBI argued that if Britain was to compete effectively in world markets, a quantum leap was required in the nation's education and training performance. It suggested that the way to achieve this was to "put individuals first": to motivate and empower individuals to improve their skills throughout their working lives. Among the measures it proposed was the quasi-market notion of a system of credits which would give all young people older than 16 a publicly-funded right to education and training, and control over the form it should take. The CBI viewed effective careers guidance as the essential means of ensuring that such individuals' decisions were well-informed. It proposed that careers guidance required "a new rationale, reinvigoration and extra investment" (CBI, 1989b, p 23).

The CBI's arguments were supported by a review of the economic benefits of careers guidance carried out by National Institute for Careers Education and Counselling (NICEC) and the Policy Studies Institute (Killeen et al, 1992). This contended that careers guidance could assist the efficient operation of the labour market in three main ways, by:

- supporting the *individual decisions* through which the labour market operated;
- reducing some of the *market failures* of the labour market;
- contributing to *institutional reforms* designed to improve the functioning of the labour market.

The second of these categories included reducing drop-outs from education and training, and reducing occupational mismatches, both of which could result in significant savings in public expenditure. The third included supporting the roles of the Training and Enterprise Councils (TECs) in activating training and employment markets.

These 'market-maker' arguments are based on the notion of guidance as a public good, in the sense of serving public as well as private purposes. They can be applied to making real markets work, but they apply even more strongly to making quasi-markets work, because of the level of public investment in such markets. The CBI's proposals to provide public support for education and training on a quasi-market basis accordingly added greatly to the force of such arguments. Howard Davies, then director-general of the CBI, suggested in an influential monograph that social markets need consumers to be given help in exercising choice effectively: this needs to include not only "better information", but also "the provision of 'buying agents' to assist the consumer in the process of choice" (Davies, 1992, p 45). In relation to individual decisions on education and training, careers guidance services would seem a classic example of such 'buying agents'.

Such arguments would appear in principle to provide a powerful case for the role of government in assuring the provision and quality of guidance services. However, it has also been contended that market principles should be applied to the delivery of guidance services themselves: that a 'market in guidance' should be established. This view was developed in a series of seminars organised by Full Employment UK (1991a; 1991b). It was argued that TECs' interest in developing guidance services for adults should move away from the notion that guidance was a free service. Instead, services should be fee-charging: in some cases, for example the unemployed, the fees would be paid by the State, in other cases by the employer, and in some cases by individuals themselves. Considerable interest was expressed in the notion of guidance credits to target the government expenditure: for some groups these credits might cover the full cost of the guidance offered, while for other groups they might provide a subsidy. One of the expressed advantages of such an approach was that it "would encourage a healthy degree of competition between different counselling providers for the custom of counselling credit-holders" (Full Employment UK, 1991a, p 29).

The CBI was attracted by these arguments, and not only adopted them in its later report, but extended them to cover young people as well as adults. It suggested that "creating an effective and informed market in careers guidance provision is the best way to guarantee that the range of individuals' needs can be satisfied, that individual choices are maximised and that customers remain the focus" (CBI, 1993b, p 22). It argued that guidance vouchers should be issued to all young people aged between 16-19, as well as to specified older groups. It saw TECs as administering the voucher system, and generally acting as the market regulator. In a subsequent report, the CBI suggested that guidance vouchers should also be issued to all students in higher education, to enable them to use services outside their own institution as well as inside it (CBI, 1994).

However, for people younger then 16 the CBI implicitly recognised that individual vouchers were inappropriate. Instead it suggested that a competitive tendering process should be adopted under which accredited providers within the local guidance market would be invited by TECs to bid for contracts for the delivery of guidance services in schools. Alternatively, it proposed that TECs might give the allocated funds directly to schools so that the schools would have autonomy in the choice of guidance provider, again possibly through a competitive tendering process (CBI, 1993b).

The view adopted by the CBI thus appeared to be that the role of guidance as market-maker could be best performed by stimulating a market in guidance. This market would include some real-market components, in the sense that some users would be expected to pay full costs. It would also include significant quasi-market components, in the sense that the costs of guidance for significant groups would be paid for by the State, but administered through quasi-market mechanisms. The favoured mechanism was guidance vouchers. The residual mechanism, for young people up to 16 years of age, was competitive tendering for contracts.

The Conservative government was strongly influenced by these ideas, but applied them tentatively, and with a different balance between the competing quasi-market mechanisms of contracts and vouchers. The next section will consider these mechanisms in more detail, along with the forms which they took in practice.

Contract option

The CBI's assertion of the importance of guidance in relation to its call for a 'skills revolution' included a proposal that "a major review be undertaken to clarify the role, responsibilities and relationships of the major guidance agencies" (CBI, 1989b, pp 23-4). Following a review set up by the government, a section on the careers service was included in the 1993 Trade Union Reform and Employment Rights Act. This removed the careers service from the mandatory control of local education authorities, and gave the Secretary of State powers to determine what form arrangements for its operation should take. Subsequently, it was announced that the model to be adopted in England was to be competitive tendering to provide careers services in specified local areas. In Scotland and Wales, by contrast, joint tenders were invited in the first instance from partnerships between education authorities and TECs (or local enterprise companies, their Scottish equivalent): competitive tendering was reserved as a fall-back option.

The statutory group covered by the careers service contracts excluded students in higher education, but included all other full-time students, as well as part-time students on courses to fit them for employment, and anyone younger than 21 who had left education up to two years previously. The contracts represented monopoly arrangements to provide free services to these client groups within the geographical area concerned. The contract option was thus applied to a much wider client group than advocated by the CBI.

Within England, invitations to tender were initially issued in autumn 1993 for three-year contracts in 13 'pathfinder' areas. Invitations to tender for five-year contracts were issued to the remaining areas in 1994 and 1995; the 13 'pathfinder' contracts were retendered in 1996. In most cases the contracts were awarded to the existing careers services, within new company structures based on various forms of partnership between local education authorities (LEAs) and TECs (and, sometimes, other partners too). However, a few contracts were awarded to *new entrants*, notably Nord Anglia, CfBT and Vosper Thorneycroft. There were also a few examples of *expansionism*, with companies based on existing services (especially Surrey) being given contracts for areas other than their own. In the retendering of the 'pathfinder' areas, three of the 13 services lost their bids (Chatrik, 1997).

Savas (1987) suggests that contracting is feasible and works well when:

1   **the work to be done is specified unambiguously;**
2   **several potential producers are available, and a competitive climate either exists or can be created and sustained;**

3   the government is able to monitor the contractor's
     performance;
4   appropriate terms are included in the contract document
     and enforced. (1987, p 109)

Experience to date with the contracting process in relation to careers services, along with the theoretical literature on public-sector contracting, suggests that problems have been experienced in four areas:

- securing and maintaining a sufficient number of providers;
- ensuring that the contracting process is cost-effective;
- defining appropriate measures for evaluating performance;
- ensuring that the contracting process encourages rather then stifles innovation and enterprise.

The problems experienced in eliciting effective competition to existing services indicates the difficulty of establishing a competitive quasi-market in this area. Professional expertise, in terms both of individual competences and organisational know-how, is concentrated in existing services. If quality standards are set at a high level, it is difficult for other organisations to meet them. If the standards are relaxed in order to encourage new entry, then the effect of the quasi-market is to drive down standards rather than to improve them. A choice may need to be made between defining the success of the quasi-market in terms of the number of new entrants it attracts to the market, or in terms of the quality of the services delivered by existing providers.

This leads to the issue of the cost-effectiveness of the contracting process itself. Davies argues that:

> **Even where there is no realistic possibility of removing the business entirely from the contractor, the discipline of the contracting process is powerful. It provides welcome opportunities for reviews of performance, which may otherwise not take place. Contracts also helpfully introduce the notion that some consequences may flow from non-performance. (1992, p 44)**

This needs to be set against the transaction costs of drafting the bids, negotiating the exchange agreements, and monitoring compliance with their terms. Bartlett and Le Grand point out that if quasi-markets

are to be more efficient than the systems they replace, any extra transaction costs they create must not be higher than any savings that may be generated by the forces of competition or by other aspects of the quasi-market. (1993, p 30)

The head of service in one of the 'pathfinder' areas estimated the costs of the bid alone at approximately one and half staff for six months and a legal bill of more than £30,000 (Chatrick, 1994).

With regards to the third issue, that of defining appropriate measures for evaluating performance, Davies (1992) argued that performance should be defined as far as possible in terms of outputs rather than inputs. However, defining the outputs of guidance is notoriously difficult (see Killeen et al, 1992). The solution adopted by the Employment Department in relation to careers service contracts was to provide 85% of the available budgets in the form of core funding, but 15% on the basis of outputs, defined as "plans of action, for clients at key points of transition, completed to quality standards acceptable to the Department" (Employment Department, 1994, p 13). Concerns were expressed that the use of action plans for this purpose could seriously undermine good practice, leading to concentration on quantity of throughput at the expense of quality and flexibility of service (see Eastwood, 1994; Chatrick, 1994), particularly when administered in a rigid 'top-down' way (Watts, 1996).

The final area of concern is the extent to which the contracting process encourages or discourages innovation and enterprise. Bartlett and Le Grand (1993) note that a purchaser which exploits its monopoly (more strictly, monopsonistic) power to drive a hard bargain "may sour relationships with providers, lower their morale and motivation, and perhaps eventually drive them out of business" (p 21). The difficulty of identifying clear output measures tends to lead to close surveillance of inputs and processes in order to assure contract compliance. This can be experienced by bidders as irksome and inhibiting. Part of the intention of the Act, as stated by ministers in the debates in Parliament, was to encourage enterprise among careers services in developing services, on a fee-charging or separately-funded basis, for non-statutory clients.[1] The initial contracting process was clearly perceived by some of the 'pathfinder' contractors as discouraging such enterprise (for example, Eastwood, 1994), and the net effect seems to have been to reduce rather than expand the services' non-statutory provision (Institute of Careers Guidance, 1996).

The problems experienced in relation to these four issues may be transitional or more chronic in nature. Contracts may solve some problems but may also cause new problems. Early evaluations of the new arrangements suggested that they had brought substantial benefits, and that these had outweighed the disadvantages (Morris and Stoney, 1996). The extent to which these benefits were due to the contracting process, or to other measures taken over the same period, is a matter of judgement.

Voucher option

In relation to guidance offered to individuals outside the careers services' statutory client-group, the strategy adopted by government has been very different in nature. It has involved two related components: market-testing, and experiments in guidance vouchers.

On market-testing, a research project was carried out by PA Cambridge Economic Consultants (1993) to examine why a self-sustaining 'market in guidance' was not already more fully developed and why public intervention and investment in the development of guidance services was needed. The report concluded that there would be difficulties in moving quickly towards a real market in guidance. It noted that many people were unclear about the nature of guidance and its benefits, and tended to associate it with the role of the Employment Service in relation to the unemployed (which is placement- rather than guidance-oriented and includes strong elements of official surveillance regarding rights to benefits). It found that most would not expect to be charged for any guidance services they might use, and that only a minority could conceive of any circumstances in which they might consider paying. The perceived need for guidance tended to be strongest among those with higher-level academic qualifications and those with higher incomes. Circumstances in which employers would consider paying for their employees to receive guidance tended to be linked to specific situations, notably redundancy and training/skills enhancement.

To test the market further, and to experiment with alternative forms of public support for guidance services, two experimental programmes were initiated by the Employment Department. The first of these, the Gateways to Learning programme, was aimed mainly at the unemployed; the second, Skill Choice, was aimed more strongly at individuals in employment. Both programmes were administered largely by TECs, and included experiments in offering guidance vouchers which individuals could take to a range of guidance providers accredited by the TEC. The vouchers provided a significant contribution towards the costs of the guidance but, particularly in the case of Skill Choice, individuals and/or their employers were also expected to meet part of the costs of the services used.

Vouchers are regarded by Savas (1987) as a more extreme level of privatisation than contracts. At least three related reasons can be advanced for this. First, they place purchasing power in the hands of individuals. Second, they make it easier to mix quasi-market and real-market elements, with varying levels of private and/or public payment for different client groups. Third, they make it possible to progress step by step towards as close to a real market as is feasible. There is an ambiguity about the extent to which quasi-markets based on vouchers are seen as a half-way house to real markets, or as a new form of social welfare provision which is likely to be more truly client-centred than the old. The two views are not mutually exclusive, but there is variation in the balance adopted between them by different advocates.

There are three main arguments put forward in favour of guidance vouchers. The *marketing* argument is that they encourage individuals to use guidance services who might not otherwise have done so. The *choice* argument is that they enable individuals to choose where they can use their voucher. The *empowerment* argument is that they empower individuals in their relationships with guidance agencies and so make it more likely that the guidance provided is designed to meet their interests.

The evaluations by Coopers & Lybrand (1994; 1995) of the Gateways to Learning and Skill Choice programmes raised doubts about the extent to which these claimed benefits were achieved. There was some evidence of marketing benefits, but little evidence of guidance clients using anything but the most basic of methods for choosing guidance providers: in the Gateways evaluation, most were largely uninformed about the benefits of using one provider rather than another, and based their decisions on criteria such as geographical location, personal recommendation or previous experience. There was also little evidence in either study that clients felt empowered by their use of guidance vouchers. The Gateways evaluation noted that the transaction costs associated with vouchers were considerable, and that there would need to be convincing evidence of the additional motivational benefits arising from their use before these costs could be justified. The Skill Choice evaluation commented that:

> **while a charitable conclusion would be that the case for or against vouchers was 'not proven', our view is that it has been adequately considered, and tested, by pilots and found to be wanting.** (Coopers & Lybrand, 1995, p 65)

According to Savas (1987), the conditions under which a voucher system will work well are when:

1   **there are widespread differences in people's preferences for the service, and these differences are recognised and accepted by the public as legitimate;**
2   **individuals have incentives to shop aggressively for the service;**
3   **individuals are well informed about market conditions, including the cost and quality of the service and where it may be obtained;**
4   **there are many competing suppliers of the service, or else start-up costs are low and additional suppliers can readily enter the market if the demand is there;**
5   **the quality of the service is easily determined by the user;**
6   **the service is relatively inexpensive and purchased frequently, so the user learns by experience.** (Savas, 1987, p 113)

The existing evidence, including the Coopers & Lybrand evaluations, casts doubt on the extent to which these conditions are satisfied in the case of guidance. It is by no means evident that individuals are currently capable of, or particularly interested in becoming capable in, making an informed choice between competing *guidance* providers. What they want is assurance of high-quality guidance to help them in making informed choices between competing *opportunity* providers. Users may have preferences for different guidance services, but this can be accommodated by collaborative referral as well as by competition. One of the most valuable perceived benefits of voucher schemes, as administered in some TEC areas, was the establishment of stronger networks between guidance agencies, which made them more aware of each other's strengths and limitations (Hawthorn, 1992): this could be developed further on a collaborative rather than a competitive basis.

Weighing up the options

The discussion in this chapter has centred around three sets of options:

- between the competing notions of guidance as market-marker and of a market in guidance;
- whether any market in guidance should be on a real-market or quasi-market basis;
- whether any quasi-market should be based on contracts or on vouchers.

This final section will give concluding comments on each of these options, in reverse order.

Contracts versus vouchers

Vouchers have considerable attractions. In addition to the points made earlier, they can offer greater flexibility than contracts in promoting equity between individuals (Osborne and Gaebler, 1992, p 185). Also, by encouraging plurality of provision, they enable consumers to exert pressure on providers through 'exit' (going elsewhere) as well as through 'voice' (consumer feedback) (Hirschman, 1970).

Nonetheless, the evidence presented in the preceding section would seem to advocate caution in relation to the CBI's proposals that guidance vouchers should be adopted for young people as well as for adults (CBI, 1993b; 1994). This is particularly the case because the voucher experiments on adults were introduced under conditions which a priori would seem relatively advantageous, in four respects. First, the range and diversity of the individual circumstances of adults means that no single service is likely to meet all of their needs. Second, there is already a wide range of guidance provision for adults, including a relatively substantial private fee-paying sector, notably in out-placement and career consultancy for executives and managers. Third, it is realistic to target guidance vouchers for adults to certain groups, and encourage some of these groups to 'top up' the value of their voucher. Fourth, sufficient public funds have never yet been made available to provide universal guidance services for adults; a quasi-market based on vouchers could provide a means for getting much closer to this goal, without all the costs being borne by the public purse.

In relation to young people, none of these conditions applies:

- young people are more homogenous in their circumstances;
- there is a narrower range of guidance providers for young people;
- the notion of targeting guidance vouchers to certain groups is not being proposed;
- universal access to guidance services for most young people is already provided by statute.

In view of all this, the Conservative government's decision to adopt the contract option for young people, plus some adults based in education, seemed preferable to the voucher option advocated by the CBI.

At the same time, it is important to recognise the tensions and links between the two distinct quasi-market thrusts of the Conservative government's policy. The awarding of large monopoly contracts to particular services could be seen as giving them a significant market advantage in relation to any voucher-based quasi-market for guidance developed for other client groups. Conversely, the development of a voucher-based quasi-market in guidance could make it easier to attract new entrants to the contractual quasi-market for the statutory client group, so solving the problem, identified earlier, of introducing genuine competition into this quasi-market.

Real market versus quasi-market

The relative merits of contract or voucher systems are linked to the wider question of whether the intention is to move as close as possible towards a real market in guidance, in which the costs are paid by individuals or employers rather than by the State, or to continue, and possibly even extend, publicly-funded provision for guidance. If the former is the case, then vouchers have strong ideological attractions regardless of any practical difficulties they may involve; if the latter is the case, then the pros and cons of contract and voucher schemes alike can be weighed more dispassionately.

Views about the relative merits of real markets and of quasi-markets vary considerably. Some argue that direct payment is the best way to assure that consumers value guidance, and that the guidance offered is designed to meet their needs. Against this needs to be set the evidence, cited earlier, of consumer resistance to payment, and the fact that many of the people who need guidance most are least able to pay for it.

There appears to be no explicit political pressure for applying real-market principles to guidance for young people or those based in education. However, in relation to other client groups, some would like to move as close as possible to a real market; others would like to move towards a statutory all-age guidance service available free of charge to all, as is the case in Germany (Watts et al, 1994).

A possible compromise offering attractions to both of these lobbies has been proposed (TEC National Council, 1994; Watts, 1994; NACCEG, 1996). This was endorsed formally by the Conservative government shortly before the end of its term of office (see Sharpe, 1996). The compromise suggests that *foundation* guidance provision, including open-access information centres and brief diagnostic guidance designed in particular to identify further guidance needs, should be made available on a universal free basis. This should be complemented by *customised* guidance provision – for example, counselling interviews, group sessions, psychometric testing – which should be provided on a charged basis to those able to pay, and on a free basis to those who cannot. This proposal acknowledges the difficulties identified earlier in securing a market in guidance, and assures the general availability of core elements of guidance as a public good; however, it also provides a base on which extended provision can be marketed to those able to pay for it, thus stimulating a market in guidance where this is feasible.

Progress along these lines could in principle make it easier to achieve policy coherence between guidance services for young people and for adults. There have hitherto been two different sets of policies in operation. Provision of a basic level of all-age guidance for all could open up new coordinated policy options. For example, provision for open-access information centres might be included in future careers service contracts, or might be run by TECs as part of a general coordinating role in assuring lifelong access to guidance (see Watts et al, 1997).

Guidance as market-maker versus market in guidance

However, the fundamental issue is the relative weight attached to the concepts of guidance as market-maker and of a market (or quasi-market) in guidance. The demands of the former are logically superordinate. If primacy is given to the public interest in guidance as a means of making the labour market, and the education and training market, operate effectively, then the notion of a market or quasi-market in guidance can only be supported to the extent that it meets this interest. Where it fails to do so, other approaches are required.

In this sense, guidance is in a different category from most other public services. The applicability of market principles has in recent years been tested in relation to most government activities. But guidance is itself a means of addressing market imperfections in relation to provision of education, training and employment – notably that of imperfect information. If a market or quasi-market in guidance proves itself to be imperfect in this respect, then, logically, further intervention is required to address this imperfection. Alternatively, it needs to be recognised that to apply market forces to guidance is to advance a bridge too far.

Note

[1] Statements made by ministers included references to "giving the careers service commercial freedoms and flexibilities", to the intention to "encourage innovation", and to hopes that "careers advice will be expanded", with "scope to assist unemployed adults, people faced with redundancy or those seeking a career change" (Hansard, 2/2/93, cols 710, 708; 17/11/92, col 179).

This chapter is an updated version of a paper published in the *British Journal and Guidance and Counselling*, 1995, vol 23, no 1, pp 69-81.

Part Seven

Television

THIRTEEN

Public television quasi-markets in New Zealand and the UK

Diana Barrowclough

Introduction

The different experiences of public broadcasting quasi-markets in New Zealand and the UK offer a rich opportunity to extend our understanding of the theory and practice of the 'quasi-market experiment'. Broadcasting shares many of the features seen in other sectors for which quasi-markets have been recommended. Like health and education, for example, it is characterised by features such as ill-defined property rights, non-rival consumption, externalities and imperfect information, as well as increasing returns to scale. Comparing the two countries' broadcasting quasi-markets can further insight into the way that these new forms of market work generally, and the likely future funding and provision of a broad range of collective services.

Radio and television broadcasting is especially suitable for this role, since it has always been the 'classic' metaphor for a public good. The recent developments in New Zealand and the UK broadcasting reforms act as a mirror, reflecting the changing economic theory pertaining to public goods, and the changing policy prescriptions these imply for State finance and provision.

The next section of this chapter shows why reform of New Zealand and UK public television took the quasi-market form, rather than the fuller deregulation or privatisation form occurring in other public sectors. Television had long been considered to be 'special', with characteristics that constrained the ways markets could, or should, provide it. This belief remained even after this decade's widespread re-evaluation of the State's role in providing public goods. Vestiges of the 'conventional wisdom' about broadcasting survived the severe buffeting that rocked the public sector. The 'quasi-market solution' emerged as an attempt to protect the traditional ideals of public service broadcasting, while still introducing the perceived benefits of markets and competition.

This is followed by a section describing the public television quasi-market introduced into the British Broadcasting Corporation (BBC) in the early 1990s, and the 'New Zealand On Air' (NZOA) quasi-market introduced in 1989. It shows how these television reforms fit the general 'quasi-market model', such as one exists, since they share the generic structures and objectives that have become familiar in quasi-markets elsewhere. While the two markets share important similarities, they have even more important differences. New Zealand has been much more committed to the 'market' element of quasi-market reform, whereas the UK has been more committed to the 'quasi' part. This analysis focuses on two key aspects of the two quasi-markets, which have important implications for the finance and provision of public goods in general, as well as for television in particular. Firstly, the central similarity in each market is analysed, namely the fact that each quasi-market still has at its core a state-owned broadcaster, and still relies on raising revenue through the hypothecated tax of the public broadcasting fee (PBF). Secondly, the fundamental difference in each quasi-market's purchaser is considered, showing crucial differences in each purchaser's powers, the nature of the competition this engenders, and the implications this has for the service to be purchased.

The section on implications concludes by summarising the findings and highlighting their wider implications. It suggests that there is no stability in either country's quasi-market 'solutions' to the pressing question of how best to finance and provide public television. In both countries the television sectors are marked by an intense degree of transition, flux and uncertainty. This reflects both the new opportunities available in ever-changing television and multimedia technology, and the fact that these new quasi-markets are constantly evolving and adapting to circumstances and experience. Each quasi-market sketched out in this case study appears likely to change in the near future, as both countries introduce still further aspects of competition, prices and markets into the finance and provision of public television. New Zealand has already 'gone further' than the UK in this respect, and further marketisation seems likely. The UK has yet to adopt the full measure of quasi-market reforms currently operating in New Zealand, and most recently its quasi-market appears more as a passing phase in the general programme of reform. However, the door is open for it to do so, and in the future it appears likely to introduce further use of markets and competition.

More generally, the developments in New Zealand and UK public television quasi-markets reflect the wider environment beyond television, where there is constant questioning of the most effective and appropriate role of the State. Television stands as an insightful metaphor, revealing widespread lack of consensus as to what the role of the State 'should be' in the 1990s and beyond. Questions that are not clearly answered in the case of public television are also not clearly answered in the wider public arena. For example, should the State continue to use taxation to finance collective goods, when 'user-pays' systems are possible? What public goods should be provided, and for whom? Should public goods be provided to large numbers of users who may not value them much; or targeted to smaller groups who value them most highly? Can markets provide substitutes for public goods, and if so what role if any is required of the State? These questions are especially topical and pertinent in the case of television, but they resonate in a much wider sphere.

Broadcasting as a public good

The conventional wisdom

Broadcasting has long been seen as the quintessential public good, with all of the characteristic features of such goods and the subsequent policy recommendation that it be organised centrally by the State. Markets were considered likely to fail, so State intervention was needed to finance, own, provide or regulate broadcasting services (see, for example, Congdon et al, 1992; Noll et al, 1973; Vogel, 1994).

These arguments rested on two key observations about the production and consumption of broadcasting. Firstly, broadcasting was traditionally non-excludable. Broadcast providers could not exclude any listeners or viewers from consuming broadcast messages, given the initial purchase of a receiving set. Secondly, broadcasting is non-rival, as consumption by one person does not reduce the consumption benefits available for others. These two features mean that markets are likely to fail, because there is no link between service provider, service user and price. Providers lack the incentives that motivate private markets, as they cannot appropriate revenue or profits earned.

A strong tradition on how to resolve these problems had already developed in economics long before broadcasting was invented at the start of the 20th century. Hume's 1739 analysis of the commons outlined the problem, correctly identifying the paralysing impact of poorly-defined property rights and non-excludability, where opportunism and freeriding would lead to collective inaction, so society would fail to provide the services desired by all. Adam Smith in 1776 showed how to resolve this failure, through the intervention by a 'higher authority'; a century later, J.S. Mill advocated financing it through a compulsory tax.

Broadcasting fitted comfortably into this conventional wisdom, and a tradition developed whereby the State was deeply involved in the financing, provision, and/or regulation of broadcasting. Even those countries that typically eschewed State intervention acknowledged the need for regulation, and a central state role became the norm in broadcasting, rather than the exception. The continued existence of New Zealand and the UK's state-owned broadcaster and hypothecated broadcasting tax, is testament to the resilience of this tradition.

Other arguments for a strong state role go beyond these technological constraints. For example, it cannot be argued that markets fail in all respects, because typically a vigorous commercial broadcasting sector occurs alongside this strong state role. Commercial broadcasters solved the problem of their non-excludable audiences by finding ways to exclude intermediate consumers instead – by charging advertisers for access to the potential customers that gathered to enjoy the programmes offered. However, it was traditionally argued that this did not negate the State's rationale, because although commercial broadcasters offered television viewers a valued service, this service was not a perfect substitute for publicly-provided broadcasting. Commercial broadcast providers' objectives were different, and hence the nature of the service provided could be expected to be different too. The State was needed to regulate the behaviour of commercial broadcasters, and to ensure the optimal quality and quantity of the broadcasting offered.

Commercially-provided broadcasting, for example, includes advertising as well as programmes which represent a non-money 'cost' to audiences. Imperfectly competitive broadcasters could be expected to supply excessive advertising – a viewer observes up to 15 minutes advertising per hour in New Zealand and the United States, compared to around seven minutes per hour in the regulated UK. Commercial broadcasting also differs in terms of its non-advertising material, with the most notable criticisms being that its programming lacks diversity and aims for the 'lowest common denominator'. The argument is, briefly, that commercial broadcasters earn greatest advertising revenue when they can attract the largest audiences, and so programmes aim to maximise audience numbers rather than audience 'satisfaction'. This stems from non-exclusion: without a price mechanism viewers cannot signal the intensity of their desires for particular services, by paying more for them, as they would in conventional markets. The only 'signal' consumers can send is that of audience size.

The effect of this is reinforced by the fact that broadcasters face increasing returns to scale, incurring little or no additional costs of broadcasting to audiences of millions, rather than to merely thousands. As viewers can signal only an 'on/off' vote, as broadcasters' costs do not rise proportionately as the numbers of viewers increases, and as advertising revenue increases as the number of viewers increases, the preferred strategy of the profit-maximising broadcaster would seem clear. It is to maximise numbers of viewers, not satisfaction, and at the least cost. This, say supporters of public broadcasting, is not all that broadcasting is, or potentially could be. Commercial broadcasting is valuable and meets a consumer need, but it fails to maximise its potential.

An especially topical argument today is whether the problem above would be solved if broadcasting was properly excludable, with a functioning price system. Technological advances in scrambling, unscrambling and computerised accounting now mean it is technologically and economically possible to make broadcasting a private good. Subscription television works by such direct payment, and the new BBC Royal Charter allows direct payment for some BBC services. However, critics argue that the price system would not work properly, even if broadcasting was excludable. One argument is that consumers cannot calculate their true values for broadcasting services. They would underestimate their true willingness to pay, because of information asymmetries, externalities of consumption and production, and myopia about their long-term interests. This position is a combination of the 'merit good' argument used by the 'father' of the BBC, Lord Reith, who famously claimed that "few [listeners] know what they want, and very few want what they need" (Briggs, 1979, p 238) and more modern Arrow-style arguments phrased in terms of experience goods, and myopia (for example, Arrow, 1963; 1970; 1971). The modern position is well summarised by Graham and Davies (1992):

> The point ... is not that television may have great power for good or evil over society as a whole, but that television has the capacity either to cramp or enrich the knowledge, experience and imagination of individuals ... if all television is elicited by the market, there is a very real danger that consumers will under-invest in the development of their own tastes, their own experiences and their own capacity to comprehend. This is not because consumers are stupid, but because it is only in retrospect that the benefits of such investment become apparent. (1992, p 174)

In most countries of the world, a strong state role in broadcasting is the norm not the exception. This role may vary from the minimal one of industry regulator, to more interventionist roles including financing, owning and providing public broadcasting. In both New Zealand and the UK there was a long tradition of a national state-owned broadcaster, which for decades represented the ideal of culture, national identity, and public service. The BBC, and the aspirations of Reith, were the pinnacle to which public broadcasters around the world aspired. New Zealand was no exception, as it followed the BBC model (even if its pragmatic needs harnessed private sector capital alongside its public sector finance and aspirations).

Challenges

In more recent years broadcasting has undergone the same powerful challenges that have assailed every other public sector. As the public sector's share of GDP rose to 40-50% in many countries,[1] criticisms that public service operators were inefficient, unresponsive to consumer needs, and excessively bureaucratic gained momentum. 'Government failure' became as feared as the 'market failure' which governments attempted to remedy, and the costs of bureaucratic capture and principal/agency divergence were emphasised. This was reinforced by renewed arguments that markets could, and in the past did, provide collective goods, or at least substitutes for them. To say that these challenges had a powerful effect throughout the public sector is an understatement (see Holtham and Kay, 1994, for an excellent overall review).

In broadcasting, these challenges converged as increased globalisation and international and national competition promised audiences dazzling new viewing choices, and exclusion was now a technical and an economic possibility. It was increasingly doubted whether broadcasting was a 'pure public good', if indeed any such thing existed. The question focused more on degrees of rivalry or excludability, rather than absolute measures (for example, Buchanan, 1965) and on the ability of the market to provide public television substitutes. The history of the other 'classic' public good, the lighthouse, was similarly revised (see Coase, 1988; Peacock, 1979) and it was increasingly argued that markets could (and in the past did) provide such public goods. If television could now be excludable, did this not undermine the traditional arguments for a state role? Why should there be market failure, and market 'gaps' of quality or diversity, if private sector providers could exclude non-payers and could charge higher prices for specialised services that minority audiences valued highly? These challenges fuelled skepticism that had always existed about the ability of 'higher authority' to know what society (or its television viewers) actually wanted. The 'preference revelation' problem was more difficult to ignore now that preferences could be revealed, through 'user-pays' television.

These challenges were most powerfully presented in the Peacock Report on the *Committee on financing the BBC* (HMSO, 1986). The effect of this watershed in conventional broadcasting economics cannot be underestimated, as its ripples have been felt far beyond the UK environment to which it was directed. Peacock recommended introducing direct payment, markets and competition into public television. These market-oriented reforms were to be complemented by a special agency that would protect the diversity and creative challenges that helped distinguish 'public service' television from that offered otherwise. The Peacock Report fell on very fertile soil in New Zealand, as it complemented the radical overhaul of economic policy that had already begun (see Easton, 1994). Its radical revision of conventional broadcasting economics and policy has permeated throughout the ethos and structure behind the New Zealand television quasi-market. Ironically, it has not been similarly received at the BBC.

The flurry towards quasi-markets can be seen as a relatively muted response to all of these challenges. The quasi-market in New Zealand and UK public television is a tempered reform when compared to the fuller privatisation or deregulation seen in other markets. This reflects a continued respect for the traditional ideals of public broadcasting described above. The quasi-market seemed to offer the benefits of competition and of markets, without having to forgo the traditional ideals inherent in state-ownership and public service. As in other quasi-markets (Le Grand and Bartlett, 1993), its 'market' elements seemed to promise enhanced efficiency of provision, responsiveness to viewers' needs, and choice of providers and services. On the other hand, its 'quasi' elements reflected a continued appreciation of the way that prices and competition in television markets could be distorted by factors such as externalities, information asymmetry, myopia, and increasing returns to scale.

Quasi-markets in television

Generic quasi-market

The 'Producer Choice' television quasi-market in the BBC and the NZOA quasi-market share the broad generic features that have now become synonymous with quasi-market reforms in other sectors throughout the world:

- broadcasting services are financed by licence fee or tax, and are not paid for directly by service users at the point of consumption, creating the third-party, agency relationship that characterises quasi-markets in other sectors; consumers are represented by a purchasing agency, which uses the broadcasting tax revenue to purchase services on their behalf;
- the purchasers of broadcasting services are separated from service providers, and their relationship is governed by the use of prices and formal contracts;
- these newly disintegrated broadcasting providers are required to compete; as in quasi-markets elsewhere, these providers comprise an unusual mixture of publicly-owned and privately-owned companies, competing against each other for a share of the public purse despite their potentially very different corporate objectives and services.

In the television quasi-market, as in quasi-markets elsewhere, it is also not easy to define precisely what the purchasing agency is supposed to purchase, or how it should compare competing providers. Buying broadcasting services is not the same as buying, for example, tomatoes, for which conventional markets work very well. It is not easy to define, measure or value the service to be provided, nor the inputs used in its

Table 6: Broadcasting production process

1	2	3	4	5
Finance	Programme production	Channel generation	Broadcast distribution	Consumption

production. Purchasers' decisions involve complex qualitative comparisons, as well as quantitative ones. Comparing providers' costs and prices does offer some insights into relative efficiency or service quality, but this insight can only be limited. For example, lower costs do not mean improved value for money if service quality is undermined. It is extremely difficult to evaluate and compare service quality, because it includes subjective elements such as taste, as well as objective standards such as technical quality. Broadcasting has not yet developed the quality adjusted life year (QALY) mechanism that is widely used to help resolve some of these problems in health markets.

Table 6 shows how the quasi-market structure fits into the overall broadcasting production process. The broadcasting production process can be divided into at least five discrete (highly stylised) sections.

Traditionally tax revenue entered the process in cell 1. It was collected (typically by the Post Office), and then granted to the state-owned broadcaster. The broadcaster's 'provider' role traditionally encompassed the three production stages in cells 2, 3 and 4. 'Programme production' in cell 2 involves a myriad of diverse resources, people and skills used to produce programme material. This completed material is then bundled together as part of a channel, given a scheduled date and time for transmission to audiences, and then marketed under a particular brand name (cell 3). This is then usually distributed (cell 4), via satellite, to receiving households where the service is finally enjoyed (cell 5). (These descriptions of an industry which employs tens of thousands of people are simplistic in the extreme, but serve to highlight the essential components of the quasi-market reforms.) It is delivered 'free-to-air' to the final consumer since payment has already been achieved via the PBF (cell 1). In the case of commercial free-to-air broadcasting finance in cell 1 comes from advertising. In subscription broadcasting, service delivery is contingent on direct payment of the subscription charges so there is a direct link between cell 1 and cell 5.

In-house production, for distribution on a recognised and national television channel, used to be an ideal of which nations were proud; it was synonymous with national identity and quality. It is only relatively recently that this has been so challenged, and provision broken down into its constituent tasks. As shown in Table 6, the basic pattern conforms to that which can be seen in quasi-markets generally. Both NZOA and Producer Choice in the UK aimed to reallocate the property rights within the integrated corporate umbrella, thus carving out the now familiar quasi-market distinctions between 'purchaser', 'provider', and 'service user' shown in the Tables 7 and 8.

However, a major country difference is that New Zealand has a much greater orientation towards the 'market' part of the quasi-market reforms than does the UK. In New Zealand, competition occurs in all of the first four cells in Table 6, whereas in the UK it occurs only within the programme production cell. These differences are described more fully below.

New Zealand and UK quasi-markets

Tables 7 and 8 extend Table 6 to incorporate the quasi-market's new purchasing agency cell 2. Provision of programmes now appears in cell 3, while channel generation and transmission services have been subsumed into cell 4. As these tables show, while New Zealand and the UK show the similarities above with the generic quasi-market model, they are also different from each other in important ways. The following discussion focuses on the different roles of the purchaser in each country, and on the nature and number of service providers.

In the UK, the 'purchaser' of broadcasting services is the Secretary of State for National Heritage, who retains key powers in the Royal Charter (HMSO, 1996) that mandates the state-owned broadcaster, the BBC. These broadcasting services are to be purchased from the BBC, using PBF revenue. The BBC also collects this revenue, thus acting as both 'agent-purchaser' for the Secretary of State and its 'provider' of broadcasting. The Secretary of State is represented at the BBC by the board of governors. (It is not always clear how the board is expected to use its powers, and its future role and ideal constituency is currently under debate.)

In New Zealand the situation is very different. A special quasi-autonomous non-governmental purchasing agency (quango) was created under the 1989 Broadcasting Act. It collects the broadcast fee, and uses it to purchase public broadcasting services. The sole role of the quango

Table 7: Quasi-market structure in UK public broadcasting

I Finance	2 Purchaser	3 Provider – programmes	4 Provider – broadcaster	5 Consumer
Public broad-casting fee	Department of National Heritage State agent: BBC	BBC resources and producers; independent resources and producers	Sole broad-caster, BBC	Receives service 'free-to-air'

Table 8: Quasi-market structure in New Zealand public broadcasting

I Finance	2 Purchaser	3 Provider – programmes	4 Provider – broadcaster	5 Consumer
Public broad-casting fee	State agent: quango NZOA	Broadcasters' resources and producers; independent resources and producers	Several broadcasters, private and state-owned	Receives service 'free-to-air'

is purchasing; unlike the UK, it is not also a provider of programming, nor a channel, nor a broadcaster. The quango, now named 'New Zealand On Air', complemented wider policy reforms that separated out the commercial objectives of state-owned enterprises from their traditional social objectives. Many state-owned enterprises were privatised, and those that were not were typically corporatised and required to pursue commercial objectives wholeheartedly, with their former social roles now being met by other agencies (see 1986 State Owned Enterprises Act). The state-owned broadcaster Television New Zealand (TVNZ) was to act like a fully commercial broadcaster, with any 'social' objectives in broadcasting being met by the purchasing agent NZOA instead. The NZOA 'purse' of public funds consists of around 13% of the total industry revenue, with the remaining revenue gained from sales of advertising and other commercial activities.

Differences in the role of each country's purchaser occur at all levels of the production process, including channel generation and broadcast distribution, as well as the provision of programming services. They reflect the different objectives imbued in each purchasing agent, and affect the level of competition that exists in the quasi-market, and the degree of purchaser choice.

In the UK the relationship between the purchaser (cell 2) and the state-owned broadcaster-provider (cell 4) is not a competitive one. The BBC is the only broadcaster receiving tax revenue from the broadcasting fee. It receives all of the net PBF, £1.9billion in fee revenue in 1987, in return for providing broadcast services throughout the UK. Other broadcaster-providers (the ITN network, Channel 4, or cable companies) in the commercial sector are not included in the quasi-market as they do not receive any of this tax revenue.[2]

However, the UK quasi-market did have competition at the level of programme production. Programme producers employed within the BBC could choose where to source inputs, hence the title 'Producer Choice'. Resources, such as costume and design, could be purchased from providers employed within the BBC or from providers in the private sector. Traditionally, BBC programme producers would always have used internal suppliers of resources, and a main objective of the producer choice reforms was to encourage producers to compare the costs and quality of services offered outside, as well as inside, the BBC. Competition was introduced within cell 3, as providers of resources and production inputs compete to sell their services to the many programme producers employed within the BBC.

Purchasers higher up the production process also decided whether to fill their channel's programming schedule with completed programmes purchased from producers in-house or from external producers. Competition existed between cell 3 and cell 4 to the extent that BBC programme producers competed against each other, and against independent producers, to sell completed programmes to the BBC broadcaster. Therefore, while the BBC faced no competition for its share of the PBF revenue as a whole, there was a lower tier of competition in terms of the decisions the BBC made about how to spend this revenue.

By contrast, the relationship between the purchaser and the various providers in New Zealand is very different. The NZOA purchaser basically acts as a subsidiser, inducing the various broadcasters to produce or broadcast 'public service' programmes rather then the more commercially-oriented programmes they would produce and broadcast otherwise. To this end the purchaser NZOA makes two types of purchasing decisions. Firstly, it purchases programmes, choosing from among competing programme producers (cell 3). These competing providers include independent programme producers, and the in-house programme producers employed by the broadcaster-providers. Traditionally, the state-owned TVNZ producers would have gained the lion's share of all PBF revenue, but now the independent sector has blossomed, so that TVNZ programme makers' share of PBF revenue has fallen from more than 80% to less than 35%. Secondly, the purchaser has choice over where the completed programmes are broadcast. In this case, the state-owned broadcaster TVNZ has also gradually lost its advantage, as it now broadcasts only about half of the programmes produced using NZOA subsidies, including its own programmes and those produced independently, while another privately-owned broadcaster, TV3, steadily increased its share.

Before the quasi-market reforms TVNZ used to take the lion's share of the PBF revenue, in much the same way as the BBC. It received the bulk of taxation revenue, and used this to finance the production and broadcasting of programmes. This revenue was used alongside revenue gained from the sale of advertising, with the private and public sources of funds being essentially mixed into the same pool. Now the two sources of finance are operationally separated. The idea is that broadcasters use advertising revenue to finance the production of commercially-viable programmes, and use the NZOA finance to pay for others. NZOA subsidies compensate the broadcaster for the lost advertising revenue or additional expenses it incurs in producing and broadcasting 'public services' style broadcasting rather than commercial broadcasting.

These structural differences reflect the different objectives with which each purchaser is imbued. In the UK, the service that the Secretary of State purchaser expects to buy for its money is laid out in the latest Royal Charter (HMSO, 1996) and numerous policy and research documents. These set out the nature of the service that is to be purchased, and the potential service users for whom it is targeted. For example, the charter states that the BBC should provide "the highest standards, probity, propriety and value for money in the use of the PBF revenue". It does not specify precise details about programme content or about how the BBC should achieve this, although the service should "reflect the needs and interests of the public". Programmes should maintain high general standards of content and quality, and provide a balanced service across a wide range of subject matter. The purchaser has also traditionally required that coverage be universal, ensuring audiences in remote or inaccessible regions of the country receive a clear signal. While the tangible elements of the service are reasonably clear, there is a fair degree of discretion allowed in how the BBC should interpret and provide the less tangible elements.

In New Zealand, the nature of the service to be purchased is defined differently. The purchaser is required by law to use tax revenue to purchase programming which reflects and promotes 'New Zealand identity and culture', and which protects the interests of minority groups such as women and the disabled. (Maori programming used to be included in this remit but is now financed separately.) The Act also sets out the criteria on which the purchaser should make these purchasing decisions. These include the extent to which funding applicants have access to other funds; the potential size of the programme's audience, and whether there is a balanced range of programmes provided. The purchaser is to consider both the particular aspects of the service in question, as well as the way that this would fit into the wider picture of other services currently, or potentially, offered. As in the UK, NZOA is required to subsidise the costs of transmission, to ensure universal coverage reaches households in remote or economically unviable regions.

In summary, New Zealand has introduced more elements of competition and markets into its television quasi-market than has the UK. Both countries have maintained a state-owned broadcaster, and have continued to use the virtually universal tax of the PBF to finance public broadcasting. However, the role of the purchaser is different, the nature of the services the purchaser aims to purchase is different, and the relationship between the purchaser and the providers is very different. New Zealand's quasi-market in public television fundamentally changed the structure of the television sector, altering the role of the state-owned broadcaster and the entire way in which taxation revenue was used to finance and provide public television. By comparison, the UK's reforms appear to be more in the nature of an internal managerial reform, initiated within the BBC, and not altering the landscape of the sector as a whole.

Implications

The introduction to this chapter argued that the television case study highlighted controversial questions that remain unresolved in the wider arena of public economics today. For example, should a virtually universal tax still be used to finance public goods, when selective user-pays mechanisms are possible? What types of public goods should be financed, and for whom? Can the market provide substitutes for public goods, and if so what role does that leave for the State? New Zealand and the UK have come up with different answers to these questions, as is revealed in the quasi-markets for television described above.

In New Zealand, the purchaser essentially acts as a gap-filler. It subsidises the marginal costs broadcasters incur in providing public-service-oriented broadcasting instead of providing commercially-oriented broadcasting, which earns advertiser revenue. Programming produced in New Zealand is more costly than imported programming, so could be underprovided by commercially-oriented broadcasters. There would also be underprovision of the production and consumption externalities associated with domestic programming. For example, an active domestic production industry may generate much 'learning by doing' human capital, which could cause spillover effects into other sectors. A strictly cost-minimising broadcast company could underestimate these external benefits, when comparing the relative costs of domestic programme production and imported programmes. Also, programming which appeals to minority audiences, rather than majority ones, incurs opportunity costs in terms of forgone advertiser revenue. The NZOA purchaser induces broadcasters to produce or broadcast 'public service' programmes rather then the more commercially-oriented services they would provide otherwise. It is not important who provides the public service, so long as it is provided.

New Zealand has refined its definition of broadcasting's 'publicness' to the smallest essential unit,[3] that of a single aspect of service, existing within a wider sea of commercial broadcasting. This definition focuses on the specific programme type, which would not be funded otherwise by the commercial sector, or the supply of transmission signals to remote regions, which commercially-oriented broadcasters would not otherwise provide. The definition of 'publicness' seems to be a marginal, market-failure one, rather than the more complex Reithian justifications which have been used in the past. It is geared towards resolving the particular market failures of inadequate diversity, inadequate domestic production, and lack of service to minority audiences. However, it does not deal with the 'failure' of excessive advertising.

By comparison, the quasi-market structure in the UK suggests that the public good aspect of broadcasting is still seen as a 'block service.' It comprises a diverse bundle of many different services, to be broadcast by the identified public institution of the BBC. Other providers may compete at the level of producing programmes, but the task of channel generation and transmission is tied to the BBC, and the BBC does not have to compete for its share of the PBF tax revenue. This suggests that the public good aspect of broadcasting is much broader than in New Zealand, since it includes the types of programmes that commercially-oriented broadcasters would provide, as well as those which they would not. Also, the identity of the public service channel providers BBC1 and BBC2 matters as much as the service they provide.

The second question asked 'for whom' should these public goods be provided. Since the BBC is explicitly not a gap-filler, it is not surprising that the BBC aims to offer something for everyone. This means a combination of majority-oriented and minority-oriented programming. However, it could be questioned whether the BBC should aim for majority audiences, given that these are already being targeted by the commercially-funded broadcasters. Broadcasting observers often focus on market share. The fact that the BBC has clawed its share of the total television market back up to a majority over the commercial ITV is sometimes seen as a justification for its receiving tax revenue. This argument is not obvious; if it means there is duplication of services with those provided commercially, then it could be argued that a gap-filling role would be preferable.

The NZOA model seems to have succeeded in meeting its objectives of promoting New Zealand programming, although interestingly it is also haunted by this same lure of market share. Does the quango's legitimacy depend on its providing a service that is consumed by the largest possible number of viewers, even though this is no longer 'gap-filling' programming? For example, as one former executive officer commented:

> **"... .the owner and profits of the broadcaster are irrelevant. It's the product that gets to the widest number of fee payers that matters ... as many people as possible get value for their broadcasting fee."**

Programmes that attract very large audiences could be financed by advertiser revenue, so why should the state purchaser subsidise them? Is the purchaser falling into the trap of behaving like competitive broadcaster providers, in seeking to maximise its audience and market share? This is perhaps not surprising as it would be difficult for a purchaser to claim 'success' for decisions that were enjoyed by only the very few, even if they valued them extremely highly. How is diversity to be protected if this happens? NZOA purchasing decisions are regularly greeted with debate of this type, and the problem has not been grasped in any systematic way. The broader lesson seems to be that improved mechanisms of monitoring and evaluating performance are useful to ensure that new forms of 'agency failure' cannot emerge, which might cost as much as the market and government failures the quasi-market aimed to remedy.

These questions of how the PBF should be spent may be side-stepped altogether, if user-pays mechanisms such as subscription funding are introduced instead of the compulsory tax. Broadcasting finance and consumption would no longer necessarily be universal, but could be selective. The Peacock Report has already called for this direct funding of public television, and the BBC's latest Royal Charter has opened the door to it. Subscription funding would mean that individual households could signal their preferences by being willing to pay more for services they valued highly, so that minority or specialist preferences should be fulfilled (assuming ability to pay).

However, it is not clear that consumers would adequately incorporate the effects of externalities, myopia, and other information asymmetries, to properly calculate their willingness to pay, let alone whether broadcasters' internal pricing systems could properly accommodate all externalities or transactions costs of broadcast production. Willingness to pay does not identify varying abilities to pay. The type of service that would survive the change to subscription would be very different from that provided by public service broadcasting now (Congdon et al, 1992). Gap-filling of the type provided by NZOA could still be appropriate, although it would require regulation that ensured the public service complemented, rather than competed with, services offered by the market.

The quasi-markets described above were introduced as a tempered response to this decade's challenges to the broadcasting sector in particular, and to the broader challenges to public funding and provision of public goods in general. The television quasi-markets have brought into sharp relief the questions described above, and this is likely to be exacerbated in the future. The quasi-markets in both countries appear to be unstable and transient in their current forms, and many new questions have been raised by the quasi-market experiment to date. Television reforms in both New Zealand and the UK are more likely to develop towards the 'market' pole of the quasi-market spectrum, rather than returning to traditional 'quasi' principles.

Acknowledgement

This work was partially funded by the Cambridge Commonwealth Trust, and Royal Economic Society.

Notes

[1] In New Zealand, at the time of the reforms, government expenditure was around 40% of GDP, with gross public debt at 75% of GDP (Dalziel and Lattimore, 1996).

[2] The BBC also earns commercial revenue but this is still a relatively small amount (£364m); an even smaller proportion of this cross-subsidised the BBC's national 'public broadcasting' services. Future projections are for this commercial revenue to increase significantly, especially if the BBC achieves its ambitions in world multimedia markets. This is likely to fuel intense debate about the BBC's future role.

[3] This echoes the way that Coasian economics refines its gaze to the single transaction, and sees the firm as being the 'island' of internal relations existing within a sea of external transactions (Coase, 1937).

Lessons from experience of quasi-markets in the 1990s

Jennifer A. Roberts, Julian Le Grand
and Will Bartlett

Introduction

The quasi-market revolution has been a defining characteristic of social policy in the 1990s. While the market reform agenda had some theoretical economic underpinning based on public choice agency theories it was laden with the political philosophy and rhetoric of the New Right. The reforms in publicly-provided services have been introduced throughout the world in developed and developing countries (Mills, 1995). This process began in Britain by privatisation of components of public provision such as cleaning and catering, but during the 1980s and 1990s core services in education, health and social care were included. Considerable research effort has focused on this experiment. This research has opened up a rich agenda and has brought together many disciplines and opened up new topics. The central theme has been to determine whether markets, primarily in provision, have overcome inefficiency in the public sector (Le Grand and Bartlett, 1993). This volume has included a selection of the best research, carried out mainly in the UK.

The context in which quasi-markets operate within the UK has changed with the coming to power, in May 1997, of the new Labour government. It is as yet too early to say whether the government's policies will steer the direction of social policy away from quasi-market models or whether it will continue in the same direction. The evidence so far suggests that the emphasis on individual responsibility for welfare will continue but with greater emphasis on equity and participation and a recognition of the structural aspects of social well-being (DfEE, 1997; DoH, 1997; 1998). There is also some evidence in health of a movement away from competitive providers (Mays and Dixon, Chapter Nine, this volume) and a movement towards a more relational network of organisations:'soft-quasi-markets' (DoH, 1997;Vincent-Jones and Harries, Chapter One, this volume). In education and social services there appears to be a tendency to reduce the autonomy of local schools and steps are to be taken to encourage greater cooperation among schools locally (Whitty et al, Chapter Five, this volume). In legal aid the quasi-market trend looks likely to continue (Bevan, Chapter Eleven, this volume). Whatever the changes that take place in the UK and elsewhere there is much to be learned about organisational structures and their development from the research reported in this volume.

A number of key themes have emerged from this research. In this conclusion the principal lessons that can be drawn from this work and the work of others who have contributed to this field, both within the research seminar programme and outside it, will be discussed. It will not be possible to cover all the issues required for a full evaluation; in any case, such an evaluation would be premature as the experiment is still evolving and entering a new era in the UK. Instead, a few ideas that seem to have particular importance and relevance for analysing and managing quasi-markets and for the future of social policy will be highlighted. The usefulness of the new institutional economics and the contribution of new institutional sociology in analysing the quasi-market experiment is discussed and consideration is given to contracting, relationships and the role of trust in mitigating against opportunism and the use of regulations. The implications of the reforms on choice and the comprehensiveness and equity of provision are examined.

Analysing quasi-markets

A great deal is already known about the problems of markets and bureaucracies in providing welfare services. There is much to learn about the problems of quasi-markets. Quasi-market solutions tend to locate bureaucratic failures in provider units and to rely on purchasers to deal with matters that the markets fail to accommodate. This would be acceptable if all the aspects of market failure in the welfare sectors could be dealt with by farsighted purchasers representing the societal perspective and if competitive disciplines could be relied on to ensure efficiency of provision (Roberts, 1997). However, the problems of providing welfare services are more systemic than such a solution would suggest.

Managing markets

If markets are used it is important that they are at least competitive. Quasi-markets are highly regulated by overall budget allocations, charter standards, and sundry government legislation and regulations that constrain professionals. Yet, oddly, market structure has received little attention. It is difficult to see why those who advocated markets in the welfare sector should be chary of extending to quasi-markets the regulations faced by other industries. Market structures should provide the external disciplinary force that propels firms to the least cost position and provide the demanded quality and range of services. Apart from local government, where compulsory competitive tendering (CCT) has been introduced (Vincent-Jones and Harries, Chapter One, this volume), there have been few attempts to ensure that contracts were placed competitively. In many of the quasi-markets there has not even been much effort to ensure that the markets were at least contestable: that there was a threat from a potential supplier.

Some early studies analysed markets for surgery using the Hirschman-Herfindahl index which tests only the potential for competition (Appleby, 1994b). Competitive tendencies have also been measured using the deviation of price from marginal cost, but given the variation in accounting conventions and the poor information available these assessments have not been conclusive (Propper, 1995). In the Philippines, Bautista (1995) found extreme price rigidity and large deviations between price and marginal costs in a well-populated marketplace that might have been expected to display features of competition. The explanation appeared to be in the disciplines exerted by professional organisations that prevented doctor 'firms' stepping out of line and by the loyalties that developed between doctors and patients. Other explanations for high prices in concentrated markets include quality competition and high search costs that give rise to monopolistic arrangements. Markets for many services in the welfare sectors are local, and size and scale provides limits to the numbers of firms that can exist. Relationships based on long-standing patterns of 'trade' and professional links are likely to be cooperative rather than competitive. Such relationships can reduce transaction costs but exchange can become sluggish and inefficient causing problems (discussed by Williamson, 1985) in the context of the 'fundamental transformation' that occurs when alternative suppliers no longer contest the market, and bilateral trade becomes the norm. The new organisational forms for health services in the UK, suggested in the

White Paper (DoH, 1997) indicate that a change of suppliers of healthcare would only be undertaken as a last resort and the control on prices is envisaged to come from the publication of a schedule of 'reference costs' which will itemise what individual treatments cost across the NHS (DoH, 1997, para 3.11). Expertise in implementing the management of such reference pricing will be needed but the resources to do this are to be capped (DoH, 1997, see para 3.10).

New institutional economics

The products produced in quasi-markets present difficulties for those wishing to trade as there are information deficiencies and imbalances, bounded rationality and uncertainties. Such issues pose problems of governance structures and agency relationships. It is not surprising, given these problems, that the perspective that has dominated the analysis is that of the new institutional economics, concentrating as it does on transaction costs (Williamson, 1985). Research on quasi-markets has indicated the usefulness and limitations of this approach.

The new institutional economics provides an explanation for organisational arrangements that extends the neoclassical optimising explanations to include costs of contracting. It provides a rationale for the extent to which organisations choose trade or hierarchy as the appropriate form for components of their business. If trade, in the estimation of the entrepreneur, is too risky because of behavioural uncertainties and bounded rationality and the scope for opportunism that this provides, then vertical integration, hierarchy, may be chosen to provide security and to reduce the costs of negotiating and monitoring contracts.

In the analysis of quasi-markets, transaction costs have been used to evaluate organisations formed by decree by governments. Research has involved scrutiny of quasi-market organisations to determine whether or not they can be seen to impose or reduce transaction costs (Rafferty et al, 1994).

Measurement of transaction costs is difficult. Transaction cost theories have much in common with the subjective cost theories in so far as it is the perception of costs rather than estimated costs that are expected to motivate entrepreneurs:

> **Transaction costs are funny things: the most important of them exist not in reality, but in realities that have been avoided,**

in worlds that have not come to be. (Buckley and Chapman, 1997, p 136)

Prediction of whether a firm would be better off buying in or making in-house becomes the central task of the entrepreneur. The organisational forms that emerge from these deliberations represent the 'optimising' solution. Transaction cost economics yields a *modus vivendi* for decision making yet has a potentially tautological outcome as survivors are by definition those that choose the optimising strategies. However, some authors coming from new institutional sociology, have challenged the view that survival of an organisation depends on it being efficient (Perrow, 1981a).

Research estimates of transaction costs in the quasi-market field have concentrated not on anticipation of the costs that might arise from adopting a particular organisational form but on the time expended by employees on the contracting process (Appleby, 1994b). Even the ex ante costs of formulating contracts to ensure compliance and guard against opportunism and the ex post costs of monitoring, interpreting and re-negotiating are difficult to estimate. In quasi-markets, such costs may depend on resources allocated to the task. These may not be optimal because of the overall budgetary pressures and the growing unease about the amount spent on management costs. The agents drawing up the contracts may not have sufficient information to anticipate the possible problems that might occur, or sufficient time or skill with which to undertake these tasks. Transactions costs do not disappear because little is spent on strategies to counter them. The transaction costs that a 'farsighted entrepreneur' would have anticipated, may, if unrecognised, be manifest in opportunistic behaviour of providers and borne by the users of services who lack the information or the bargaining power to deflect them (Milgrom and Roberts, 1992). Suggestions such as the proposals for the reform of the health system in the UK, discussed above, to reduce the management costs of transactions in a quasi-market, while rightly concerned with reducing costs of billing, neglect the much more important aspects of transaction costs that require more insightful management.

Transaction costs as a determinant of the efficient organisational form are concerned only with the minimisation of costs to the organisation. Most of the welfare sectors that have been placed in the quasi-market environment have external effects which might be immediate, for example, the effect of school exclusions on crime or the effect of an infection acquired in a hospital, or ones that may occur in the longer term, affecting the environment or the social and economic capital of society. Efficient organisational forms that emerge if well-informed manager entrepreneurs minimise production and transaction costs may still be inefficient social organisations unless those negotiating contracts take steps to internalise these external effects and manage any public good aspects of services in the contracting process (see Barrowclough, Chapter Thirteen, this volume). Choices made by purchasers and providers may not consider external effects, may involve inappropriate time horizons and may not represent the preferred choices of those who consume the services.

Transaction costs and change

It is not clear who, among those who orchestrated the quasi-market changes in the UK health services of 1989, undertook the task of locating the organisational efficiency locus or who was to maintain it (Dugger, 1983). Purposeful transaction cost minimisation did not feature strongly in decisions to adopt quasi-market strategies but it was expected that managers of provider units would subsequently minimise production and transaction costs. Managers operating in quasi-markets have only attenuated property rights, being subject to budgetary constraints, regulations and government interventions. Hughes et al (1997) question the independence of managers in the quasi-markets and thus their capacity to adopt optimising strategies. They suggest quasi-markets are being in government control, being formed and likely to be changed by decree.

Some developments have occurred. Contracts did evolve to meet provider, purchaser and user needs and amalgamations did take place to minimise risk or rationalise services (Lapsley and Llewellyn, Chapter Seven, this volume). In Chapter Nine Mays and Dixon indicated a great divergence among arrangements for purchasing in fundholding practices that have property rights and which stand to gain professionally and financially from these arrangements. Interesting diversity has also been reported in Italy in the context of regional structures within the federal state (France, Chapter Eight, this volume). In the UK, LAs adopted different strategies for managing contracts won by in-house contestants (Vincent-Jones and Harries, Chapter One, this volume).

Changes in organisations have been ascribed to coercive forces, normative pressures or imitative processes (Hughes et al, 1997). Coercive forces are the dominant mode and consist in the health sector of annual revenue allocations, annual contracting timetables, 'cost improvement' percentages, pricing rules, standardised returns, conciliation procedures, charter standards and long-term strategic targets (Hughes et al, 1997, p 266). Normative change arises from professionals exerting common standards of conduct. Imitative pressures have been apparent in the development of administrative procedures and the form of contracts.

It is unclear how far organisational forms will converge, as some of the isomorphic theories suggest, or whether diversity will continue. Such diversity may arise either as an adaptive response to different contexts or as purposeless flux in immature systems that fail to develop because of organisational uncertainties, frequent intervention by governments and lack of financial or cultural 'property rights' of the participants.

In the UK, it would appear that future developments in quasi-markets will become more relational in health and education; it is unlikely that quasi-markets in social care, the most resistant to quasi-market pressures so far, will develop further along market lines. It is expected that individual property rights will be attenuated further. Local groups, schools and professionals will be encouraged to cooperate and participate in community programmes which they will be able to develop and use in common.

Contracts, relationships, altruism and trust in quasi-markets

Simple contracting is rare in areas of welfare because bounded rationality and uncertainties prevail. There is scope for opportunism. There are situations in which contracts will need to specify in great detail the procedures to be followed; in other situations general clause contracts with 'reopener' clauses may be more suitable. Some sensitive contracting has been described by Lapsley and Llewellyn in Chapter Seven, but few contracts incorporate strategies to cope with particular types of ex ante or ex post opportunism that may arise (Allen, 1995; Hughes et al, 1997; Bartlett, 1991; 1994; Roberts, 1997; Maher, 1997).

However, it is the relationships that develop among the trading parties that provide the best guard against opportunism. Such relationships supplement contracts and may give rise to hybrid organisational forms, networks, neither market nor hierarchy but some mix that is more 'collaborative and trusting' than 'combative and competitive' (Di Maggio and Powell, 1991; Ferlie and Pettigrew, 1996; Hughes et al, 1997; Vincent-

Jones and Harries, Chapter One, this volume). The movement away from the strict behavioural assumption of individual self-interest in neoclassical economics is discussed in Chapter Two by McMaster. This movement arose from a greater appreciation that the agency relationship is embedded in cultural norms and customs. The norms and routines give guidance for acceptable behaviour in normal trading relationships. This provides the goodwill trust that exists between the parties (Sako, 1992). These issues seem to have been appreciated in proposals to reform the NHS (DoH, 1997).

Trust has been seen as an externality that diminishes behavioural uncertainty and so increases efficiency (Arrow, 1974). It is a characteristic of a trading partnership that would not indulge in opportunistic behaviour. Trust enables governance costs to be reduced. Trust takes time to build up but can be demolished in an instant and may be impossible to re-establish (Dasgupta, 1988). The nature of trust and its role in the operation of market relationships has been discussed many times (Arrow, 1974; Dasgupta, 1988; Deakin and Michie, 1997a; 1997b; Sako, 1992; Williamson, 1993). The theme is discussed in the context of quasi-markets in Chapter Two. Lyons and Mehta (1997), who distinguish 'self-interested trust' and 'social oriented trust', point to the danger of economists and sociologists adopting polar positions concerning trust. Burchell and Wilkinson (1997) documented aspects of trust that were important in business relationships.

For economists, trust is instrumental and its benefits calculable; for sociologists and anthropologists trust is embedded in social arrangements. Patterns of behaviour may be ingrained and represented by routines and ceremony. Both perspectives are valid. The transaction costs perspective needs support from other perspectives in particular from new institutionalism in sociology. Trust must involve mutual value systems. These mutual social and group value sets both mould and are moulded by the interaction between structures and individual agents (Bhasker, 1994). This perspective stresses the interdependence and continuing interplay between structures and agents in an emancipatory cycle (personal communication, Corry-Roberts, 1997). Lyons and Mehta (1997) recognise the interplay and argue that trust is unstable and can be manipulated. In formulating policy it is important to be aware of the dynamics of these interactions since policy may impose pressures that can undermine traditional patterns and disrupt functioning long-term relationships.

Lining up in contrast to the spectre of the self-interested agent is the altruistic agent (Di Maggio and Powell, 1991; Le Grand, 1997; McMaster, Chapter Two, this volume; Roberts, 1997). Whynes (1993) points out that individuals in many public services genuinely care and as such are willing to offer more than they need. This is an extension of the belief that all contractual relations for employment include potential gifts (Akerlof, 1982). This 'gift' is embodied in the culture of the organisation. The norms and customs may become embedded in routines and procedural conventions that reduce moral hazard since peer groups monitor, discipline and sanction group members who deviate from them. Altruistic behaviour can be affected by attempts to impose external control. Changes in existing conventions may be seen to infringe 'property rights' unfairly. Monitoring and regulation may be seen as signals of distrust. Resistance to controls may lead agents to ignore arrangements and base their decisions on the professional integrity and the interests of the client or patient or they may alienate workers who may become slack and inefficient. Monitoring potentially 'crowds out' work effort (Frey, 1993, quoted by McMaster in Chapter Two of this volume). This aspect of monitoring should be borne in mind by those who implement the new efficiency approach in the NHS in the UK (DoH, 1997)

Relationships that underpin contracts can be fractured by staff changes or by the establishment of new patterns of behaviour (Ferlie and Pettigrew, 1996). Many of the quasi-market experiments led to the importation of personnel from industry who brought to the new organisations new codes of ethics and behaviour. Hughes et al (1997) show how arrangements between trading partners can be discontinued as agents are replaced. The frequent staff changes, that have been a feature of many quasi-market developments, have often eaten away at the corporate memory. Recently an infectious disease ward, set up to control the spread of an antimicrobial resistant infection, was closed to meet pressing contractual arrangements for elective surgery. No one could recall the bleak scenario that had led to the opening of the ward. Changes in personnel can of course improve as well as destroy working relationships and facilitate better agreements (Hughes et al, 1997).

Relationships are many layered and interlocking; tasks are jointly conducted and interdependent. The central task is to manage these agency relationships. There are two approaches: one attempts to motivate agents to fulfil the objectives of the principal; the other attempts to protect those providing the services from the exigencies of the contract. The attempt to protect social workers from finance was picked up by Lewis (1994). Evidence of the professional ethic dominating the placing of contracts for care by social workers, who tend to place quality above price, is reported in Chapter Six by Mannion and Smith. The insulation of proximate providers from financial influences, advocated by Bevan (1952) on the setting up of the NHS, has been replaced (mainly as a result of the moral panics engendered by the possibilities of supplier-induced demand) by devolving management in initiatives such as 'resource management' that make clinical directorates financially and professionally responsible for services provided. Some movement in this direction preceded quasi-markets but this devolution of control in new public management structures has gained an increased momentum subsequently. Financial responsibility has been placed on headteachers and school governors and in some areas social workers have budgetary responsibility for clients. GP fundholders were rewarded indirectly for accepting financial responsibilities by having discretion to use surpluses to enhance the value of their practice.

Introductions of quasi-markets initially concentrated on so-called peripheral and separable functions such as cooking and cleaning. Ascher (1987) showed that tasks performed by ward maids and cleaners contributed to the management and monitoring of patients and to the provision of ancillary comforts and aids that contributed to patient well-being. Ascher also pointed out the loss of operating synergies that arise from dislocation of services by hiving off services such as cleaning. The complexity of interactions of many different agencies may be dealt with at the organisational level by evolving networks (Ferlie and Pettigrew, 1996). However, organisational networks may be insensitive to the need for close interaction among the people providing services. This needs to be addressed if gaps in services and demarcation disputes are to be avoided. The proposed involvement of staff at all levels in framing policy in the NHS recognises some of these issues (DoH, 1997).

The length of the agency chain and the dislocation of the proximate or end user from those involved in the contracting process in quasi-markets leads to problems. In Chapter One, Vincent-Jones and Harries showed that the standards of cleanliness, for example, are often determined by those not actively engaged in the day-to-day management of units being cleaned. This distancing of the contractors from the users of services is a problem common to many quasi-markets.

Choice in quasi-markets

Choice of provider or clients was to be the driving force of the quasi-market experiment but choice of trading partner seems illusory in most quasi-markets in the UK. The rhetoric of the New Right is heavily laden with a general distrust of professionals. Professionals find their professional discretion limited either by external constraints, protocols or contracts, the National Curriculum and OFSTED (Office for Standards in Education) (Broadbent and Laughlin, 1997). It is consumer choice, the feature anticipated in the legislation and rhetoric of quasi-markets, that appears to have been most compromised. The triangular relationship between end user, purchaser and provider of care limits choice in quasi-markets. Because of information biases the choice of agent is a factor determining the quality of the product in health, welfare or education. Choice of doctor is rarely exercised and choice of school is frustrated by capacity constraints and by selection procedures. The choice seems to be increasingly made by the school, not the parent or the child.

The external monitoring devices and financial payment structures have provided incentives for this development. Costs of disruptive pupils are greater than payment for taking them on. Performance indicators reinforce the tendency to search for education capital by adopting selection processes that further enhance the disparities and the choices on offer to parents and children (see also Chapter Four in this book by Vandenberghe). Schools have been able to 'walk away' from the disruptive and the less able. Schools that have been over subscribed can rarely expand to meet the demand so the unsuccessful are forced to move elsewhere. Such schools have characteristics of 'positional goods' and cannot because of their nature be used by all those wishing to join (Hirsch, 1977). The administrative arrangements associated with choice of GPs in the UK were eased but the inertia in the system is such that little movement takes place. Even if a choice of GP is made it is difficult for those choosing to know the full implications of that choice on arrangements for secondary care. In Chapter Nine, Mays and Dixon showed that more information is available if a managed care programme is chosen in the USA. In Chapter Eight, France describes the element of direct choice of secondary provider that is exercised by the patient in the Italian health sector. In Chapter Six, Mannion and Smith discuss how choice of care is exercised to a greater extent in the field of social services where the importance of individual in choice of services is recognised.

Whereas in most businesses expansion, development of new products, new markets, new sources of revenue is a driving force, in quasi-markets the opposite sometimes seems to be the case. Choice is increasingly restrained by budgetary pressure that makes 'rationing' and 'prioritising' the primary focus of choice. The agenda seems to be dominated by restricting the range of services offered. Cost neutral change (to imitate only those changes that have no impact on the overall budget) appears to be the pervading objective of those managing quasi-markets. This links the whole initiative back to the central philosophy of rolling back the state, supporting Whiteside's view (Chapter Ten of this book) that quasi-markets potentially provide a buffer for central authorities, deflecting responsibility from governments.

Sharing of capital investment with the private sector potentially both provides funds and offers the opportunity for expansion. However, mixed ownership of highly specific assets poses risks for both parties engaging in public financing initiatives. In the early shedding of assets and in some joint ventures it appeared that the private sector was more adept in risk limitation than the public sector (Roberts, 1993b). In more recent partnerships, private funders seem to face more risks and appear more wary of partnerships. Complex long-term franchising arrangements are likely to feature strongly if quasi-markets are to attract private sector capital investment.

Equity in quasi-markets

Resources are distributed by central governments to purchasing authorities. The financial arrangements used have compromised equity in some sectors. Arrangements for financing fundholding practices (Dixon et al, 1994), and directly managed schools (Barrow, Chapter Three, this volume), appear to have been biased towards those adopting the changes. It is still to be seen whether changes in the UK will remedy these inequities.

Adverse selection within the quasi-market undermines equity of access. This, highlighted by Scheffler (1989) as likely to prove the Achilles' heel of the NHS reforms, has occurred, although the potential gains from adverse selection or risk-sharing have not been fully exploited. The opportunism that arose from redefining a unit of hospital care as a 'consultant episode', so inflating the apparent throughput, has already been explored (Clarke and McKee, 1992; Magsaganis and Glennerster,

1994). Schools may embark on dual adverse selection by using exclusion to divest themselves of 'problem' children and selection to ensure an adequate supply of high achievers to enhance the school's league table performance and so add further inequities. As Bevan has shown in Chapter Eleven, legal aid is increasingly given to winnable cases.

Information imbalance has been a major constraint in the welfare sector. This imbalance can be reduced as consumers using new information technologies become as well informed about issues as some professionals. This suggests that new relationships with professionals may develop where discourse replaces direction. Information may not be accessible to all and thus a new equity problem may arise.

Budgetary pressures are likely to be a constant feature of quasi-markets so long as we are collectively unwilling to pay for the services that we individually wish to consume. Initiatives to reduce budgetary pressures include the introduction of user charges either for specific products previously included in the welfare sector, such as the transfer of drugs to over-the-counter provision or, as shown by France in Chapter Eight, as top up payments used in Italy to purchase services from providers that charge above the regional reimbursement levels. The introduction of user fees to fund services in many developing countries has given rise to concerns over equity of access (Abel-Smith, 1991), but these have been countered by claims that revenue collected from fees has provided services that otherwise could not have been funded (Vogel, 1988).

Summary

It is too early in the experiment for a comprehensive appraisal of the social costs and benefits of quasi-markets to be undertaken. Given the state of flux that exists evaluation will also be difficult. The emphasis on individual responsibility and choice that has dominated policy since the 1980s has deflected attention from structural problems, externalities that spill over from individual decisions and the public good aspects of welfare that require community initiatives. Social costs and benefits are not decreed away by the adoption of market policies.

Problems inherent in welfare sectors may not change as systems change but they may change as the underlying constraints yield to changed circumstances. Some impediments that relate to information may be removed as information becomes more widely available and the imbalance between the parties is reduced. Information systems should make monitoring easier and reduce the opportunity for moral hazard and risk selection.

Quasi-markets need management that is responsive – adjusting to correct anomalies (Enthoven, 1988). This management should involve the management of contracts, agents and market structures to ensure effectiveness and equity of services that are also comprehensive and offer choice (Roberts, 1993a). As Mays and Dixon point out in Chapter Nine, if consumers are to exercise any choice about what is purchased on their behalf then they should either be able to choose among providers themselves, as is the case of social services, or have the ability to elect or choose those making purchases on their behalf.

Management of market structures is undeveloped. The evidence so far shows little finesse has been used to formulate or monitor contracts. Management must address the complex aspects of the motivation of those working in the welfare sector, recognising that value systems of professionals can foster altruistic behaviour while also being aware that altruism may be tempered by self-interest. The appropriate balance between horizontal controls, based on convention, routines and processes monitored by peers, and vertical regulation, by protocol, charter targets, league tables and financial penalties enforced by external authorities, has not been addressed. If the economic approach is too crude then it is important not to be blinded by faith in relationships (Croxson, 1997). There is a tightrope that has to be walked in the management of agents providing social welfare. A more reflexive approach that allows for adjustment to be made as agency relationships and structures develop is required.

With the coming to power of a new Labour government in the UK in 1997 the quasi-market system of welfare provision is coming under close scrutiny. New directions in policy are opening up that will be shaped and constrained by the experience so far of operating quasi-markets. These assessments will be informed by the increasing number of research studies that are beginning to appear on these issues. Meanwhile, to gain the most benefit from quasi-markets they must be managed.

If it is decided to end the experiment in quasi-markets, losses may occur during the period of planning blight that might open up. It is important to be cautious:

> **the empirically important point is that opportunistic behaviour can be expected to re-emerge if ever the prospect**

**of an end to profitable exchange between particular partners
is expected in the near future. For dissembling, self-interested
individuals, history doesn't matter once the end of a
relationship looms large. (Lyons and Mehta, 1997, p 254)**

Emerging policies in the UK

The policies that are emerging from the various government departments
in the UK since the election appear to have several common themes. There
is a continuation of the theme of individual responsibility for welfare that
has been retained from the policy initiatives of the previous administration.
The implications of this for the various services is as yet unclear, but it
seems likely that responsibilities will be accompanied by support and
access to information and guidance. However, in the context of the
Welfare-to-Work philosophy, in particular, adopting such policies in a
less than buoyant labour market is likely to be both expensive to manage
and unlikely to reduce inequalities suffered by less advantaged workers.

The provision of information in the form of access to new
communication technologies in schools and the health sector and the
provision of advisory services in the health sector will do much to deal
with information imperfections. It is a positive and progressive aspect of
reforms in social policy. However, having provided people with
information it is necessary to ensure opportunities are available for them
to exercise choice. Patient surveys and expert opinion to assess good
practice is not likely to compensate those locked into a local purchasing
group that does not share their priorities.

Transaction costs have been perceived mainly as billing costs (which
are unnecessarily large and contravene Bevan's dictum that if everyone is
entitled to healthcare then there is no need for bits of paper flowing
around the country to prove it [1952]). Management was never entirely
absorbed in this activity and the need to achieve a well-informed national
service that is efficient, responsive and equitable requires good
management. The cuts in management, where managers are doing the
appropriate tasks, may be ill-advised. The idea of a contract for health
that recognises structural impediments to achieving good health is a
significant departure from trends towards the individualisation of welfare
(DoH, 1998).

In higher education there have been greater moves towards
individualisation and self-funding which embody the notion that benefits

of education go primarily to those educated at this level. Education for younger children is receiving greater attention and there is some retrenchment in the market structures that were developing as a result of greater autonomy enjoyed by opted out schools. Social care was the area that had seen least quasi-market developments in the allocation of resources although the provider market became largely private. In terms of legal aid, the quasi-market trajectory seems set to continue, and care needs to be given to the criteria adopted for aid if this trend is not to compromise both distributional equity and justice.

The challenge for the Labour administration, in reforming the welfare state, is to achieve distributional equity, security and efficiency without losing the goodwill and trust of both those who provide and those who receive services. Lessons from the early experiences of quasi-markets should not be ignored.

Bibliography

Abbott, P. and Wallace, C. (eds) (1990) *The sociology of the caring professions*, Brighton: Falmer Press.

Abel-Smith, B. (1991) 'Financing health for all', *World Health Forum*, vol 12, pp 191-200.

Agenzia Sanitaria Italiana (1996) 'Proposta di linee guida sui criteri di applicazione del processo di accreditamento', *Agenzia sanitaria Italiana*, vol 16, 22 April, pp 6-10.

Akerlof, G.A. (1970) 'The market of "lemons": quality, uncertainty and the market mechanism', *Quarterly Journal of Economics*, no 84, pp 488-500.

Akerlof, G.A. (1982) 'Labor contracts as partial gift exchange', *Quarterly Journal of Economics*, vol 94, pp 543-69.

Alchian, A.A. and Demsetz, H. (1972) 'Production, information, and economic organisation', *American Economic Review*, vol 62, pp 777-95.

Alchian, A.A. and Woodward, S. (1988) 'The firm is dead: long live the firm: a review of Oliver E. Williamson's "The economic institutions of capitalism"', *Journal of Economic Literature*, vol 26, pp 65-80.

Allen, P.W. (1995) 'Contracts in the NHS internal market', *Modern Law Review*, vol 58, pp 321-42.

Appleby, J. (1994a) 'The reformed National Health Service', *Social Policy and Administration*, vol 284, pp 345-358.

Appleby, J. (1994b) 'Monitoring managed competition', in R. Robinson and J. Le Grand (eds) *Evaluating the NHS reforms*, London: The King's Fund Institute, pp 24-53.

Arcangeli, L., Falcitelli, N. and Langiano, T. (1996) 'Rassegna dei provvedimenti regionali di determinazione delle tariffe delle prestazioni di assistenza ospedaliera', *Salute e Territorio*, XVII(94-95), pp 50-8.

Arnott, M., Bullock, A. and Thomas, H. (1992) 'Consequences of local management: an assessment by head teachers', Paper presented to the ERA Research Network, 12 February.

Arrow, K.J. (1963) 'Uncertainty and the welfare economics of medical care', *American Economic Review*, vol 53, pp 941-73.

Arrow, K.J. (1970) 'The organisation of economic activity: issues pertinent to the choice of market versus non-market allocation', in R.M. Haveman and J. Margolis (eds) *Public expenditure and policy analysis*, Chicago, IL: Markham.

Arrow, K.J. (1971) 'Political and economic evaluation of social effects and externalities', in M. Intriligator (ed) *Frontiers of quantitative economics*, Amsterdam: North Holland.

Arrow, K.J. (1974) *The limits of organisation*, New York. NY: Norton.

Artoni, R. and Saraceno, P. (1995) 'Federalismo e finanziamento della sanità', *Prospettive Sociali e Sanitarie*, vol 1, pp 10-17.

Ascher, K. (1987) *The politics of privatisation: Contracting out public services*, Basingstoke: Macmillan.

Assobiomedica (1995) *Tempi medi di pagamento delle unità sanitarie locali: Dati regionali*, Milan: Assobiomedica-Confindustria.

Association of Metropolitan Authorities (1994) *Reviewing local management of schools*, consultation document, London: AMA.

Audit Commission (1994) *Taking stock: progress with community care*, London: HMSO.

Audit Commission (1996) *What the doctor ordered: A study of GP fundholders in England and Wales*, London: HMSO.

Banting, K. (1995) 'The welfare state as statecraft: territorial politics and Canadian social policy', in S. Leibfried and P. Pierson (eds) *European social policy: Between fragmentation and integration*, Washington, DC: Brookings Institution.

Barber, M. (1997) 'Education leadership and the global paradox', in P. Mortimore and V. Little (eds) *Living education*, London: Paul Chapman.

Bariletti, A. and France, G. (1994) 'Riforme pro-concorrenziali per il settore sanitario ed economia dell'organizzazione', *Giornale degli Economisti e Annali di Economia*, vol 53, pp 51-80.

Bariletti, A. and France, G. (1996) 'Transaction cost economics and efficiency in health reform: the case of Italy', *Studi e Discussioni*, Florence: Dipartimento di Scienze Economiche, University of Florence.

Barrow, M. (1997) 'The Further Education Funding Council's new funding methodology', *Education Economics*, vol 5, no 2, pp 135-51.

Bartlett, W. (1991) *Quasi-markets and contracts: A market and hierarchies perspective on NHS reform*, Studies in Decentralisation and Quasi-markets No 3, Bristol: SAUS Publications.

Bartlett, W. (1992) *Quasi-markets and educational reforms: A case study*, Studies in Decentralisation and Quasi-markets, No 12, Bristol: SAUS Publications.

Bartlett, W. (1993) 'Quasi-markets and educational reforms', in J. Le Grand and W. Bartlett (eds) *Quasi-markets and social policy*, London: Macmillan.

Bartlett, W. and Le Grand, J. (1993) 'The theory of quasi-markets', in J. Le Grand and W. Bartlett (eds) *Quasi-markets and social policy*, London: Macmillan.

Bartlett, W., Propper, C., Wilson, D. and Le Grand, J. (eds) (1994) *Quasi-markets in the welfare state: The emerging findings*, Bristol: SAUS Publications.

Batley, R. and Stoker, G. (eds) (1991) *Local government in Europe: Trends and developments*, London: Macmillan.

Bautista, M.C.G. (1995) 'Markets in health care: An analysis of demand and supply and the market structure of primary care in the Philippines', PhD thesis London: London University.

Beale, H. and Dugdale, T. (1975) 'Contracts between businessmen: planning and the use of contractual remedies', *British Journal of Law and Society*, vol 2, pp 45-60.

Bénabou, R. (1996) 'Equity and efficiency in human capital investment: the local connection', *Review of Economic Studies*, vol 63, no 2, pp 237-64.

Bevan, A. (1952) *In place of fear*, London: Heinemann.

Bevan, G. (1996) 'Has there been supplier-included demand for legal aid?', *Civil Justice Quarterly*, vol 15, pp 98-114.

Bevan, G. and Price, C. (1990) 'Roles of case-mix measures in managing use of resource', in R. Leidl, P. Potthoff and D. Schwefel (eds) *European approaches to patient classification systems*, London: Springer-Verlag, pp 35-51.

Bevan, G., Holland, T. and Partington, M. (1996) 'Organising cost-effective access to justice', in A.A. Paterson and T. Goviely (eds) *Resourcing civil justice*, Oxford: Oxford University Press, pp 281-303.

Bevan, G., Fenn, P. and Rickman, R. (1998) *Contracting for legal services with different cost rules*, London: LCD, Research Series no 3/98.

Beveridge, W. (1924) Initially published in the *Atheneum*, this formed the basis for *Insurance for All and Everything*.

Bhasker, R. (1994) *Plato etc*, London: Verso.

Billiet, J. (1977) *Secularisering en verzuiling in het onderwijs: Een sociologisch onderzoek naar de vrije schoolkeuse als legitimatie schema en als sociaal proces*, Leuven, Belgium: Leuven University Press.

Binmore, K. and Samuelson, L. (1994) 'An economist's perspective on the evolution of norms', *Journal of Institutional and Theoretical Economics*, (Symposium on New Institutional Economics: Bounded Rationality and the Analysis of State and Society), vol 150, pp 45-63.

Black, D.G., Birchall, A.P. and Trimble, I.M.G. (1994) 'Non-fundholding in Nottingham: a vision of the future', *British Medical Journal*, vol 309, pp 930-2.

Bland, R., Bland, R., Cheetham, J., Lapsley, I. and Llewellyn, S. (1992) *Residential homes for elderly people: Their cost and quality*, London: HMSO.

Blank, R. (1990) 'Educational effects of magnet high schools', in W.H. Clune and J.F. Witte (eds) *Choice and control in American education*, vol 2, London: Falmer Press.

Blankenberg, E. (1992) 'Comparing legal aid schemes in Europe', *Civil Justice Quarterly*, vol 11, pp 106-14.

Blankenberg, E. (1995) 'Access to justice and alternatives to courts: European procedural justice compared', *Civil Justice Quarterly*, vol 14, pp 176-89.

Bonus, H. (1986) 'The co-operative association as a business enterprise', *Journal of Institutional and Theoretical Economics*, vol 142, pp 310-39.

Borland, J. (1994) 'On contracting out: some labour market considerations', *Australian Economic Review* (Policy Forum on Competitive Tendering), 3rd Quarter, pp 86–90.

Bosi, P., Giarda, P., Morcaldo, G. and Tabellini, G. (1994) 'Gli squilibri della finanza pubblica italiana', in Ministero del Tesoro, Comitato Tecnico per la Spesa Pubblica (ed) *Il Controllo della Spesa Pubblica: Interpretazioni e Proposte*, Rome: Istituto Poligrafico e Zecca dello Stato.

Bowe, R. and Ball, S. with Gold, A. (1992) *Reforming education and changing schools*, London: Routledge.

Bowles, S. and Gintis, H. (1993) 'An economic strategy for democracy and equality', Mimeo, Amherst, MA: Department of Economics, University of Massachusetts.

Bradach, J.L. and Eccles, R.G. (1991) 'Price, authority and trust: from ideal types to plural forms', in G. Thompson, J. Francis, R. Levačić, R. and J. Mitchell (eds) *Markets, hierarchies and networks: The coordination of social life*, London: Sage Publications.

Bramley, G. (1993) 'Quasi-market and social housing', in J. Le Grand and W. Bartlett (eds) *Quasi-markets and social policy*, London: Macmillan.

Breton, A. (1987) 'Towards a theory of competitive federalism', *European Journal of Political Economy*, vol 3, 263-329.

Breton, A. and Wintrobe, R. (1982) *The logic of bureaucratic conduct: An economic analysis of competition, exchange, and efficiency in private and public organisations*, Cambridge: Cambridge University Press.

Briggs, A. (1979) *The history of broadcasting in the United Kingdom*, vol 4, Oxford: Oxford University Press.

Broadbent, J. and Laughlin, R. (1997) 'Contracts and competition? A reflection on the nature and effects of recent legislation on modes or control in schools', *Cambridge Journal of Economics*, vol 21, pp 277-90.

Brock, W.A. and Durlauf, S.N. (1995) *Discrete choice with social interactions I: theory*, Working Paper No 5291, Cambridge, MA: National Bureau of Economic Research.

Brooks-Gunn, J., Duncan, G.J., Klebanov, P.K. and Sealand, N. (1993) 'Do neighborhoods influence child and adolescent development?', *American Journal of Sociology*, vol 99, pp 353-95.

Bryk, A.S., Lee, V.E. and Holland, P.B. (1993) *Catholic schools and the common good*, Cambridge, MA: Harvard University Press.

Buchanan, J.M. (1965) 'An economic theory of clubs', *Economica*, vol 32, pp 1-14.

Buckley, P.J. and Chapman, M. (1997) 'The perception and measurement of transaction costs', *Cambridge Journal of Economics*, vol 21.

Bullock, A. and Thomas, H. (1994) *The impact of local management of schools: Final report*, Birmingham: University of Birmingham.

Burchell, B. and Wilkinson, F. (1997) 'Trust, business relationships and the contractual environment', *Cambridge Journal of Economics*, vol 21, pp 217-37.

Bush, T., Coleman, M. and Glover, D. (1993) *Managing autonomous schools*, London: Paul Chapman.

Campbell, D. and Harris, D. (1993) 'Flexibility in long-term contractual relationships: the role of co-operation', *Journal of Law and Society*, vol 20, pp 166-91.

Carnaghan, R. and Bracewell-Milnes, B. (1993) *Testing the market: Competitive tendering for government services in Britain and abroad*, London: Institute for Economic Affairs.

Carr-Hill, R.A. (1992) 'The measurement of patient satisfaction', *Journal of Public Health Medicine*, vol 14, pp 236-49.

CBI (Confederation of British Industry) (1989a) *Towards a skills revolution – a youth charter*, interim report of the Vocational Education and Training Task Force, London: CBI.

CBI (1989b) *Towards a skills revolution*, report of the Vocational Education and Training Task force, London: CBI

CBI (1993a) *Routes of success*, London: CBI.

CBI (1993b) *A credit to your career*, London: CBI.

CBI (1994) *Thinking ahead: Ensuring the expansion of higher education into the 21st century*, London: CBI.

CERI (Centre for Educational Research and Innovation (1994) *School: A matter of choice*, Paris: CERI, OECD.

Chandler, A.D. (1977) *The visible hand: The managerial revolution in American business*, Cambridge, MA: Harvard University Press.

Chandler A.D. and Daems, H. (1979) 'Administrative coordination, allocation and monitoring: a comparative analysis of the emergence of accounting and organisations in the USA and Europe', *Accounting, Organisations and Society*, vol 4, pp 3-20.

Chatrick, B. (1994) *Careers change*, London: Youthaid/UNISON.

Chatrick, B. (1997) 'Who's running the careers service now?', *Working Brief*, vol 81, pp 17-20.

Chubb, J.E. and Moe, T.M. (1990) *Politics, markets and America's schools*, Washington, DC: The Brookings Institution.

Clark, C. with Asquith, V. (1985) *Social work and social philosophy: A guide for practice*, London: Routledge and Kegan Paul.

Clarke, A. and McKee, M. (1992) 'The consultant episode: an unhelpful measure', *British Medical Journal*, vol 304, pp 1307-88.

Clewell, B.C. and Joy, M.F. (1990) *Choice in Montclair, New Jersey*, Princeton, NJ: ETS.

Clune, W.H. and Witte, J.F. (eds) (1990) *Choice and control in American education*, vol 1 and 2, The Stanford Series on Education and Public Policy, London: The Falmer Press.

Coase, R.H. (1937) 'The nature of the firm', *Economica*, vol 4, pp 386-405, reprinted in O.E. Williamson, S.G. Winter (eds) (1991) *The nature of the firm*, Oxford: Oxford University Press.

Coase, R. (1988) 'The lighthouse in economics', reprinted in *The firm, the market and the law*, Chicago: University of Chicago Press.

Coleman, J.S., Campbell, E.Q., Hobson, C.F., McPartland, J. Mood, A.M., Weifeld, F.D. and York, R.L. (1966) *Equality of educational opportunity*, OE-38001, Washington, DC: US Office of Education, US Department of Health, Education and Welfare.

Coleman, J.S., Hoffer, T. and Kilgore, S. (1982) *High school achievement: Public, catholic and private schools*, New York, NY: Basic Books.

Congdon, T., Sturgess, B., NERA, Shew, W.B., Graham, A. and Davies, G. (1992) *Paying for broadcasting: The handbook*, BBC, London: Routledge.

Coopers & Lybrand (1988a) *Strategy for competition: A model for the 1990s*, London: Coopers & Lybrand.

Coopers & Lybrand (1988b) *Local management of schools: A report to the Department of Education and Science*, London: Coopers & Lybrand.

Coopers & Lybrand (1994) *Gateways to learning national evaluation: Final report*, London: Coopers & Lybrand.

Coopers & Lybrand (1995) *National evaluation of skills choice: Final report*, London: Coopers & Lybrand.

Corcoran, M., Gordon, R., Laren, D. and Solon, G. (1990) 'Effects of family community background on economic status', *American Economic Review*, vol 80, pp 362-6.

Cousins, M. (1993) 'Civil legal aid in France, Ireland, The Netherlands and the United Kingdom – a comparative study', *Civil Justice Quarterly*, vol 12, pp 154-66.

Cousins, M. (1994) 'The politics of legal aid – a solution in search of a problem?', *Civil Justice Quarterly*, no 18, pp 111-32.

Croxson, B. (1997) *Co-operation, competition and the NHS internal market*, Discussion Paper 2/97, Aberdeen: Health Economics Research Unit, Department of Public Health and Economics.

Dalziel, P. and Lattimore, R. (1996) *The New Zealand macroeconomy: A briefing on the reforms*, Melbourne: Oxford University Press.

Dasgupta, P. (1988) 'Trust as a commodity', in D. Gambetta (ed) *Trust: Making and breaking co-operative relations*, Oxford: Basil Blackwell.

Davies, H. (1992) *Fighting Leviathan: Building social markets that work*, London: Social Market Foundation.

Davies, R. (1995) 'Workers and medical services', in J. Edwards, *Tinopolis*, Llanelli Historical Society.

Davis, L.E. and North, D.C. (1971) *Institutional change and American economic growth*, Cambridge: Cambridge University Press.

De Alessi, L. (1983) 'Property rights, transaction costs, and X-efficiency', *American Economic Review*, no 73, pp 64-81.

Deacon, A. (1977) *In search of the scrounger*, London: LSE.

Deakin, S. and Michie, J. (eds) (1997a) *Contracts, cooperation and competition: Studies in economics, management and law*, Oxford: Oxford University Press.

Deakin, S. and Michie, J. (1997b) 'Contracts and competition: an introduction', *Cambridge Journal of Economics*, vol 21, no 2, pp 121-5.

Deakin, S. and Wilkinson, F. (1996) 'Contracts, cooperation and trust: the role of the institutional framework', in D. Campbell and P. Vincent-Jones (eds) *Contract and economic organisation: Socio-legal initiatives*, Aldershot: Dartmouth.

Dei Ottati, G. (1994) 'Trust, interlinking transactions and credit in the industrial district', *Cambridge Journal of Economics*, no 18, pp 529-46.

Desideri, C. and Santantonio, V. (1996) 'Building a "third level" in Europe: prospects and difficulties in Italy', *Journal of Regional and Federal Studies*, vol 6, no 2, pp 96-116.

DfE (1992) *Choice and diversity*, White Paper, Cm 2021, London: HMSO.

DfE (1993) *A common funding formula for self-governing (GM) schools*, consultation paper, London: HMSO.

DfE (1994a) *Statistical Bulletin 8*, London: HMSO.

DfE (1994b) *The disparity in funding between primary and secondary schools*, Select Committee on Education, HC 45-I, London: HMSO.

DfEE (Department for Education and Employment) (1996a) *National funding for GM schools*, Discussion paper, London: HMSO.

DfEE (1996b) *Self-government for schools*, White Paper, Cm 3315, London: HMSO.

DfEE (1997) *Excellence in schools*, London: HMSO.

Di Biase, R. and Citoni, G. (1994) 'Italy', in OECD (ed) *The reform of health care systems: A review of seventeen OECD countries*, Paris: OECD.

Di Maggio, P. and Powell, W. (1991) 'The iron cage revisited: institutional isomorphism and collective rationality in organisational fields', *American Sociological Review*, vol 35, pp 147-60.

Dingwall, R. and Fenn, P. (1987) 'A respectable profession? Sociological and economic perspectives on the regulation of professional services', *International Journal of Law and Economics*, vol 7, pp 51-64.

Dirindin, N. (1995) 'La riforma del finanziamento del sistema sanitario', paper presented at the *IV Riunione della Società Italiana di Economia Pubblica*, Pavia, 6-7 October.

Dixon, J. and Glennerster, H. (1995) 'What do we know about fundholding in general practice?', *British Medical Journal*, vol 311, pp 727-30.

Dixon, J., Dunwoodie, M., Hodson, D., Dodd, S., Pottorak, T., Garret, C. Rice, P., Doncaster, I. and Williams, M. (1994) 'Distribution of NHS funds between fundholding and non-fundholding practices', *British Medical Journal*, vol 309, pp 30-4.

Dobra, J.L. (1983) 'Property rights in bureaucracies and bureaucratic efficiency', *Public Choice*, vol 40, pp 121-40.

DoH (Department of Health) (1989a) *Working for patients*, Secretaries of State for Health, Wales, Northern Ireland, Scotland, Cm 555, London: HMSO.

DoH (1989b) *Caring for people: Community care in the next decade and beyond*, Cm 849, London, HMSO.

DoH (1991) *Purchase of service: practice guidance and practice material for SSDs and other agencies*, London: HMSO.

DoH (1994a) *Developing NHS purchasing and GP fundholding*, EL(94)79, Leeds: NHSE; accompanying booklet: *Developing NHS purchasing and GP fundholding. Towards a primary care-led NHS*, Leeds: NHSE.

DoH (1994b) *An accountability framework for GP fundholding: Towards a primary care-led NHS*, EL(94)92, Leeds: NHSE.

DoH (1996) *Choice and opportunity: Primary care the future*, Cm 3390, London: HMSO.

DoH (1997) *The new NHS: Modern, dependable*, Secretary of State for Health, London: The Stationery Office.

DoH (1998) *Our healthier nation: A contract for health*, Cm 3852, London: HMSO.

Domanico, R.J. (1990) *Restructuring New York City's public schools: The case for public school choice*, Education Policy Paper No 3, New York, NY: Manhattan Institute for Policy Research.

Domberger, S., Hall, C. and Li, E.A.L. (1995) 'The determinants of price and quality in competitively tendered contracts', *Economic Journal*, vol 105, pp 1454-70.

Domberger, S., Meadowcroft, S.A. and Thompson, D.J. (1986) 'Competitive tendering and efficiency: the case of refuse collection', *Fiscal Studies*, vol 7, pp 69-84.

Domberger, S., Meadowcroft, S.A. and Thompson, D.J. (1987) 'The impact of competitive tendering on the costs of hospital domestic services', *Fiscal Studies*, vol 8, pp 39-55.

Doyal, L. and Gough, I. (1991) *A theory of human need*, London: Macmillan.

Dreyfus, M., Kott, S., Pigenet, M. and Whiteside, N. (1998) 'Les bases multiples du syndicalisme en Allemagne, France et Grande Bretagne', in A. Prost and J.L. Robert (eds) *L'invention des syndicalismes en Europe occidentale*, Paris: Presse de la Sourbonne.

Dugger, W.M. (1983) 'The transaction cost economic of Oliver E. Williamson: a new synthesis?', *Journal of Economic Issues*, vol 17, pp 95-114.

Duncan, G.J. (1994) 'Families and neighbors as sources of disadvantage in the schooling decisions of white and black adolescents', *American Journal of Education*, no 103, pp 20-53.

Dunleavy, P.J. (1991) *Democracy, bureaucracy, and public choice: Economic explanations in political science*, London: Harvester Wheatsheaf.

Dunsire, A., Hartley, K.J., Parker, D. and Dimitriou, B. (1988) 'Organisational status and performance: a conceptual framework for testing public choice theories', *Public Administration*, vol 66, pp 363-88.

Dynarski, M., Schwab, R.M. and Zampelli, E. (1989) 'Local characteristics and public production: the case of education', *Journal of Urban Economics*, vol 26, pp 250-63.

Earl, P. (1983) *The economic imagination: Towards a behavioural analysis of choice*, New York, NY: Sharpe.

Easton, B. (1994) 'Economic and other ideas behind the New Zealand reforms', *Oxford Economic Review of Economic Policy*, vol 10, pp 78-94.

Eastwood, M. (1994) 'High planes drifter blazing a trail...', *Careers Guidance Today*, vol 2, pp 14-16.

Edwards, T., Fitz, J. and Whitty, G. (1989) *The state and private education: An evaluation of the assisted places scheme,* London: Falmer Press.

Employment Department (1994) *Prospectus for the provision of careers services from April 1995,* London: Employment Department.

Enthoven, A.C. (1987) 'The health care economy in the USA', in G. Teeling Smith (ed) *Health economics: Prospects for the future,* London: Croom Helm.

Enthoven, A.C. (1988) 'Managed competition: an agenda for action', *Health Affairs*, vol 7, pp 25-47.

Evans, R.G. (1981) 'Incomplete vertical integration: the distinctive structure of the health care industry', in J. Van der Gaag and M. Parlman (eds) *Health, economics, and health economics,* Proceedings of the World Congress on Health Economics, Leiden, The Netherlands, September 1980, Amsterdam: North Holland.

Evans, R.G. (1987a) 'Hang together, or hang separately: the viability of universal health care system in an aging society', *Canadian Public Policy*, vol xiii, pp 165-80.

Evans, R.G. (1987b) 'Public purchase of health insurance: the collective provision of individual care', *Health Policy*, vol 7, pp 115-34.

Evans, W.N., Oates, W.E. and Schwab, R.M. (1992) 'Measuring peer group effects: a study of teenage behavior', *Journal of Political Economy*, vol 100, pp 966-91.

Ezzamel, M. and Wilmott, H. (1993) 'Corporate governance and financial accountability: recent reforms in the UK public sector', *Accounting, Auditing and Accountability Journal*, vol 6, pp 109-33.

Fama, E.F. and Jensen, M.C. (1983) 'Agency problems and residual claimants', *Journal of Law and Economics*, vol 26, pp 327-50.

Feintuck, M. (1994) *Accountability and choice in schooling,* Buckingham: Open University Press.

Ferlie, E. and Pettigrew, M. (1996) 'Managing through networks: some issues and implication for the NHS', *British Journal of Management*, vol 7, Special Issue, March, S81-S99.

Fitz, J., Halpin, D. and Power, S. (1993) *Grant maintained schools: Education in the marketplace*, London: Kogan Page.

Fliegel, S. with Macguire, J. (1990) *Miracle in East Harlem: The fight for choice in public education*, New York, NY: Random House.

Fowler, M. (1993) *Factors influencing choice of secondary schools*, Christchurch: University of Canterbury.

Fox, A. (1974) *Beyond contract: Work, power and trust relations*, London: Faber and Faber.

France, G. (1996) 'Governance of two national health services: Italy and the United Kingdom compared', in G. Pola, G. France and R. Levaggi (eds) *Developments in local government finance: Theory and policy*, Cheltenham: Edward Elgar.

France G. (1997) 'L'introduzione di riforme pro-concorrenziali nel Servizio sanitario nazionale: vorrei e non vorrei', *L'Assistenza Sociale*, nos 1-2, pp 73-89.

Frantz, R.S. (1988) *X-efficiency: Theory, evidence and applications*, Boston, MA: Klumer.

Frantz, R.S. (1992) 'X-efficiency and allocative efficiency: what have we learned?', *American Economic Review* (Papers and Proceedings), no 82, pp 434-8.

Frey, B.S. (1993) 'Does monitoring increase work effort? The rivalry with trust and loyalty', *Economic Inquiry*, vol 31, pp 663-70.

Friedman, M. (1962) 'The role of government in education', in M. Friedman, *Capitalism and freedom*, Chicago: University of Chicago Press.

Full Employment UK (1991a) *Investing in skills, Part Four*, London: Full Employment UK.

Full Employment UK (1991b) *Investing in skills, Part Seven: Developing fee-charging adult guidance services*, London: Full Employment UK.

Gamoran, A. and Nystrand, M. (1994) 'Tracking, instruction and achievement', *International Journal of Educational Research*, vol 21, pp 217-31.

Geddes, M. (ed) (1994) *La salute degli Italiani – Rapporto 1993*, Rome: La Nuova Italia Scientifica.

Gewirtz, S., Ball, S.J. and Bowe, R. (1995) *Markets, choice and equity*, Buckingham: Open University Press.

Glenn, C.L. (1989) *Choice of school in six nations: France, Netherlands, Belgium, UK, Canada, West-Germany*, Washington, DC: Office of Educational Research and Improvement.

Glennerster, H. (1991) 'Quasi-markets for education ?', *Economic Journal*, vol 101, pp 1268-76.

Glennerster, H. and Le Grand, J. (1994) 'The development of quasi-market in welfare provision', *Comparing Social Welfare Systems in Europe* (MIRE, Recontres et Recherches).

Glennerster, H. and Le Grand, J. (1995) 'The development of quasi-markets in welfare provision in the United Kingdom', *International Journal of Health Services*, vol 25, pp 203-18.

Glennerster, H., Cohen, A. and Bovell, V. (1996) *Alternatives to fundholding*, Discussion Paper WSP/123, Welfare State Programme, London: Suntory and Toyota International Centres for Economics and Related Disciplines, LSE.

Glennester, H., Matsaganis, M., Owens, P. with Hancock, S. (1994) *Implementing GP fundholding*, Buckingham: Open University Press.

Goldberg, V.P. (1980) 'Relational exchange: economics of complex contracts', *American Behavioural Scientist*, vol 23, pp 337-52.

Goldsmith, M. and Willetts, D. (1988) *Managed health care: A new system for a better health service*, London: Centre for Policy Studies.

Goodin, R.E. (1982) 'Freedom and the welfare state: theoretical foundations', *Journal of Social Policy*, vol 11, vol 2, pp 149-76.

Gordon, L. (1994) '"Rich" and "Poor" Schools in Aotearoa', *New Zealand Journal of Educational Studies*, vol 29, pp 113-25.

Goriely, T. (1992) 'Legal aid in the Netherlands: a view from England', *Modern Law Review*, vol 55, pp 803-21.

Graffy, J.P. and Williams, J. (1994) 'Purchasing for all: an alternative to fundholding', *British Medical Journal*, vol 308, pp 391-4.

Graham, A. and Davies, G. (1992) 'The public funding of broadcasting', in T. Congdon et al, *Paying for broadcasting: The handbook*, BBC, London: Routledge, pp 167-221.

Granovetter, M. (1985) 'Economic action and social structure: the problem of embeddedness', *American Journal of Sociology*, vol 91, pp 481-510.

Granovetter, M. and Swedberg, R. (1992) *The sociology of economic life*, Oxford: Westview Press.

Gray, A. (1991) 'A mixed economy of health care', in A. McGuire et al (eds) *Providing health care: The economics of alternative systems of finance and delivery*, Oxford: Oxford University Press.

Gray, A. (1994) 'The reform of legal aid', *Oxford Review of Economic Policy*, vol 10, pp 51-67.

Gray, J. (1993) *Beyond the New Right: Markets, government and the common environment*, London: Routledge.

Ham, C. (1996) *Public, private or community – what next for the NHS?*, London: Demos.

Ham, C. and Shapiro, J. (1995) *Integrating purchasing: Lessons from experience*, Discussion Paper 35, Birmingham: Health Services Management Centre, University of Birmingham.

Harris, J. (1977) *William Beveridge*, Oxford: Oxford University Press.

Harris, J. (1986) 'Political ideas and the debate on social welfare', in H.J. Smith, *War and Social Change*, Manchester: Manchester University Press.

Hartley, K.J. (1990) 'Contracting out in Britain: achievements and problems', in J. Richardson (ed) *Privatisation and deregulation in Canada and Britain*, Dartmouth: Institute for Research on Public Policy.

Hawthorn, R. (1992) 'Guidance vouchers for adults: how effective are they?', *Newscheck*, vol 2, pp 8-10.

Health Service Journal (1996) 'Flavour of the month' [by M. Limb], 14 March, p 18.

Henderson, V., Mieszkowski, P. and Sauvageau, Y. (1978) 'Peer group effects and educational production functions', *Journal of Public Economics*, vol 10, pp 97-106.

Henig, J.R. (1994) *Rethinking school choice: Limits of the market metaphor*, Princeton, NJ: Princeton University Press.

Hill, P.T., Foster G.E. and Gendler, T. (1990) *High schools with character*, Santa Monica, CA: RAND.

Hirsch, F. (1997) *Social limits to growth*, London: Routledge and Kegan Paul.

Hirschman, A.O. (1970) *Exit, voice and loyalty: Response to decline in firms, organizations and states*, Cambridge, MA: Harvard University Press.

HMSO (1926) Royal Commission on National Health Insurance (RCNHI), Report and Evidence, Cmd 2596, Evidence Appendix I, section 8, p 10.

HMSO (1986) *Report on the Committee on Financing the BBC*, Cmnd 9824 (Chairman Professor Alan Peacock), London: HMSO.

HMSO (1996) *Royal Charter for the continuance of the British Broadcasting Corporation*, Cmnd 3248, London: HMSO.

HMSO (1998) *New ambitions for our country: A new contract for welfare*, London: HMSO.

HMSO Beveridge Committee (1942) *Social insurance and allied services*, Cmd 6404/1942.

Hodgson, G.M. (1991) *After Marx and Sraffa: Essays in political economy*, Basingstoke: Macmillan.

Holtham, G. and Kay, J. (1994) 'The assessment: institutions of policy', *Oxford Review of Economic Policy*, vol 10, pp 1-16.

Hope, M. (1997) *Expenditure on legal services*, Research Series No 9/97, London: LCD.

Horne, M. (1987) *Values in social work*, Aldershot: Ashgate.

Hudson, B. (1994) *Making sense of markets in health and social care*, Sunderland: Business Education Publishers.

Hughes, D. (1991) 'The reorganisation of the National Health Service: the rhetoric and the reality of the internal market', *Modern Law Review*, no 54, pp 88-103.

Hughes, D., Griffiths, L. and McHale, J. (1997) 'Do quasi-markets evolve? Institutional analysis and the NHS', *Cambridge Journal of Economics*, vol 21, pp 259-76.

Hughes, G. (1990) 'The economics of contracting out', in R.G. Milne (ed) *Competitive tendering and the public sector*, Proceedings of a Conference, Glasgow: Centre for Urban Regional Research, University of Glasgow, April.

Institute of Careers Guidance (1996) *Careers guidance for adults*, Stourbridge: Institute of Careers Guidance.

Istituto Nazionale di Statistica (1994a) *Le regioni in cifre – 1994*, Rome: Istituto Nazionale di Statistica.

Istituto Nazionale di Statistica (1994b) *Conti economici regionali*, Rome: Istituto Nazionale di Statistica.

Istituto Nazionale di Statistica (1995) *Le regioni in cifre – 1995*, Rome: Istituto Nazionale di Statistica.

James, E. (1986) 'Public subsidies for private education: the Dutch case', in D.C. Levy (ed) *Private education. Studies in choice and public policy*, New York, NY: Oxford University Press.

Jencks, C. and Meyer, S.E. (1987) 'The social consequences of growing up in poor neighborhoods', in L.E. Lynn and M.G.H. MacGeary (eds) *Inner-city poverty in the United States*, Washington, DC: National Academy Press.

Kahnemann, D., Knetsch, J.L. and Thaler, R.H. (1986) 'Fairness as a constraint on profit seeking: entitlements in the market', *American Economic Review*, no 76, pp 728-41.

Kay, N.M. (1982) *The evolving firm: Strategy and structure in industrial organisation*, London: Macmillan.

Khalil, E.L. (1994) 'Trust', in G.M. Hodgson, W.J. Samuels and M.R. Tool (eds) *The Elgar companion to institutional and evolutionary economics*, Aldershot: Edward Elgar.

Killeen, J., White, M. and Watts, A.G. (1992) *The economic value of careers guidance*, London: Policy Studies Institute.

Klein, R.E. (1991) 'The American health care predicament. Spending more and feeling worse', *British Medical Journal*, vol 303, pp 259-60.

Knapp, M.R.J. (1986) 'The relative cost effectiveness of public, voluntary, and private providers of residential child care', in A.J. Culyer and B. Jonsson (eds) *Public and private health services*, Oxford: Blackwell.

Labour Party (1995) *Renewing the NHS: Labour's agenda for a healthier Britain*, London: Labour Party.

Laffont, J. and Tirole, J. (1993) *A theory of incentives in procurement and regulation*, Cambridge, MA: MIT Press.

Lancaster, K.J. (1966) 'A new approach to consumer theory', *Journal of Political Economy* no 74, pp 132-57.

Lansley, J. and Whittaker, T. (1994) 'Structural issues in befriending and advocacy: evaluation of a befriending scheme for elders in residential care', *Generations Review*, vol 4, no 1, pp 8-10.

Lapsley, I. and Llewellyn, S. (1995) 'Real life constructs: the exploration of organizational processes in case studies', *Management Accounting Research*, vol 6, pp 223-35.

Lauder, H., Hughes, D., Waslander, S., Thrupp, M., McGlinn, J., Newton, S. and Dupuis, A. (1994) *The creation of market competition for education in New Zealand*, Smithfield Project, Wellington: Victoria University of Wellington.

LCD (Lord Chancellor's Department) (1995) *Legal aid – targeting need*, Green Paper, Cm 2854, London: HMSO.

LCD (1996) *Striking the balance – the future of legal aid in England and Wales*, White Paper, Cm 3305, London: HMSO.

Le Grand, J. (1991) 'Quasi-markets and social policy', *Economic Journal*, vol 101, pp 1256-67.

Le Grand, J. (1997) 'Knights, knaves or pawns? Human behaviour and social policy', *Journal of Social Policy*, vol 26, pp 149-64.

Le Grand, J. and Bartlett, W. (eds) (1993) *Quasi-markets and social policy*, London: Macmillan.

Le Grand, J. and Estrin, S. (1989) *Market socialism*, Oxford: Clarendon Press.

Lee, V.E. and Bryk, A.S. (1993) 'Science or policy argument?' in G. Rassell and R. Rothstein (eds) *School choice: Examining the evidence*, Washington, DC: Economic Policy Institute.

Leibenstein, H. (1966) 'Allocative efficiency vs 'X-efficiency'', *American Economic Review*, vol 56, pp 392-415 [also in Leibenstein, H. (1989)].

Leibenstein, H. (1975) 'Aspects of the X-efficiency theory of the firm', *Bell Journal of Economics*, vol 6, pp 580-606 [also in Leibenstein, H. (1989)].

Leibenstein, H. (1976) *Beyond economic man: A new foundation for microeconomics*, Cambridge, MA: Harvard University Press.

Leibenstein, H. (1979) 'A branch of economics is missing: micro–micro theory', *Journal of Economic Literature*, vol 17, pp 477-502 [also in Leibenstein, H. (1989)].

Leibenstein, H. (1984) 'On the economic conventions and institutions: an explanatory essay', *Journal of Institutional and Theoretical Economics*, vol 140, pp 74-86.

Leibenstein, H. (1987) 'On some economic aspects of a fragile input: trust', in G.R. Feiwel (ed) *Arrow and the foundations of the theory economic policy*, Basingstoke: Macmillan.

Leibenstein, H. (1989) *The collected essays of Harvey Leibenstein: Volume II; X-efficiency and micro–micro theory*, Aldershot: Edward Elgar.

Leibenstein, H. and Maital, S. (1994) 'The organisational foundations of X-inefficiency: a game-theoretic interpretation of Argyris' model of organisational learning', *Journal of Economic Behaviour and Organisation*, vol 23, pp 251-68.

Leroy-Audouin, C. (1995) *Les modes de groupement des élèves à l'école primaire, catalyseurs des performances*, Cahier de l'Iredu No 95009, Dijon: Iredu.

Levačić, R. (1992a) 'An analysis of differences between historic and formula school budgets: evidence from LEA LMS submissions and from detailed study of two LEAs', *Oxford Review of Education*, vol 18, pp 75-100.

Levačić, R. (1992b) 'Local management of schools: aims, scope and impact', *Educational Management and Administration*, vol 20, pp 16-29.

Levačić, R. (1995) *Local management of schools: Analysis and practice*, Milton Keynes: Open University Press.

Lewis, J. (1994) 'Care management and the social services: reconciling the irreconcilable', *Generations Review*, vol 4, pp 2-4.

Liberal Democrat Party (1995) *Building on the best of the NHS: Proposals to reform the National Health Service*, Policy Paper 14, London: Liberal Democratic Party.

Link, C.R. and Mulligan, J.G. (1991) 'Classmates' effects on black student achievement in public school classrooms', *Economics of Education Review*, vol 10, pp 297-310.

Lipsky, M. (1980) *Street level bureaucracy: Dilemmas of the individual in public services*, New York, NY: Russell Sage Foundation.

Little, S. (1995) 'GPs to seize buying role for whole district', *Fundholding*, 24 January, p 5.

Llewellyn, S. (1998) 'Pushing budgets down the line: ascribing financial responsibility in the UK social services', *Accounting, Auditing and Accountability Journal*, forthcoming.

Local Government Management Board (1995) *CCT information service*, London: LGMB.

Long, A.F. and Sheldon, T.A. (1992) 'Enhanced, effective and acceptable purchaser decisions: overview and methods', *Quality in Health Care*, vol 1, pp 74-6.

Loughlin, M. (1994) 'The re-structuring of central–local government relations', in J. Jowell and D. Oliver (eds) *The changing constitution*, Oxford: Clarendon.

Lyons, B. and Mehta, J. (1997) 'Contracts, opportunism and trust, self-interest and social orientation', *Cambridge Journal of Economics*, vol 21, pp 239-57.

Macaulay, S. (1963) 'Non-contractual relations in business: a preliminary study', *American Sociological Review*, vol 28, pp 55-67.

Macneil, I. (1978) 'Contracts: adjustment of long-term economic relations under classical, neo-classical, and relational contract law', *Northwestern University Law Review*, vol 72, pp 854-905.

Macneil, I.R. (1982) 'Economic analysis of contractual relations', in R. Burrows and C.G. Veljanovski (eds) *The economic approach to law*, London: Butterworths.

Magsaganis, M. and Glennerster, H. (1994) 'The threat of cream skimming in the post-reform NHS', *Journal of Health Economics*, vol 13, pp 331-60.

Maher, M. (1997) 'Transaction cost economics and contractual relations', *Cambridge Journal of Economics*, vol 21, pp 147-70.

Mannion, R. and Smith, P. (1997a) 'How purchasing decisions are made in the mixed economy of care', *Financial Accountability and Management*, vol 13, no 3, pp 243-60.

Mannion, R. and Smith P. (1997b) 'Trust and reputation in community care: theory and evidence', in P. Anand and A. McGuire (eds) *Changes in healthcare: Reflections on the NHS internal market*, London: Macmillan.

Mapelli, V. (1995a) 'Cost-containment measures in the Italian healthcare system', *Pharmaeconomics*, vol 8, pp 85-90.

Mapelli, V. (1995b) 'Ipotesi di riforma regionale del SSN', *Prospettive Sociali e Sanitarie*, vol 2, pp 2-9.

Mason, A. and Morgan, K. (1995) 'Purchaser–provider: the international dimension', *British Medical Journal*, vol 310, pp 231-5.

Matthews, R.C.O. (1991) 'The economics of professional ethics: should the professions be more like a business?', *Economic Journal*, vol 101, pp 737-50.

Mays, N. and Dixon, J. (1996) *Purchaser plurality in UK health care*, London: King's Fund Publishing.

Mays, N., Goodwin, N., Bevan, G. and Wyke, S. (on behalf of Total Purchasing National Evaluation Team) (1997) *Total purchasing: A profile of national pilot projects*, London: King's Fund Publishing.

McGuire, A., Henderson, J. and Mooney, G. (1988) *The economics of health care*, London: Routledge and Kegan Paul.

McMaster, R. (1995) 'Competitive tendering in UK health and local authorities: what happens to the quality of services?,' *Scottish Journal of Political Economy*, vol 42, pp 409-27.

Migue, J.L. and Belanger, G. (1974) 'Towards a general theory of managerial discretion', *Public Choice*, vol 17, pp 27-47.

Milgrom, P. and Roberts, J. (1992) *Economics, organisation and management*, London: Prentice Hall.

Mills, A. (1995) *Improving the efficiency of public sector health services in developing countries, bureaucratic versus market approaches*, PHP Papers No 17, London: London School of Hygiene and Tropical Medicine.

Milne, R.G. and McGee, M. (1992) 'Compulsory competitive tendering in the NHS: a new look at some old estimates', *Fiscal Studies*, no 13, pp 96-111.

Ministère de l'éducation, de la recherche et de la formation (Ministry of Education) (1993) *Annuaire Statistique 1991-92*, Bruxelles: Services des Statistiques, Communauté Française de Belgique.

Ministero della Sanità (1994a) *Rendiconti trimestrali delle unità sanitarie locali – Dati analitici – 4 trimestre 1993*, Rome: Servizio Centrale della Programmazione Sanitaria.

Ministero della Sanità (1994b) *Attività gestionali ed economiche delle unità sanitarie locali – Anno 1992*, Rome: Servizio Centrale della Programmazione Sanitaria.

Ministero della Sanità (1995) *Attività gestionali ed economiche delle unità sanitarie; locali – Anno 1993*, Rome: Servizio Centrale della Programmazione Sanitaria.

Ministry of Health (1939) *National Health Insurance and contributory pension insurance*, London: HMSO.

Miron, G. (1993) *Choice and the use of market forces in schooling: Swedish education reforms for the 1990s*, Stockholm, Sweden: Institute of Education, Stockholm University.

Moe, T. (1994) 'The British battle for choice', in K.L. Billingsley (ed) *Voices on choice: The education reform debate*, San Francisco, CA: Pacific Institute for Public Policy.

Mooney, G. (1994) *Key issues in health economics*, London: Harvester Wheatsheaf.

Moore, D. and Davenport, S. (1990) 'School choice: the new improved sorting machine', in W. Boyd and H. Walberg (eds) *Choice in education*, Berkeley, CA: McCutchan.

Morris, M. and Stoney, S. (1996) *An evaluation of the performance of pathfinder careers services*, QADU RD12, London: Choice and Careers Division, DfEE.

Mueller, D.C. (1989) *Public choice II: A revised edition*, Cambridge: Cambridge University Press.

NACCEG (National Advisory Council for Careers and Educational Guidance) (1996) *Consultation paper on a national strategy for adult guidance,* London: RSA.

National Association of Community Health Councils for England and Wales (1995) *The accountability of fundholding,* Health News Briefing, London: NACHCEW.

National Audit Office (1987) *Competitive tendering for support services in the National Health Services,* London: HMSO.

Nelson, R.R. and Winter, S.G. (1982) *An evolutionary theory of economic change,* Cambridge, MA: Harvard University Press.

Niskanen, W.A. (1968) 'Non-market decision making: the peculiar economics of bureaucracy', *American Economic Review* (Papers and Proceedings), vol 58, pp 293-305.

Niskanen, W.A. (1971) *Bureaucracy and representative government,* Chicago, IL: Aldine-Atherton.

Noll, R., Peck, M. and McGowan, J. (1973) *Economic aspects of television regulation,* Washington, DC: The Brookings Institution.

Nooteboom (1992) 'Towards a dynamic theory of transaction', *Journal of Evolutionary Economics,* vol 2, pp 281-99.

North, D.C. (1994) 'Economic performance through time', *American Economic Review,* no 84, pp 359-68.

OECD (1992a) *The reform of health care: A comparative analysis of seven OECD countries,* Paris: OECD.

OECD (1992b) *OECD economic surveys – Italy,* Paris: OECD.

Office for Public Management (1994) *The North East Westminster locality purchasing project: An evaluation,* London: Kensington Chelsea and Westminster Commissioning Agency/Office for Public Management.

Orzechowski, W. (1977) 'Economic models of bureaucracy: survey, extensions and evidence', in T.E. Borcherding (ed) *Budgets, and bureaucrats: The sources of government growth,* Durham, NC: Duke University Press.

Osborne, D. and Gaebler, T. (1992) *Reinventing government,* Reading, MA: Addison-Wesley.

Ouchi, W.G. (1977) 'The relationship between organisational structure and organisational control', *Administrative Science Quarterly*, vol 22, pp 95-113.

Ouchi, W.G. (1979) 'A conceptual framework for the design of organisational control mechanisms', *Management Science*, vol 25, no 9, pp 833-8.

Ouchi, W.G. (1980) 'Markets, bureaucracies, and clans', *Administrative Science Quarterly*, vol 25, pp 129-41.

Ouchi, W. (1991) 'Markets, bureaucracies and clans', in G. Thompson, J. Frances, R. Levačić and J. Mitchell (eds) *Markets, hierarchies and networks: The co-ordination of social life*, London: Sage.

Ouchi, W.G. and Price, R.L. (1978) 'Hierarchies, clans and theory Z: a new perspective of organisation development', *Organisational Dynamics*, Autumn, pp 25-44.

PA Cambridge Economic Consultants (1993) *Research on the labour market need for advice and guidance services: Final report*, Cambridge: PACEC.

Paterson, A. (1991) 'Legal aid at the crossroads', *Civil Justice Quarterly*, vol 10, pp 124-37.

Paton, C. (1993) 'Devolution and centralism in the National Health Service', *Social Policy and Administration*, vol 27, pp 83-108.

Peacock, A. (1979) *The economic analysis of government and related themes*, Oxford: Robertson.

Peacock, A.T. (1983) 'Public X-inefficiency: informational and institutional constraints', in H. Hanusch (ed) *The anatomy of government deficiencies*, Berlin: Springer-Verlag.

PEP (Political and Economic Planning) (1937) *Report on the National Health Services*, London: PEP.

Perlman, H.H. (1975) 'Self determination: reality or illusion', in F.E. McDermott, *Self-determination in social work*, London: Routledge and Kegan Paul.

Perrow, C. (1981a) 'Markets, hierarchies and clans', *Administration Science Quarterly*, vol 25, pp 129-40.

Perrow, C. (1981b) 'Markets, hierarchies and hegemony', in A. van de Ven and W.F. Joyce (eds) *Perspectives on organisation and design and behaviour*, Wiley.

Pierson, P. (1994) *Dismantling the welfare state? Reagan, Thatcher and the politics of retrenchment*, Cambridge: Cambridge University Press.

Plank, S., Schiller, K.S., Schneider, B. and Coleman, J.S. (1993) 'Effects of choice in education', in E. Rassell and R. Rothstein (eds) *School choice: Examining the evidence*, Washington, DC: Economic Policy Institute.

Pollard, S. (1995) *Schools, selection and the Left*, London: Social Market Foundation.

Powell, M.A. (1996) 'The ghost of health services past', *International Journal of Health Services*, vol 26, no 2.

Powell, W.W. (1990) 'Neither market nor hierarchy: network forms of organisation', *Journal of Organisational Behaviour*, vol 12, pp 295-336, as adapted in G. Thompson, J. Frances, R. Levacic and J. Mitchell (eds) *Markets hierarchies and networks*, London: Open University Press/Sage Publications.

Power, S., Fitz, J. and Halpin, D. (1994) 'Parents, pupils and grant maintained schools', *British Educational Research Journal*, vol 20, no 2, pp 209-26.

Propper, C. (1992) *Quasi-markets, contracts and quality*, Studies in Decentralisation and Quasi-Markets No 9, Bristol: SAUS Publications.

Propper, C. (1995) 'Regulatory reforms of the NHS Internal Markets', *Health Economics*, vol 4, pp 77-83.

Public Record Office (1925a) Correspondence and papers on file PIN 3/117.

Public Record Office (1925b) Papers and correspondence on file ACT 1/247.

Public Record Office (1930) Note on draft of Cmd 3458, no 5 (nd), PIN 4/11.

Public Record Office (1932) Epps to Kinnear, 23 May: on file, ACT 1/485.

Public Record Office (1933) Paper on file PIN 4/33.

Public Record Office (1934) A survey of the recent history of the National Health Insurance, by Sir Walter Kinnear: on file, PIN 3/41.

Putnam, R.D., Leonardi, R. and Nanetti, R. (1985) *La pianta e le radici: il radicamento dell'istituto regionale nel sistema politico Italiano*, Bologna: Il Mulino.

Rafferty, J., Mulligan, J., Forrest, S. and Robinson, R. (1994) *Third national review of contracts, 1994-95*, Leeds: NHS Executive.

Raywid, M.A. (1994) 'Focus schools: a genre to consider', Urban Diversity Series No 106, New York, NY: ERIC Clearinghouse on Urban Education, Columbia University.

Reed, M. and Anthony, P. (1993) 'Between an ideological rock and an organisational hard place: NHS management in the 1980s and 1990s', in T. Clarke and C. Pitelis (eds) *The political economy of privatisation*, London: Routledge.

Rees, R. (1985) 'The theory of principal and agent part 1: the theory of principal and agent part 2', *Bulletin of Economic Research*, vol 37, pp 3-26 and 75-95.

Roberts, J.A. (1993a) 'Managing markets in the reformed NHS', *Journal of Public Health Medicine*, vol 4, pp 1-7.

Roberts, J.A. (1993b) 'Public Eye November 5 and 12 1993 – Review', *British Medical Journal*, November 22, vol 37, pp 1364-5.

Roberts, J.A. (1997) *Journeying to Agathotopia: Scope for opportunism and altruism in reformed health sectors*, London: Department of Public Health and Policy, London School of Hygiene and Tropical Medicine.

Robinson, J.C. and Casalino, L.P. (1996) 'Vertical integration and organizational networks in health care', *Health Affairs*, no 15, pp 7-22.

Robinson, R., Appleby, J. et al (1991) 'Who's playing Monopoly?', *The Health Service Journal*, vol 101, no 5245, pp 20-2.

Rodwin, M.A. (1993) *Medicine, money and morals: Physicians' conflicts of interest*, New York, NY: Oxford University Press.

Rojek, C., Peacock, G. and Collins, S. (1988) *Social work and received ideas*, London: Routledge.

Rossell, C.H. and Glenn, C.L. (1988) 'The Cambridge controlled choice plan', *Urban Review*, vol 20, pp 75-94.

Rothbard, M. (1977) *Power and market*, Kansas City, KS: Sheed Andrews and McMeel.

Rowann, J. (1993) 'Legal aid in New Zealand', *New Zealand Law Journal*, pp 396-401.

Rowley, C.K. and Elgin, R. (1985) 'Towards a theory of bureaucratic behaviour', in D. Greenaway and G.K. Shaw (eds) *Public choice, public finance, and public policy: Essays in honour of Alan Peacock*, Oxford: Blackwell.

Rumberger, R.W. and Willms, J.D. (1992) 'The impact of racial and ethnic segregation on the achievement gap in California high schools', *Educational Evaluation and Policy Analysis*, vol 14, pp 377-96.

Sako, M. (1991) 'The role of "trust" in Japanese buyer-supplier relationships', *Ricerche Economiche*, vol 45, pp 449-74.

Sako, M. (1992) *Price, quality and trust*, Cambridge: Cambridge University Press.

Salmon, P. (1987) 'Decentralization as an incentive scheme', *Oxford Review of Economic Policy*, vol 3, pp 24-43.

Savas, E.S. (1987) *Privatisation: The key to better government*, Chatham, NJ: Chatham House.

Schanze, E. (1991) 'Symbiotic contracts: exploring long-term agency structures between contract and corporation', in C. Joerges (ed) *Franchising and the law: Theoretical and comparative approaches in Europe and the United States*, Baden-Baden: Nomos.

Scheffler, R. (1989) 'Adverse selection: the Achilles' heel of the NHS reforms', *Lancet*, vol 1, pp 950-2.

Schramm, C.J. and Gabel, J. (1988) 'Prospective payment. Some retrospective observations', *New England Journal of Medicine*, no 318, pp 1681-6.

Seal, W. and Vincent-Jones, P. (1996) *Accounting and trust in the enabling of long-term relations*, School of Financial Studies and Law Working Paper, Sheffield: Sheffield Hallam University.

Services des Statistiques (1993) *Annuaire Statistiques 1991-92,* Bruxelles: Ministère de l'éducation, de la recherche et de la formation, Communauté Française de Belgique.

Sexton, S. (1987) *Our schools – a radical policy*, Warlingham: Institute of Economic Affairs, Education Unit.

Sharpe, T. (1996) *The learning society: The role of adult guidance*, CRAC/ NICEC Conference Briefing, Cambridge: CRAC.

Shen, T.Y. (1985) 'Worker motivation and X-efficiency', *Kyklos*, vol 38, pp 392-411.

Shen, T.Y. (1992) 'Towards a general theory of X-efficiency', *Journal of Socio-Economics*, vol 20, pp 277-95.

Shleifer, A. (1985) 'A theory of yardstick competition', *Rand Journal of Economics*, vol 16, no 3, pp 319-27.

Simon, H.A. (1991) 'Organisations and markets', *Journal of Economic Perspectives*, vol 5, pp 25-44.

Smith, C. (1996) 'A health service for a new century: Labour's proposals to replace the internal market in the NHS', speech by the Shadow Health Secretary, 3 December, London: Labour Party.

Smith, K.B. and Meier, K.J. (1995) *The case against school choice: Politics, markets and fools*, Armonk, NY: M.E. Sharpe.

Smith, K.B. and Wright, K. (1994) 'Principals and agents in social care: who's on the case and for whom?', Discussion Paper 123, York: Centre for Health Economics.

Smith, S.R. and Lipsky, M. (1993) *Nonprofits for hire*, Cambridge, MA: Harvard University Press.

Smith, T. and Noble, M. (1995) *Education divides: Poverty and schooling in the 1990s*, London: Child Poverty Action Group.

Starey, N., Bosanquet, N. and Griffiths, J. (1993) 'General practitioners in partnership with management: an organisational model for debate', *British Medical Journal*, vol 306, pp 308-10.

Stephen, F.H., Love, J.H. and Paterson, A.A. (1994) 'Deregulation of conveyancing markets in England and Wales', *Fiscal Studies*, vol 15, pp 102-18.

Stewart, J. (1993) 'The limitations of government by contract', *Public Money and Management*, vol 13, no 3, July-September, pp 7-12.

Stigler, G. (1976) 'The X-istence of X-efficiency', *American Economic Review*, vol 66, pp 213-16.

Stiglitz, J.E. (1991) 'Symposium on organisations and markets', *Journal of Economic Perspectives*, vol 5, no 2, pp 15-24.

Stinchcombe, A. (1985) 'Contracts as hierarchical documents', in A. Stinchcombe and C. Heimer (eds) *Organization theory and project management*, Oslo: Norwegian University Press.

Strong, P. and Robinson, J. (1990) *The NHS – under new management*, Milton Keynes: Open University Press.

Summers, A.A. and Wolfe, B.L. (1977) 'Do schools make a difference?', *American Economic Review*, vol 67, pp 639-52.

Szymanski, S. and Wilkins, S. (1993) 'Cheap rubbish? Competitive tendering and contracting out in refuse collection', *Fiscal Studies*, vol 14, pp 109-30.

TEC National Council (1994) *Individual commitment to lifetime learning*, London: TEC National Council.

The Guardian (1996) 'Labour tilts to GP fundholding' [by D. Brindle], 9 March.

The Guardian (Society) (1996) 'Picking and mixing' [by C. Ham], 29 May.

The Times Educational Supplement (1988) 'Peers back policy on open enrolment' [by L. Blackburne], 13 May.

Thomas, H. and Bullock, A. (1992) 'School size and local management funding formulae', *Educational Management and Administration*, vol 20, no 1, pp 30-7.

Thorelli, H. (1986) 'Networks: between markets and hierarchies', *Strategic Management Journal*, vol 7, p 37.

Timms, N. (1983) *Social work values: an enquiry*, London: Routledge and Kegan Paul.

Tirole, J. (1994) 'The internal organisation of government', *Oxford Economic Papers*, vol 46, pp 1-29.

Tooley, J. (1995) 'Markets or democracy? A reply to Stewart Ranson', *British Journal of Educational Studies*, vol 43, pp 31-4.

Vandenberghe, V. (1996) *Functioning and regulation of educational quasi-markets*, unpublished PhD dissertation, CIACO, Nouvelle Serie No 283, Louvain-la-Neuve, Belgium: IRES, Université Catholique de Louvain.

Vincent, C., Evans, J., Lunt, I. and Young, P. (1995) 'Policy and practice: the changing nature of special educational provision in schools', *British Journal of Special Education*, vol 22, pp 4-11.

Vincent-Jones, P. (1994a) 'The limits of contractual order in public sector transacting', *Legal Studies*, vol 14, pp 364-92.

Vincent-Jones, P. (1994b) 'The limits of near-contractual governance: local authority internal trading under CCT', *Journal of Law and Society*, vol 21, p 214-37.

Vincent-Jones, P. (1996) 'Hybrid organisation, contractual governance and CCT in the provision of local authority services', Paper presented to ESRC seminar on 'Contracts and Competition', University of Essex, June.

Vincent-Jones, P. and Harries, A. (1996a) 'Limits of contract in internal CCT transactions: a comparative study of buildings cleaning and refuse collection in Northern Metropolitan', in D. Campbell and P. Vincent-Jones (eds) *Contract and economic organisation: Socio-legal initiatives*, Aldershot: Dartmouth.

Vincent-Jones, P. and Harries, A. (1996b) 'Conflict and cooperation in local authority quasi-markets: the hybrid organisation of internal contracting under CCT', *Local Government Studies*, vol 22, pp 187-209.

Vogel, H. (1994) *Entertainment industry economics: A guide for financial analysis*, 3rd edn, Cambridge: Cambridge University Press.

Vogel, R. (1988) *Cost recovery in the health sector: Selected costing studies in West Africa*, World Bank Technical Paper No 82, Washington, DC: The World Bank.

Walford, G. (1992) 'Educational choice and equity in Great Britain', *Educational Policy*, vol 6, pp 123-38.

Walsh, K. (1991) 'Quality and public services', *Public Administration*, no 69, pp 503-14.

Walsh, K. (1995) 'Competition for white-collar services in local government', *Public Money and Management*, vol 11, pp 11-18.

Walsh, K. and Davis, H. (1993) *Competition and service: The impact of the Local Government Act 1988*, London: HMSO.

Waslander, S. and Thrupp, M. (1995) 'Choice, competition and segregation: an empirical analysis of a New Zealand secondary school market 1990-93', *Journal of Education Policy*, vol 10, no 1, pp 1-26.

Watts, A.G. (1991) 'The impact of the "New Right": policy challenges confronting careers guidance in England and Wales', *British Journal of Guidance and Counselling*, vol 19, no 3, pp 230-45.

Watts, A.G. (1994) *A strategy for developing careers guidance services for adults*, CRAC Occasional Paper, Cambridge: CRAC.

Watts, A.G. (1996) 'Measuring the impact of the careers service', *Newscheck*, vol 6, pp 7-8.

Watts, A.G., Guichard, J., Plant, P. and Rodriguez, M.L. (1994) *Educational and vocational guidance in the European Community*, Brussels: Commission of the European Communities.

Watts, A.G., Hawthorn, R., Hoffbrand, J., Jackson, H. and Spurling, A. (1997) 'Developing local lifelong guidance strategies', *British Journal of Guidance and Counselling*, vol 25, no 2, pp 217-27.

Webster, C. (1985) 'Health, welfare and unemployment during the depression', *Past and Present*, no 109.

Wells, A.S. (1993) *Time to choose: America at the crossroads of school choice policy*, New York, NY: Hill and Wang.

Whiteside, N. (1983) 'Private agencies for public purposes: some new perspectives on policy making in health insurance between the wars', *Journal of Social Policy*, vol 12, pp 165-93.

Whiteside, N. (1987) 'Counting the cost: sickness and disability among working people in an era of industrial depression', *Economic History Review*, vol xl, pp 228-46.

Whiteside, N. (1988) 'Unemployment and health: an historical perspective', *Journal of Social Policy*, vol 17, pp 177-94.

Whiteside, N. (1992) *Bad times: Unemployment in British social and political history*, London: Faber and Faber.

Whitty, G., Edwards, T. and Gewirtz, S. (1993) *Specialisation and choice in urban education: The City Technology College experiment*, London: Routledge.

Whynes, D.K. (1993) 'Can performance monitoring solve the public services' principal–agent problem?', *Scottish Journal of Political Economy*, no 40, pp 434-46.

Williamson, O.E. (1975) *Markets and hierarchies*, New York, NY: Free Press.

Williamson, O.E. (1985) *The economic institutions of capitalism: Firms, markets, and relational contracting*, New York, NY: Free Press.

Williamson, O.E. (1990) 'The firm as a nexus of treaties: an introduction', in M. Aoki, B. Gustafsson, and O.E. Williamson (eds) *The firm as a nexus of treaties*, London: Saga, pp 1-25.

Williamson, O.E. (1991a) 'Comparative economic organization: the analysis of discrete structural alternatives', *Administrative Science Quarterly*, vol 269, no 36, pp 269-96.

Williamson, O.E. (1991b) 'The logic of economic organisation', in O.E. Williamson and S.G. Winter (eds) *The nature of the firm: Origins, evolution and development*, Oxford: Oxford University Press.

Williamson, O.E. (1993) 'Calculativeness, trust and economic organisation', *Journal of Law and Economics*, vol 4, pp 53-86.

Williamson, O.E. and Ouchi, W.G. (1981) 'The markets and hierarchies and visible hands perspectives', in A. van de Ven and W.F. Joyce (eds) *Perspectives on organisational design and behaviour*, Chichester: Wiley.

Willms, D.J. and Echols, F. (1992) 'Alert and inert clients: the Scottish experience of parental choice of schools', *Economics of Education Review*, vol 11, pp 339-50.

Winkler, D.R. (1975) 'School peer composition', *The Journal of Human Resources*, vol 10, pp 189-201.

Witte, J.F., Thorn, C.A., Pritchard, K.M. and Claibourn, M. (1994) *Fourth year report: Milwaukee Parental Choice Program*, Madison, WI: Department of Public Instruction.

Wohlstetter, P., Wenning, R. and Briggs, K.L. (1995) 'Charter schools in the United States: the question of autonomy', *Educational Policy*, vol 9, no 4, pp 331-58.

World Health Organisation (1996) *Health care systems in transition: Sweden, Copenhagen,* World Health Organisation, Regional Office for Europe.

Worthman, L. and Cretin, S. (1986) *Review of the literature on diagnosis-related groups,* Santa Monica, CA: Rand.

Wylie, C. (1994) *Self managing schools in New Zealand: The fifth year,* Wellington: New Zealand Council for Educational Research.

Wylie, C. (1995) 'Contrary currents: the application of the public sector reform framework in education', *New Zealand Journal of Educational Studies,* vol 20, pp 149-64.

Zucker, L.G. (1986) 'Production of trust, institutional sources of economic structure, 1840-1920', *Research in Organisational Behaviour,* pp 53-111.

Index

Please note: figures/tables are indeicated by italics, unless there is related text on the same page.

A

Abbott, P. 138
Abel-Smith, B. 287
ability gap
    in Belgian study 82, 94
accountability
    in NHS purchasing 189-90
activity plasticity 53, 54, 57
Agenzia Sanitaria Italiana 170
Akerlof, G.A. 51, 220, 221, 283
Alchian, A.A. 48, 53
Allen, P.W. 281
allocative efficiency 5
altruism 4, 283, 288
    see also Hippocratic ethos;
        professionals; social work
        ethos
ancillary services (health) 284
    and Hippocratic ethos 50-2,
        54-6
annual maintenance grant (AMG)
    for GM schools 66
Anthony, P. 50, 52
Appleby, J. 277, 279
APQT bundles 45
    in ancillary health services 51-
        2
    and ex ante specification 53-5,
        56, 57
arbitration 22
    in Eastmet 28-9, 41n17

Arcangeli, L. 173n12
Arnott, M. 100
Arrow, K.J. 47, 219, 261, 282
Artoni, R. 172n6
Ascher, K. 50-1, 52, 284
Asquith, V. 137
asset specificity
    in contracting 135, 224
assisted places scheme (APS) 96,
    107
    New Zealand equivalent 98
Assobiomedica 169
Association of Metropolitan
    Authorities 76
Audit Commission 121, 189

B

Banting, K. 172n6
Barber, Michael 108
Bariletti, A. 161, 171n1
Barrow, Michael 6, 63-77, 286
Barrowclough, Diana 15, 257-74,
    280
Bartlett, Will
    on quasi-markets 1-16, 79, 80,
        101, 112, 156, 275-9
    in education 64, 102
    performance criteria 155,
        212, 246-7, 264
Batley, R. 171
Bautista, M.C.G. 277

BBC
  as public good 261, 262, 269-70, 272
  as quasi-market 258, 266, *267,* 268, 274n2
  Producer Choice 264, 266, 268
Beale, H. 23
behaviour
  and choice 115
  and organisations 134, *135,* 278
  see also bounded rationality; opportunism
Belanger, R. 43
Belgium
  education quasi-markets 79-80, 91-2
    and ability segregation 6-7, 80-6
    peer effects 87-8, 89
    regulation 89-91
Bénabou, R. 87
Best Value framework 37-8
Bevan, A. 284, 289
Bevan, Gwyn 13-14, 219-35, 276, 287
Beveridge, W. 206
  Report (1942) 202, 203, 204, 211, 213
Bhasker, R. 282
bilateral contracting 22, 23, 36, 37
  example: Eastmet (1990-) 29-32
Billiet, J. 79
Birmingham University LMS study 100-1
Black, D.G. 187
Bland, R. 138, 139
Blank, R. 99
Blankenberg, E. 226

Bonus, H. 53
Borland, J. 53
Bosi, P. 172n5
bounded rationality 3
  in choice/decision making 10, 115, 142, 150
  in contracting 53, *135,* 140, 224, 281
  and legal aid 13, 224
  in organisations 134, *135,* 278
Bowe, R. 101, 102
Bowles, S. 79, 89
Bracewell-Milnes, B. 52, 53
Bradach, J.L. 114
Bramley, G. 3
Breton, A. 52, 171
Briggs, A. 261
Broadbent, J. 285
broadcasting
  challenges to 262-4
  commercial 260-1
  direct payment 261, 263, 273
  as public good 257, 259-62, 263
  as quasi-market 257-8, 264-5, *267*
    in New Zealand cf UK 266-74
Broadcasting Act (NZ, 1989) 266
Brock, W.A. 87
Brooks-Gunn, J. 88
Bryk, A.S. 105
Buchanan, J.M. 263
Buckley, P.J. 279
Bullock, A. 64, 100
Burchell, B. 282
Buros voor Rechtshulp 231, 232
Bush, T. 103

C

Campbell, D. 23
Canada
    healthcare financing 172n6
care *see* community care; social care
care managers
    and budgeting 9-10, 121-2,
        130-1, 141, 144, 152
    ethics *see* social work ethos
careers guidance 14-15
    contracts 244-8, 252
    as market-maker *vs* market in
        guidance 242-4, 253-4
    real *vs* quasi-market 252-3
    voucher system 244, 248-52
Carnaghan, R. 52, 53
Carr-Hill, R.A. 127
Casalino, L.P. 194
cash protection: for GM schools 66,
    68
CBI (Confederation of British
    Industry)
    on careers guidance 242, 243-
        5, 251
CERI (Centre for Educational
    Research and Innovation) 80
Chandler, A.D. 134
Chapman, M. 279
Chatrick, B. 245, 247
choice, provider *see* provider choice
Chubb, J.E. 79, 89, 105
Citoni, G. 161
city technology colleges (CTCs)
    97, 102
'clan' culture 136, 140
Clark, C. 137
Clarke, A. 286
class sizes

reduction 77
cleaning, buildings
    case studies 23, 24-36
Clewell, B.C. 104
Clune, W.H. 79
Coase, R.H. 39n3, 134, 232, 263,
    274n3
Coleman, J.S. 87, 105
collective goods 240
common funding formula (CFF) 63,
    64, 67-9, 75, 76
    vs LMS 6, 70-2
community care 111, 112-13
    fieldwork: method 115-16
    as market 113, 115
    provider choice
        decisions 128-31
        financial issues 117-18, 121
        LA preferences 124-8
        local market 118-20
        organisation 120-2
        politics 120
        and population needs 116-
            17
        user preferences 122-4
    quality assessment 125, 131
community schools 76, 108
competitiveness
    measurement 277
compulsory competitive tendering
    (CCT) 4-6, 43, 49, 52-4
    abolition 37-8
    activities, defined 39n4, 49
    for careers guidance 244, 245
    case studies
        in contracting 24-37
        conflictual 25-9
        cooperative

bilateral 29–32, 36, 37
trilateral 32–7
organisation, effects on 19–24
and X-efficiency 49–58
Conditional Fee Agreements 234
conflict(s)
contractual 24, 39n2
case study 25–9
and inefficiency 38n2
of interest
in NHS purchasing 190
Congdon, T. 259, 273
Conservatives
and careers guidance 244
and central state power 40n9
and legal aid changes 226–7
social policies 1–2, 15, 16
consumer choice 285–6
in community care 122–4
in healthcare 11, 184–5
in legal aid 228
contracts/contracting 245–6
behavioural assumptions 53, *135,* 140, 224, 281
in careers guidance 244–8, 252
for CCT 20
case studies *see under* compulsory competitive tendering
uses/displacement 22–3, 31, 35–6
and conflict 24, 39n2
case study 25–9
enforceability in internal markets 39n5
form in community care 122
management, effective 42n23
officers 140–1, 150
in social care 136, 151, 281, 284

'soft' 136, 151, 281
transaction costs 246–7, 279
variations 36, 41n21
conventions
as 'clan' culture 136, 140
and effort 46–7, 49, 51
and employment 'gifts' 51, 283
public service ethos 4, 283
and trust 47–9, 54, 55
see also Hippocratic ethos; professionals; social work ethos
Co-operative Approved Society 210
Coopers & Lybrand 25, 65, 249–50
Corcoran, M. 87
corporate culture 136, 140
Corry-Roberts, S. 282
cost centres: in CCT 20, 52, 53
Cousins, M. 225, 226
cream skimming
and legal aid 13
in schools *see under* schools
Cretin, S. 235n7
Croxson, B. 288

D

Daems, H. 134
Dalziel, P. 274n1
Dasgupta, P. 48, 282
Davenport, S. 99
Davies, G. 261–2
Davies, Howard 241, 242, 246, 247
Davies, R. 209
Davis, H. 21, 40n5, 42n23
Davis, L.E. 155–6
De Alessi, L. 59n1

Deacon, A. 203
Deakin, S. 3, 39n2, 282
decentralisation: effects 4
Demsetz, H. 48
Department for Education and
    Employment (DfEE)
    (1996) 64, 69–70, 73
    (1997) 7, 108, 275
Department for Education (DfE)
    67, 68, 70, 71
Department of Employment 247
Department of Health (DoH)
    (1989) 122, 175
    (1991) 112
    (1994) 178, 180, 182, 186, 189
    (1996) 190, 194
    (1998) 2, 13, 275, 276, 278, 284,
    289
    (1997: *The new NHS*) 12, 197–
    9, 278, 282, 283
Department of the Environment,
    Transport and the Regions
    (DETR) 37, 40n8
Department of the Environment
    (DoE) 40n6/8/12
Desideri, C. 165
Di Biase, R. 161
Di Maggio, P. 281, 283
Dingwall, R. 235n1
direct payments
    in broadcasting 261, 263, 273
    to care users 124
Dirindin, N. 172n6
dissimilarity index 82, 93
Dixon, Jennifer 11, 171, 175–99,
184, 276, 280, 285, 286, 288
Dobra, J.L. 59n4
Dobson, Frank 215
Domanico, R.J. 104

Domberger, S. 44, 52, 53, 55
domiciliary care, monitoring 119
Dorrell, Stephen 180
Doyal, L. 116
Dreyfus, M. 208
Dugdale, T. 23
Dugger, W.M. 280
Duncan, G.J. 87, 88
Dunleavy, P.J. 50, 52
Dunsire, A. 54
Durlauf, S.N. 87
Dynarski, M. 87

E

Earl, P. 114, 115
Eastmet 41n14
    contracting: case studies
        conflictual (1988–90) 25–9,
        41n17
        cooperative (1990–) 29–32,
        42n22
Easton, B. 263
Eastwood, M. 247
Eccles, R.G. 114
Echols, F. 87
Economy Act (1925) 207
education: market 63–4, 70–6, 100–3
    in Belgium 79–80, 91–2
        and ability segregation 6–7,
        80–91
    funding reforms 64–70, 76–7, 89,
    96–7
    incentives 72–4, 89–91
    and new Labour 7, 76–7, 107–8,
    289–90
    and parental choice: in
        England/USA/New Zealand
        7, 95–108

see also schools
Education Bill (May 1998) 76
Edwards, T. 96
efficiency 5
  of NHI 212
  as performance indicator 155, 158, 212
  and trust 5, 38n2, 55-6, 283
  see also X-efficiency
effort
  and conventions 46-7, 49, 51
elderly people
  residential care study 138-52
Elgin, R. 47
Employment Department 247
Enthoven, A.C. 228, 288
environment: for market 116-22, 128, 155-6
equity 55, 286-7
  as performance indicator 155, 158, 212
  between schools (funding) 75, 76, 101
Estrin, S. 241
ethos *see* conventions; Hippocratic ethos; professionals; social work ethos
European Union
  welfare 16
Evans, R.G. 223, 235n2/3/4
Evans, W.N. 87
ex ante specification
  in CCT 53-5
exclusion(s)
  of broadcasting audiences 262-3
  of school pupils 73
experience good, broadcasting as 261-2

Ezzamel, M. 136

F

Fama, E.F. 44, 49
Feintuck, M. 102
Fenn, P. 235n1
Ferlie, E. 281, 283, 284
first mover advantage 225
Fitz, J. 103
Fliegel, S. 105
focus schools (USA) 98-9
foundation schools 76, 108
Fowler, M. 103
Fox, A. 45, 47, 52, 57
France, George 10, 11, 155-73, 280, 285, 287
Frantz, R.S. 45, 46, 47, 53-4, 56, 57, 59n1
freeriding 47, 51, 59n2
Frey, B.S. 54, 55, 56, 283
Friedman, M. 79
Full Employment UK 243
'fundamental transformation' 224-5, 277-8
Further Education Funding Council 77

G

Gabel, J. 222
Gaebler, T. 241, 251
Gamoran, A. 88
Gateways to Learning 248-50
Geddes, M. *169*
general practitioners (GPs)
  commissioning *176,* 178, 180, 184, 187
  as future policy 192, 193, 196

fundholding 2, 11, 175, 280, 284
  under new Labour 12,
    180
  vs HA purchasing 11, 175,
    176-7, 178, *179,* 181-91
  and patient choice 11, 184-5,
    198, 285
Germany
  health insurance 204, 207, 208
  legal aid spending 226
Gewirtz, S. 101, 103
'gifts'
  in employment 51, 283
Gintis, H. 79, 89
Glenn, C.L. 79, 104
Glennerster, H. 2, 79, 102, 184, 213,
  230, 286-7
Goldberg, V.P. 48
Goldsmith, M. 195
Goodin, R.E. 240
Gordon, L. 104
Goriely, T. 220, 231, 232
Gough, I. 116
Graffy, J.P. 184
Graham, A. 261-2
Granovetter, M. 114, 135
grant maintained (GM) schools 97,
  102-3, 108
  funding 63, 64, 65-7
    and CFF 6, 67-9, 75
    and NFF 70
  opportunism: examples 73-4
Gray, A. 202, 220
Gray, J. 241
Guardian/Society 180, 183

H

Halpin, David 7, 95-108

Ham, C. 184, 195
Hampshire: school meals 74
Hansard 254n1
Harries, Andrew 4-5, 19-42, 59n3,
  276, 277, 280, 282, 284
Harris, D. 23
Harris, J. 202, 208
Hartley, K.J. 50, 52
Hawthorn, R. 250
health authorities (HAs)
  purchasing
    cf GPs 11, 175, *176,* 178,
      179, 181-91
    in *The new NHS* 197, 198
Health Service Journal 180
healthcare 10-13, 277-8
  in Italy 10-11, 156, 160-70
  in UK *see* general practitioners;
    health authorities; National
    Health Service
Henderson, V. 87, 88
Henig, J.R. 104, 105, 106-7
Herfindahl index 81, 92n1
hierarchy/hierarchies 21-2
  and markets 22-3, 40n10, 134-
    8, 278
  case studies
    strong (Westmet) 32-6
    weak (Eastmet) 25-32
Hill, P.T. 98
Hippocratic ethos 50-2
  and CCT effects 54-5, 56, 58
Hirsch, F. 285
Hirschman, A.O. 183, 251
Hirschman–Herfindahl index 277
HMSO
  (1926) 204, 207, 210
  (1989) 163
  (1996) 266, 269

(1998) 215
(1942: Beveridge Report) 202,
203, 204, 211, 213
(1986: Peacock Report) 263,
273
Hodgson, G.M. 59n1
Holland *see* Netherlands
Holtham, G. 262
home care, monitoring 119
homo economicus: traits 43, 54
Hope, M. 219, 226
Horne, M. 136
housing 3
Hudson, B. 112
Hughes, D. 163, 280, 281, 283
Hughes, G. 53
Hume, David 260
hybrid organisation
    in quasi-markets 19-22, 39n3,
    281-2
    governance 22-3, 41n7

I

ineqality *see* equity
information
    asymmetry 3, 43-4, 53, 220, 221
    and new technologies
    287, 289
    in NHS purchasing 182-3
    via care networks 127
inspection *see* monitoring
Institute of Careers Guidance 247
institutional environment 116-22,
    128, 155-6
Istituto Nazionale di Statistica *168*
Italy
    healthcare reforms 10-11, 162-
    5

background   156,
    160-2
    and inter-regional
    diversity 10, 165-7,
    168-9, 170

J

James, E. 79
Jencks, C. 87
Jensen, M.C. 44, 49
Joy, M.F. 104
Judicare 219-20
    economics: lunch analogy
    220-2
    as model for reform 229-32

K

Kay, J. 262
Kay, N.M. 60n6
Khalil, E.L. 48
Killeen, J. 242, 247
King's College London: studies
    101-2
Knapp, M.R.J. 44

L

Labour Party 180 *see also* new
    Labour
Laffont, J. 113
Lambeth schools: and NFF 70
Lancaster, K.J. 114
Land Planning Act (1980) 49
Lansley, J. 138
Lapsley, Irvine 9, 133-52, 280, 281
Lattimore, R. 274n1
Lauder, H. 103
Laughlin, R. 285

LCD (Lord Chancellor's Department) 219, 220, 225, 226, 227, 228-9
Le Grand, Julian
  on quasi-markets 1-16, 43, 79, 101, 112, 275-90
    performance criteria 155, 212, 246-7, 264
    politics/environment 156, 213
    and vouchers 241
Lee, V.E. 105
legal aid 13-14, 219-20, 225-9, 232-3, 290
  economics: lunch analogy 220-2
  market failure: analysis 223-5
  reform options/proposals 229-32, 234
Legal Aid Board (LAB) 223
legal aid practitioners (LAPs) 232
Leibenstein, H.
  on X-efficiency 44, 45, 55, 59n2
    and conventions/trust 46-7, 48-9, 52, 54, 55
Leroy-Audouin, C. 88
Levačić, R. 64, 95-6, 100
Lewis, J. 137, 284
Liberal Democrat Party 180
Link, C.R. 88
Lipsky, M. 125, 196
Little, S. 185
Llewellyn, Sue 9, 133-52, 151-2, 280, 281
Lloyd George, David 203, 207
local authorities (LAs)
  and CCT 4-5, 19-24, 36-7, 49, 58

case studies 24-36
  and welfarist ethos 50, 52
community care provision 111, 112-13, 115-28
funding 117
social care: purchasing 133-4
Local Government Acts (LGAs)
  (1988: on CCT) 25, 38n1, 39n4, 40n6/12, 111-12
    secondary legislation 41n18, 42n24
  (1992) 49
Local Government Management Board 38n1
local management of schools (LMS) 24-5, 64-5, 76, 97
  Birmingham University study 100-1
  vs CFF 6, 70-2
London Compositors (union) 210
Long, A.F. 183
Lord Chancellor's Department (LCD) 223
Loughlin, M. 40n9
loyalty
  of workers 46, 51
'lunch'
  Judicare analogy 220-2
Lyons, B. 282, 289

M

Macaulay, S. 23
Macneil, I.R. 23, 48
macro-environment
  for market 116-22, 128, 155-6
magnet schools
  in USA 91
Magsaganis, M. 286(-7)

Maher, M. 281
Maital, S. 44
Major, John 97
Mannion, Russell 8, 9, 111–31, 284, 285
Mapelli, V. 161, 172n6
market socialism 241
markets
   vs hierarchies 134–8
   see also quasi-markets
Mason, A. 184, 189
Matthews, R.C.O. 224, 235n1
Mays, Nicholas 11, 171, 175–99, 276, 280, 285, 288
McGee, M. 44
McGuire, A. 224
McKee, M. 286
McMaster, Robert 5–6, 8, 43–60, 55, 282, 283
Medicare 219, 222
Mehta, J. 282, 289
Meier, K.J. 106
menu auction 55, 59n5
'merit goods' 261
Meyer, S.E. 87
Michie, J. 3, 282
Middleton, Sir Peter 234
Migue, J.L. 43
Milgrom, P. 223, 279
Mill, J.S. 260
Mills, A. 275
Milne, R.G. 44
Milwaukee experiment (private school choice) 105–6
Ministère de l'éducation 81
Ministero della Sanità *168,* 171n3, 172n9, 173n11
Ministry of Health 204
Miron, G. 80

Moe, T.M. 79, 89, 96, 99, 105
monitoring 54, 59n4
   in CCT case studies
      Eastmet 28–9, 31–2
      Westmet 35
   of community care 126–7
   and distrust 48–9, 54, 55–6, 283
Mooney, G. 230
Moore, D. 99
moral hazard
   of insurance 223
   see also opportunism
Morgan, K. 184, 189
Morris, M. 248
Mueller, D.C. 43
Mulligan, J.G. 88

N

National Advisory Council for Careers and Educational Guidance (NACCEG) 253
National Association of Commissioning GPs 187
National Association of Community Health Councils 189
National Audit Office 56
National Curriculum 96
   in New Zealand 98
national funding formula (NFF) 64, 69–70, 75, 76, 77
National Health Insurance (NHI) 13, 202, 203–6, 212–14
   administration costs 210–12
   central regulation 207–9, 214–15
   inequality 210, 212
National Health Service (NHS)
   ancillary services and CCT 50–2, 54–6, 284

equity of access 186, 286
and monitoring 54, 55-6, 195-
6, 283
New Labour policy 12-13,
180, 197-9, 277-8, 282
purchasing 11-12, 175, *176-7,*
178, *179,* 180-1
policy options 191-6
process: requirements 181-
90
National Health Service and
Community Care Act (1990) 112
National Institute for Careers
Education and Counselling
(NICEC) 242
needs assessment
for community care 116-17
of NHS patients 181-2
Nelson, R.R. 52, 55
Netherlands
education 79
legal aid 226, 231-2
'new economic sociology' 114
new institutional economics 39n3,
278-80
New Labour policies 1, 215-16
Best Value framework 37-8
on education 7, 76-7, 107-8,
289-90
on healthcare 12-13, 180, 197-
9, 277-8, 282
on quasi-markets 2, 16, 275-6,
288, 289-90
on social care 151-2
New NHS 12, 197-9, 278, 282, 283
New Right 241, 275, 285
New Zealand
education reforms 97-8, 99, 100

Smithfield Project 103,
104
legal aid rationing 229-30
state broadcasting 262, 270, 271
New Zealand On Air (NZOA) 258,
264, 272-3
as purchaser 266-7, 268-9, 270,
271
Niskanen, W.A. 43, 240
'no win, no fee': in law 234
Noble, M. 103
Noll, R. 259
Nooteboom 54
North, D.C. 54, 155-6
Northern Metropolitan
case study 42n19/20
nursery voucher scheme 107
Nystrand, M. 88

O

OECD 160
Office for Public Management 184
opportunism 3, 134, *135,* 278, 281
in education 73-4, 76
and legal aid 13, 224
ordinary least squares results: in
Belgian study 82, *84-5*
organisational change
and behaviour assumptions 134,
135, 278
for quasi-markets 280-1
see also hierarchy; hybrid
organisation
Orzechowski, W. 43
Osborne, D. 241, 251
Ouchi, W.G. 23, 55, 134, 136, 140
output-based formula: as schools
incentive 89-90

P

PA Cambridge Economic Consultants 248
Paterson, A. 219, 220, 223, 225, 229, 230-1, 232
patients, NHS
    choice 11, 184-5, 198, 285
    needs assessment 181-2
Paton, C. 163
PCAT 43, 49, 54
    and X-efficiency 43-5, 57-8
Peacock, A.T. 43, 263
Peacock Report 263, 273
peer effects: in education 87-8, 89
PEP (Political and Economic Planning) 210, 211
Perlman, H.H. 138, 142
Perrow, C. 136, 279
Pettigrew, M. 281, 283, 284
Philippines
    health market 277
Pierson, P. 171n4
Plank, S. 104
plasticity, activity 53, 54, 57
Policy Studies Institute 242
politics
    and quasi-markets 120, 208, 213-14, 241
    see also Conservatives; new Labour
Pollard, S. 96
population needs see needs assessment
Powell, M.A. 201
Powell, W. 281, 283
Powell, W.W. 39n3, 114
Power, Sally 7, 95-108
Price, C. 235n7

Price, R.L. 136
primary care groups (PCGs) 197-9
principal/agent problem
    in legal services 223
Prisoners' Dilemma 59n2
private good, broadcasting as 261
Producer Choice 264, 266, 268
professionals
    values 136, 151, 288 see also Hippocratic ethos; social work ethos
Propper, C. 225, 277
provider choice
    decision making 128-31
    models
        behavioural 115, 128
        neoclassical 113, 129, 131
        sociological 114-15, 131
    as performance indicator 155, 158, 212
    and purchasing environment 128, 129
        macro 116-22, 128
        micro 122-8
    vs consumer choice 285-6
public broadcasting fee (PBF) 258, 266, 267
Public Choice Agency Theory see PCAT
public good(s) 240-1
    broadcasting as 257, 259-62, 263
    in New Zealand/UK 266-74
Public Record Office 205, 206, 207, 208, 212
purchaser–provider split 20-1, 121
    in healthcare funding 175
Putnam, R.D. 169

Q

quasi-markets 1, 95-6
    in decentralised country 156-
        60
    development (1990s) 1-16, 275
    evaluation 276-89
    government control 96, 214-
        15, 280
    hard 4, 5, 20-1, 23
        case study: Eastmet 25-9
    interwar (NHI) 201-16
    and new Labour 2, 16, 275-6,
        288, 289-90
    performance criteria 155, 212,
        246-7, 264
    rationale 80, 239-41 *see also*
        PCAT
    soft 4-5, 20, 21, 276
        case studies 29-36
    see also careers guidance;
        education; healthcare; legal
        aid; social care

R

race
    in education 88, 99-100
Rafferty, J. 278
Raywid, M.A. 98
Reed, M. 50, 52
Rees, R. 223
Reith, Lord 261, 262
relationships, agency 281-2, 283-4,
        288
        see also trust
remoteness
    and X-efficiency 50, 56
residential care purchasing

study 138-42, 150-1
    and costs 142-5
    information: use 145-7
    market orientation 147-9
residential homes
    inspection 126
responsibility
    under new Labour 107, 215,
        275, 289
responsiveness of markets 155, 158,
        212
Roberts, J. 223
Roberts, Jennifer A. 1-16, 275-90
Robinson, J. 50
Robinson, J.C. 194
Rodwin, M.A. 190
Rojek, C. 130
Rossell, C.H. 104
Rothbard, M. 240
routineness and X-efficiency 57
Rowann, J. 229
Rowley, C.K. 47
Rumberger, R.W. 82

S

Sako, M. 125, 282
Salmon, P. 171
Santantonio, V. 165
Saraceno, P. 172n6
Savas, E.S. 240, 241, 245-6, 249, 250
Schanze, E. 39n3
Scheffler, R. 286
schools
    Belgian and ability segregation
        6-7, 80-8, 89
    cream skimming/selectivity 7,
        86, 101-4, 106, 285, 287
        deterrence 89, 90

funding
    equity 75, 76, 101
    reforms 63-76
    see also common funding formula; grant maintained (GM) schools; local management of schools; national funding formula
    incentives 72-4, 89-90
    under new labour 76-7, 107-8
    in New Zealand 97-8, 99, 103
    opportunism 73-4, 76
    primary *vs* secondary (funding) 70-2, 76
    pupil exclusion 73
    sixth form provision 72-3, 77
    in USA 79, 98-9, 104-6
Schramm, C.J. 222
Scotland
    NHI policy 208-9
Seal, W. 39n2
segregation, ability *see under* Belgium
self-determination, client 137-8, 141, 142, 150
SEN children
    discrimination 101-2
services for CCT 39n4, 49
Servizio Sanitario Nazionale (SSN) 161, 172n6
Sexton, S. 97
Shapiro, J. 184
Sharpe, T. 253
Sheldon, T.A. 183
Shen, T.Y. 45, 47
Shleifer, A. 90
Simon, H.A. 45, 46, 48, 51, 136
site: in quasi-markets 59n3
sixth form provision 72-3, 77

Skill Choice 248-9, 250
skills mix
    for NHS purchasing 188-9
Smith, Adam 260
Smith, C. 180, 192
Smith, K.B. 106, 130
Smith, P. 8, 9, 111-31, 284, 285
Smith, S.R. 196
Smith, T. 103
Smithfield Project 103, 104
social care
    market 8-10, 112, 133-4, 290
        contracts 136, 151, 281, 284
        M and H perspective 134-8
        prospects under new Labour 151-2
    see also community care; residential care
social interaction
    in education (peer effects) 87-8, 89
social markets *see* quasi-markets
social work ethos 130, 136-8
    vs market 8, 9-10, 136-7, 140, 150, 284
'soft contracting' 136, 151, 281
special transitionary grant (STG) 117-18
specification
    in CCT 53-5
staff changes 283
'stakeholding' 215
standard spending assessment (SSA) 67, 69, 117
Starey, N. 194
State Owned Enterprises Act (NZ, 1986) 267

Stephen, F.H. 228
Stewart, J. 144
Stigler, G. 59n1
Stiglitz, J.E. 134
Stinchcombe, A. 39n3
Stoker, G. 171
Stoney, S. 248
Strong, P. 50
subscription television 261, 273
Summers, A.A. 87
'super-DSOs' 20-1, 22, 23-4
    case study: Eastmet Trading
    Services 26
        vs ESCA 27-9, 41n17
sustainability in NHS purchasing
    188
Sutton schools and NFF 70
Swedberg, R. 114
Sweden
    health reforms 171
synergy/synergies 55, 60n6
Szymanski, S. 44

T

television
    as quasi-market 15, 257, 258-
    9, 264-6
        in New Zealand/UK 266-
    74
Television New Zealand (TVNZ)
    267, 269
Thomas, H. 64, 100
Thorelli, H. 39n3
Thrupp, M. 103, 104
Times 97
Times Educational Supplement 100
Timms, N. 136
Tirole, J. 55, 113

Tooley, J. 106
Trade Union Reform and Employ-
    ment Rights Act (1993) 245
trade union societies 210
traditions *see* conventions
Training and Enterprise Councils
    (TECs) 243, 244
National Council 253
transaction costs 39n3, 114, 232, 246-
    7
    in federal settings 157, 171n2
    in legal aid 223-5
    measurement/perception 278-9,
    280, 289
    in NHS purchasing 186-7
    and trust 282
trilateral contracting 21, 23, 36-7
    case study: Westmet 32-6
trust 3-4, 8-9, 45-9, 131, 282
    in community care 125-6
    and Hippocratic ethos 52
    loss 6
        in hard quasi-market 27,
        42n19
        through monitoring 48-9,
        54, 55-6, 283
        and X-inefficiency 5, 38n2,
        55-6, 58, 283

U

unemployment
    and NHI 208-9
Unemployment Insurance Fund
    bankruptcy 205, 209
USA
    education reforms 79, 98-9, 100,
    106-7
        research 104-6

'user-pays' television *see* direct payment

V

Vandenberghe, Vincent 6-7, 79-94, 285
vertical integration *see* hierarchy
Vincent, C. 102
Vincent-Jones, Peter 4-5, 19-42, 39n2, 59n3, 276, 277, 280, 281-2, 284
Vogel, H. 259
Vogel, R. 287
vouchers 241, 249, 250
    for careers guidance 244, 248-50
        vs contracts 251-2
    nursery 107

W

Walford, G. 103
Wallace, C. 138
Walsh, K. 19, 21, 40n5, 42n23, 51, 53
Waslander, S. 103, 104
Watts, A.G. 14, 239-54
Webster, C. 203
Welfare to Work 289
welfarist ethos *see* Hippocratic ethos
Wellington Evening Post 98
Wells, A.S. 98
Westmet 40n11
    and CCT: case study 23, 32-6, 42n22
Weston-super-Mare: sixth form provision 77

Whiteside, Noel 13, 201-16, 203, 208, 286
Whittaker, T. 138
Whitty, Geoff 7, 95-108, 276
Whynes, D.K. 51, 53, 54, 283
Widows, Orphans and Old Age Pensions Act (1925) 207
Wilkins, S. 44
Wilkinson, F. 39n2, 282
Willetts, D. 195
Williams, J. 184
Williamson, O.E.
    on market behaviour 53, 134-5, 140, 151, 282
    on markets/hierarchies 9, 39n3, 136
    on transaction costs 114, 223-5, 277, 278
Willms, D.J. 87
Willms, J.D. 82
Wilmott, H. 136
Winkler, D.R. 88
Winter, S.G. 52, 55
Wintrobe, R. 52
Witte, J.F. 79, 105
Wohlstetter, P. 99
Wolfe, B.L. 87
Woodward, S. 53
World Health Organisation 171
Worthman, L. 235n7
worthy goods 240-1
Wright, K. 130
Wylie, C. 98, 103, 104

X

X-efficiency 5, 43, 44, 59n1
    and CCT 49-58

and monitoring/specification
48-9, 53-6, 59n4
and PCAT 43-5, 57-8
and trust 45-9, 52, 58

Y

yardstick competition (schools) 90

Z

zoning: in USA 79-80
Zucker, L.G. 39n2, 47